THE TIGER CLUB:
A TRIBUTE

VOLUME I 1957-1966

This isn't a history of the Tiger Club. It could never be. At the best it's a *pot pourri* of the growth of the most remarkable flying Club that's ever been and seen through one pair of eyes. Happily biased.

WITH A NEW FOREWORD BY DESMOND PENROSE

CIRRUS ASSOCIATES

PUBLISHED BY:
Cirrus Associates (S.W.),
Kington Magna,
Gillingham,
Dorset,
SP8 5EW UK.

ISBN 1 902807 15 4

REPRINTED IN ENGLAND BY:
Cats Solutions Ltd.
2 Rushy Platt
SWINDON
Wilts
SN5 8WQ

COVER & PHOTO SCANNING BY:
International Graphics Services Ltd.
24-31 Fourth Avenue
Westfield Trading Estate
Radstock
BATH
BA3 4XE.

DISTRIBUTORS:
Cirrus Associates (S.W.)
Kington Magna
Gillingham
Dorset
SP8 5EW UK.

ORIGINAL COVER: Tigerprint, London.

TO NORMAN JONES
1905-1991

ACKNOWLEDGEMENTS

To Michael and Norvela Jones, for their encouragement in this venture, and to Michael in particular for his contribution of the Appendix. To Bob Pooley for suggesting the title and his unwavering support. To Trudi, my wife, for her patient hours of typing, proof-reading, cups of tea and her love.

To Jack Nusbaum for his guidance in the production of the first edition of this book, and to Betty Monk and Lauretta Dives my very especial thanks.

I am deeply indebted to John Blake for many of the photographs used. His generosity in this field is legendary. Sadly, time has obscured the origins of some of the others, and if I omit a rightful credit I ask forgiveness.

For this new edition may I also acknowledge the kindness of Desmond Penrose, that exceptional pilot, vintage aircraft stalwart and good friend, for agreeing to write the Foreword.

And finally, my thanks to Peter Campbell for his enthusiasm and perseverance in preparing this reprint.

FOREWORD

by DESMOND PENROSE

'The best flying Club in the world.' Such was a description of the Royal Air Force in the 1930s. That appellation could rightly have been applied to the Tiger Club in the 1960s.

How was it that a civilian organisation with limited funds came to have such an international reputation? To answer that question we must look to two founding members and their ethos.

Norman Jones had served in minesweepers in the 1939-45 war. He ran the Club with an occasionally eccentric but tightly reined hand, and was adept at choosing the right people; he had no fear of delegation (a good RN trait).

C.A. Nepean Bishop (Bish) was the Chief Flying Instructor, an inspired choice. Bish had known the founder of modern flying training, Robert Smith-Barry and, in so many ways, emulated Smith-Barry's style, viz the apparent casualness but individually well-practised style of Club flying. Which other Club engaged in air racing, aerobatics, formation flying, and that most unique of display acts – 'standing on the wing'? All with the minimum of incident and a great deal of pleasure – because it was self-disciplined.

The Tiger Club was eclectic in its membership. There were serving officers, doctors, lawyers, airline pilots, bankers, professional comedians, princes and, no doubt, paupers and test pilots, all with one consuming love: that of flying. Particularly that of flying in the enthusiastic and sometimes daring company of like-minded individuals.

It was my good fortune in 1962 to be asked by John Cunningham to care for Cirrus Moth G-EBLV; John, that most courteous of mortals, always couched his instructions as requests. That instruction resulted in Bish proposing me for Club membership. I was honoured.

I am still proud to have been a member of the 'best flying Club in the world.'

Desmond Penrose
January 2003

PREFACE

by LEWIS BENJAMIN

This book was originally started back in the eighties to satisfy Tiger Club friends who were for ever suggesting a record of all the fun we had flying in the fifties and sixties. There was no thought of a wider circulation.

And yet here I am in the early months of 2003 preparing a second edition destined to introduce Tiger Club adventures to a generation probably not born when so much of the action occurred.

The Tiger Club is still with us: albeit it is now knocking on half a century since the founder, the late Norman Jones, set things in motion. It is memories of our enterprising flying from those early years that now reach out to warm friends, wherever they may be: viewed with forgiving hindsight, they were vintage moments.

Times change of course: what was permitted, even tolerated, all those years ago wouldn't be 'on' today. And yet . . . even as I write these words a tiny inner voice whispers: "don't you believe it – that adventurous spirit is still around." That voice heartens me but I digress.

When this volume was published in 1988 it was unexpectedly bought by a curious and enthusiastic public who must have scratched their heads at the scant information and familiarity of the script, so I was forced to hastily prepare an additional explanatory slip to insert. It read:

'The Tiger Club, now based at Headcorn in Kent, is arguably the world's biggest and best known all-pilot flying Club.

It gained its unique air sporting reputation in the sixties and seventies when thousands flocked at the weekends to enjoy unforgettable airshows, all performed in open aeroplanes at speeds more akin to motoring: the chance to wave to pilots in their gaily coloured mounts, and to the pretty girl standing on the wing, and for them to wave back, often overlooked in the fun of the moment, the skill of the pilots, some of the finest in Europe.

The Tiger Club has always attracted a calibre of men and women who sought to extend their ability; a unified company of friends in what was once described as the university of the air, for nowhere else are the arts of aerobatics, formation, display and air racing practised regularly on Club aircraft.

The world-wide membership tends to maintain a low profile, but there is pleasure in admitting to the inclusion of several royal princes, and, when in 1988 the Duchess of York joined, we welcomed a royal princess too . . .'

This edition benefits from some decent editing – not the words of course, they remain as they were originally written – but mainly in the tedious detail of punctuation and the occasional addition of surnames to clarify personalities. You see, the book was printed in Spain where Trudi and I then lived, and proofing was a nightmare. Miguel Angel the wonderously patient compositor spoke no English, and I no Spanish. We spent our time in animated pantomime. How the original book ever reached fruition is something approaching a miracle.

Anticipating the immensity of the subject I restricted *Volume I, A Tribute* to the first ten years, 1957–1966. The call of time produced *Volume II, The Exuberant Years 1967–1976* in 1999, and a few years later in 2002 Michael Jones completed the trilogy with his *Redhill Saga 1977–1989*.

May you enjoy our story as much as we enjoyed our flying.

CONTENTS

1966

$$- 0 - 0 - 0 - 0 - 0 -$$

THE TIGER CLUB AIMS

1. To provide the means of meeting for those who take an active interest in light aeroplane racing, displays, aerobatics and other forms of competition.
2. To provide its members with good sporting flying at the lowest possible cost.
3. To work for improvement in standards of light aeroplane flying, aerobatics and private flying generally.

THE TIGER CLUB CHARTER

As a member of the Tiger Club I undertake:

1. Always to go out of my way to assist other members in aeronautical matters.
2. Always to fly with courtesy and with especial attention to the safety and comfort of others.
3. Never to use an aeroplane for any disreputable or unworthy purpose.

1957-58

THE VR, OURSELVES AND BISH

"Write a book," said someone. "Write a book," said another.

"I will, I will," I replied. "I'll start tomorrow." I'd like a pound for everytime I put it off.

I spotted the brief reference in an October 1957 issue of *The Aeroplane*. The Tiger Club had a few vacancies for pilot members. The minimum qualification 100 hours as pilot in charge of a light aircraft. Please contact the CFI, C.A. Nepean Bishop. Not that I had a clue what the Tiger Club stood for, but presumably they flew Tiger Moths and, come to think of it, who didn't at that time? It was enough that they flew, it was local, and I needed to fly again. I wrote off at once.

The Tiger Club couldn't have arrived on the scene at a more propitious moment for me. I had just been chucked out of that wonderfully exclusive flying club, the Royal Air Force Volunteer Reserve. Even in the fifties there couldn't have been many organisations that actually paid its members to fly for the fun of it, and the closing of the schools – a direct result of Government economies – was indeed a sad occasion for many of us. Not all the VR flying had been fun, of course, there had been a serious side, and stooging up and down the Devon coastline giving the Army radar interception practice, although worthwhile for them, was considered something of a bore, at least until we were no longer able to do it.

But the economies had not only closed down the RAF Volunteer Reserves but at the same time wound up the Auxiliary Squadrons too. These were our up-market brethren who flew first- (or near first) line aircraft. Both closures were to have a direct bearing on the birth of the Tiger Club.

The VR had for me been something special and the memories of some early morning sorties will ever linger. Each year we did a compulsory two weeks' summer camp. Best remembered were those near Exeter. At times, and way before the CO was about, we'd wheel out the aircraft and all go bouncing around the dew-covered grass of the airfield collecting mushrooms. I can still hear the staccato roar of the Gipsy Major engines bursting on my ears as we flew around in our DH Chipmunks like so many grasshoppers, a few feet from the ground, mushroom spotting, and abruptly the sudden silence broken only by a diminishing whistle as the aircraft sank to rest beside the crouching delicacy, then the rush to clamber over the side to be the first to pick and stuff them down battledress blouses. About 8 o'clock we'd be back in the mess urging sleepy white-coated stewards to take our treasure back out to the cook to have them reappear on our plates along with the eggs and bacon.

I was accepted as an Associate Member of the Tiger Club on the last day of 1957. I still hadn't a clue what I was letting myself in for, except that the Club had to be something special if it only sought qualified pilots. Looking back I can only now begin to appreciate the effect that decision, prompted by an unknown columnist (it was probably the late Harry Cooper), was to have on the rest of my life. If I would have bothered since to ponder what alternatives life could have offered me over the years, I reckon I'd be hard pressed to have come up with anything as satisfying or as entertaining as the membership of this remarkable Club. It offered a unity of friends and an integrity of purpose that never wavered. Everything in fact that a restless chap of thirty-two needed to put his energy into. It was the direction I needed and I embraced the flying and the Boss's leadership with all my natural enthusiasm.

Perhaps the first document the Club ever produced was: ABOUT OURSELVES. It was written by Bish – C.A. Nepean Bishop, to give him his full title – who had only recently been asked by Norman Jones to accept the position of Hon. Secretary.

ABOUT OURSELVES   Spring 1957

This introductory article is primarily intended for the interest of those who have joined the Club during the past few months and who, owing to the fact that the Honorary Secretary never seems to have much spare time and can only type with two fingers anyway, have not heard very much of the Club's activities since the end of last season's flying.

Briefly, the background purpose of THE TIGER CLUB is to provide Tiger Moth pilots with opportunities for competitive sport with the aircraft, whether it be racing, aerobatic or other facets of flying. It has been formed by an experienced band of racing pilots whose aim it is to endeavour to help the ordinary club pilot to gain the necessary experience to enjoy first-class sport at as little cost to himself or herself as possible.

To this end, two branches of the Club have been established, the first at Fair Oaks Airfield and the second at Croydon Airport, and at the time of writing there are three aircraft at each place. Flying at Croydon is under the supervision of Mr C. Nepean Bishop, who has Mr. W. V. Fitzmaurice to assist him, whilst at Fair Oaks Mr Norman Jones, founder of the Club, is in charge, instruction being looked after by Captain D.W. Phillips.

THE TIGER CLUB does not undertake flying tuition in the normal sense, being only concerned with the finer points of flying – that of bringing up the prospective aerobatic pilot along the right lines, and providing others with opportunities for racing as mentioned above, but particular emphasis is also placed on formation practice, for when the Club visits other airfields it is intended to do so *en masse* and arrive over its destination looking tidy.

Due to the present petrol position, flying at the moment is only carried on at weekends but, should conditions improve, it is hoped that a certain amount of midweek flying may be arranged. In the case of Croydon, bookings for Club aircraft should be made through Mr Fitzmaurice at Rollason Aircraft & Engines Ltd, during normal working hours, or through Mr Nepean Bishop on weekday evenings. Members wishing to fly at Fair Oaks should contact Mr Norman Jones at his London office in the afternoons, or at home in the evenings.

The hourly hire-rate of Club aircraft is being kept down to an absolute minimum, in fact they may be said to be unique in the annals of postwar flying. In view of this fact, entry to THE TIGER CLUB is not automatic, each application being judged on the merits of the individual concerned. Every applicant for membership has to make a declaration (a) that 'he will always go out of his way to assist other members of THE TIGER CLUB in aeronautical matters,' (b) that 'he will always fly with courtesy and with especial attention to the safety of others,' and (c) that 'he will never use an aeroplane for any disreputable or unworthy purpose.'

Such, then, are the aims and ideals of your Club; the aircraft and instructors are, within the aforesaid limitations of petrol, there for the asking. Use them, improve your flying and pave the way for a happy and successful racing season both for yourself and your fellow members.

FLYING RATES FOR CLUB AIRCRAFT

Current flying rates for TIGER CLUB aircraft are as follows:

Tiger Moths	45/- per hour
Hornet Moths	50/- per hour
The Jackaroo	55/- per hour on all private flights

DUTY flying on all aircraft is at the rate of 30/- per hour, which is also the rate for all flying carried out in the Turbulent.

All Members in their flying returns *must* show against their times either the word 'duty' or 'private.' The definition of duty flying is that carried out under instruction, or as part of the TIGER CLUB activities. All other forms of flying is rated as private. The times of taking off and landing must also be shown as we have been instructed by M.T.C.A. that this is vital . . .

No one is now quite sure how the Club began. It is 90% probable that Norman had proposed the idea of a club to race Tigers – of which he had plenty at the time – at an Air Racing Dinner at the Royal Aero Club on the 24th of January 1956. Among his guests were Jimmy Denyer, Basil

Maile, The Hon Peter Vanneck and Beverley Snook, who eventually became the Founder Members without demur. Chris Wren later used to claim he was there too and sketched out the Club's emblem that night, but then all agreed anything could be true of an evening on the town in such cheerful company.

But one thing is sure, the first official Tiger Club flight in a Tiger Club aircraft was on January 20th 1957 at Croydon, when Bish took 'Fitz' Fitzmaurice up in Tiger Moth G-AOAA. Tiger 'AA is still with the Club some thirty years later, having at last reverted to its original two-seat form after many years as an aerobatic single-seater.

The Tiger Club when I first joined was then based at Croydon, an airfield of infinite weariness, clinging to its nostalgia of 'tween-war years greatness and yielding as little as it could to the ugly progress of housing development and the encroachment of light industry. It was of course a losing battle, but still some flying clubs struggled on there in spite of the increasing restrictions – but their days were numbered. Even so in 1958 it was still a great place to fly from. The Tiger Club was closely associated right from the start with the aviation engineering firm of Rollasons of which Norman Jones had recently become both Chairman and Managing Director. They had the use of a big hangar hard by the edge of the main grass runway, all very handy for the minimum of taxying and the inducement of the briefest of landings.

On that crisp Sunday morning in January '58 the Club's Chief Flying Instructor Bish led me to an old Tiger with the legend G-ACDC writ large in silver on her maroon side. I was reverently told that she was the oldest on the register. This claim has been perpetuated until this very day regardless of the fact that she has since been sorely damaged on several occasions and rebuilt with numerous other parts. Fortunately only an heretic would question how much, if any, of the original remained. Long may 'CDC continue be the oldest surviving de Havilland 82A, to give just once her correct designation.

My first impression of our CFI did him less than justice. Had someone told me that Bish was a church organist or a species of schoolmaster I'd have accepted it. However, with all the arrogance of relative youth, I didn't think he measured up to my concept of a flying man and certainly was not the type to run the Club. After all, he looked a bit of a nobody, an illusion he was never at any pains to avoid. I never saw him dressed for flying in anything but a dirty old mac and a couple of yards of woollen scarf he'd wrap around himself, finally stuffing the ends inside his coat. His old bike was as tired-looking as himself. Nor do I ever recall Bish taking off his cycle clips, at least not until much later on when he bought an old car, and even then I believe he wore them to keep the draught out. And yet this bespectacled, ruddy faced, white-haired man was an extraordinarily able pilot and instructor. I suppose Bish must have been in his late fifties, but his honest zest for flying knew no bounds. He didn't attempt to put me in my place during that initial 45-minute check. He didn't touch the controls. Later I began to appreciate that it was not his way to fly in any other way than modestly, but something in his confidence warned me from the word go that here was a man who mattered.

The following Sunday I first met my fellow members. It was bitterly cold hanging around outside the draughty hangar and we moved restlessly up and down, stamping our feet to keep warm. The three Tigers we were to fly were already lined up, rocking slightly under the gusts of wind that howled around the corner of the building. We were waiting for Bish to lead the formation and I had been invited to go along for the ride – my pilot being Clive Elton. When eventually Bish wobbled up on his bike, Bev Snook began to tease him playfully for his lateness. Bish got very angry and, rounding on Bev, berated him soundly. Bev, who was only teasing, burst out laughing whereupon Bish lost his temper and kicked the nearest thing to him – the blameless rudder of 'CDC. A shocked silence ensued, for no one had ever seen Bish lose his temper before. Bish himself was obviously mortified. He seemed to think on it awhile, and suddenly it was as though the sun had broken through cloud: he grinned boyishly and all was well again.

The boys started each other's aircraft and we taxied out for our formation flight. We flew as usual eastwards down the narrow free lane that led along the Caterham valley and on into Kent. The flight is recorded in my logbook; I wrote: 'Detling, 30 mins.' I was to see a lot of Detling in the coming months.

CROYDON, A LOOK BACK AND GLIDER TOWING

There was no Clubroom at Croydon in 1958. We used the Rollasons offices on the first floor of the hangar, alway pausing before we climbed the stairs to glance into the engineers' room adjacent to the hangar to peer inside to see what new glamorous pin-ups they'd acquired. I had never before seen such a magnificent collection of beauties, but then censorship was a bit prudish in those days. The Rollason hangar would have gladdened the eyes of present-day vintage aircraft enthusiasts, perhaps even more than it did ours then. Along one wall leaned dozens and dozens of war-surplus Tiger fuselages, their fragile wings folded beside each fuselage for all the world like so many sleeping butterflies, an illusion heightened by the drab browns and yellows of wartime camouflage. On the floor of the workshop were strewn Tigers in every state of rebuild and everywhere the smell of dope hung heavily in the air. By the big doors clustered the finished Tigers, which were ours to use until they were sold.

In the hangar next door the Ministry of Aviation's Investigation Branch would every now and then pile in the wreckage of some appalling crash, and then try in their painstaking way to solve the mystery of its loss by reconstructing as far as they could the bits and pieces into a sad resemblance of the original. I would sometimes peer in and wonder at it all, and never fail to look up to a line of eight scars in the lintels above the hangar office windows which in turn looked down into that vast arena, and I'd grin in guilty memory.

Back in 1942, when I was an inquisitive cadet in the Air Training Corps, two of us had brazened our way into the airport on the strength of our blue uniforms and makeshift identification papers to see what we could see. Croydon in those days was a natural draw for all of us youngsters who lived and dreamed flying. The place was always packed with dozens of new and exciting types to drool over. On this day we were not disappointed, for outside of this very hangar we found a rare find indeed, a Grumman Avenger, and by squeezing inside through the tiny gap left between those massive sliding doors, we also found a lonely Spitfire, the sole occupant of that huge hangar. My fellow Sergeant, by name of Sutherland, quickly climbed into the cockpit to get the feel of it all and I wandered around the graceful wing, reverently brushing the leading edge with my hand. I wanted nothing more in life than to join the RAF and to fly one of these beautiful things. My reverie was shattered by the concerted blast of eight Browning machine guns, the nearest smoking barrel of which was only a foot further along the wing from me. The din, and then the blessed echoey silence that followed, stopped time in its tracks. In this speechless state I was aware of movement and, looking up, saw white frightened faces appear at the windows. They were staring down unbelievingly though the dust that was falling from the jagged holes in the brickwork above them. Sutherland stepped out of the cockpit, tumbled down the wing in a state of frightened shock, and we hurriedly made ourselves scarce.

Many years later there arose a rumour, still recounted every once in a while, that an ATC cadet by the name of Benjamin flew his first solo on a Spitfire at Croydon. Not so; he nearly got killed by one, that's all.

Detling was then the home of the Kent Gliding Club, a disused RAF airfield perched high on the windswept North Downs overlooking Maidstone. It was there that I was introduced by Bish to glider-towing. The object of the exercise was to tow the glider aloft on the end of a 200 ft nylon rope and try if possible to position your Tiger and the glider into an advantageous spot in the sky, where on releasing the glider its pilot would immediately find the lift all soaring pilots dream of. At least that was the theory. I soon learned to aim for a nice fat cloud, and when we were right underneath it hope the glider pilot would cast off, leaving the power pilot to break to the right and return as quickly as possible to the start line. Incidentally, if there were no likely-looking lift-worthy clouds about and the wind was in the right quarter, we'd tug our companion to the edge of the escarpment to let him seek his fun there. We lightheartedly thought the glider pilots crazy casting themselves adrift at Newton's mercy, and without the obvious benefit of an engine. I once heard gliding described as a crash looking for a place to happen. Of course on the other hand the glider boys thought us a hamfisted lot, and quite unable to appreciate the delicacy and finesse of a pilot able and willing to master the elements unhindered by the noisy smelly fan up the front. It was a timeless and friendly banter.

I was an apt pupil, and after the requisite ten tows under supervision I was allowed off to tow anyone aloft who cared to hook up to me. I soon learned that not every glider pilot was as experienced as those chosen pilots on my first ten tows. The best position for the glider – which always got airborne first – was just above the tug, and providing he kept his position the actual towing was no more effort than if he weren't there. But just as though there were rookie tug pilots, I soon learned that there were even more rookie glider pilots. It was a hard school and never dull, and more important to me, a poorly paid Assistant Manager at a London suburban departmental store, the whole exercise was free. The glider pilots did all the paying and, since they were invariably as broke as we were, the best tug pilot in their eyes was the one who got swiftly to the right spot in the sky and who got down again smartly. Minutes counted at 1/6 a time (around 8p today).

There is a certain limiting factor in losing altitude smartly when one's Tiger Moth is connected to a snaking nylon rope. Dive too fast and the rope whips viciously and ties itself into knots, always difficult to undo. The other factors, to be honest, only applied when aerobatting on the way down. I had better explain. It wasn't that glider towing was dull but any journey could be more exciting if, whilst on the way down, you could also have some fun. Anyway there was an element of competition among the tug pilots not only as to who could be down the quickest but also who could best entertain the others *en route*. We normally lost our tow around 2,000 ft, and it was soon proved that the fastest way down without tangling the rope was to spin the Tiger. The routine was to cast off, close the throttle and whip the nose up for a bit more altitude, then boot on rudder at the right moment and start counting the turns. Five turns in a spin were plenty, and all too soon you found yourself at 700 ft or so, nicely placed for the run-in. An acknowledged variation was a slow roll either way, but no one ever attempted a loop, because we believed the rope might curl around and foul the controls. Just for the record we were wrong, others have done it since.

There were two schools of thought too, about releasing the rope after the tow and prior to landing. The first was a slow run in at 30 feet to release the rope and if possible plonk it neatly in front of the next glider all ready for the hook up. The second, because some thought the extra circuit, no matter how brief, a waste of valuable time, was to land with rope still attached. This needed a most precise touch. It was considered *infra dig* to taxy about with the rope dragging behind like some pigtail. One's landing had to be so short that all one had to do – at least in theory – when one rolled to a stop was to move the glider forward a few feet to hook up. Trouble was that since the prudent glider pilot wanted as long a run as possible, he'd position his machine as near to the hedge as he could, and the Tiger's landing run had to be very very short indeed, if he were to score.

A friendly rivalry always existed between the boys with fans and those without. It was fair game too if by a little judicial manoeuvring the tug pilot could be induced – if we were fool enough to allow it happen – to overcook his approach. And it happened occasionally. It is a simple fact that the slower one flew – and the Tiger could be encouraged to fly very slowly – the more the end of the rope would dangle (colloquially the "angle of dangle" perhaps) – aided and abetted by the metal ring at its end. To drag the rope through a tree or a hedge could prove disastrous. One was, or should have been, extremely conscious of the danger. On one of my earlier trips I misjudged everything and dragged my rope not only through a hedge but between a couple having a picnic at the field's edge. The ring whipped away the cloth and goodies as neatly as any conjuror. The two were so shattered by this disappearing act that, by the time I'd run across to apologise, they'd started their motor-cycle and fled.

From then on my every free moment was spent glider-towing, dashing from work on every half day and over every weekend in my haste to get airborne as soon as I could, and to fly eastwards down the familiar A25 road that wound its way along the valley of the North Downs. Like every other self respecting seat-of-pants navigator I only deserted the road for the ease of following a railway line. It was a tiny single track that was a vital link in bad weather. It started at Westerham and, as though it didn't know where it was going, petered out in a northwards direction at Sevenoaks. Here the trio of lakes made an excellent landmark. At weekends there was a lot of dinghy sailing going on, and a little mild strafing was permitted, provided one adhered to the airman's unwritten law – and the only known counter to getting caught – of 'one low pass and never circle for another.' The law of averages being what it is, the chance of being reported for low flying on the strength of one vigorous beat-up is remote indeed. Besides it never did any harm to let one's hair down on occasion, or so I used to think at the time.

Somehow that short thirty-odd mile trip to Detling always seemed to encourage bad weather, and with the coming of the winter clag there were always those adrenalin-consuming moments no matter how

18

familiar one was with the terrain. I recall one awful time when, with light failing and desperately wanting to get back to Croydon, I imprudently set off. Somehow I found that crucial single track and followed it westward beneath a lowering 300 ft cloud base in murky, drizzly conditions that no right-minded pilot should ever be out in. In moments that became worse, so stealthily did the weather deteriorate. I can still see in my mind's eye the dark hill ahead of me, across which splashed cars, their headlights fighting for a share of wavering visibility, the whole scene a dark threatening blur, as with one hand I tried to hold steady a wind-buffeted biplane and with the other wiped my goggles incessantly in a losing attempt to keep them free of the driving rain. I crossed the drenched river that was a road, and a bright red neon sign swam beneath, a warm comforting sight and quickly identified. *Regal*, it said. This is Purley, I reasoned, and the airfield could only be just over the hill. Low over its wet brow and on over nameless fields, and then suddenly beneath my wheels slipped a hedge and a large white numeral that could only have marked the threshold of an unseen grass runway. I gratefully cut the throttle and settled quickly, and taxied on across a field that could have been anywhere, so featureless was it. And then, like the opening bars of a piece of music you can't quite put a title to, through the fog came the faint but just recognisable outline of familiar hangars and that never-to-be-forgotten control tower. I motored in slowly allowing the excitement to die away and the tensions to dissipate as one by one my muscles relaxed. I could see figures crouching in the lea of the hangar waiting to help us in. In moments the Tiger was silent but my ears continued to roar with noise. I never asked Bish who was among those waiting and who made no reproach, or the late Jacko Jackson who had been my silent passenger, what they thought of that particular pilot. I think we were all just content to count our blessings and go and get a cup of tea.

EARLY LETTERS, 'A' LICENCE, SHOREHAM AND ME

It was a long time before I got to meet many of my fellow Club members. I knew for instance that Club members also flew from Fair Oaks, a grass airfield near Woking. I only went there once in 1958, and then only *en route* to the Royal Aeronautical Society Garden Party which was rained off, as it often seemed to be. For me it was always Croydon, Bish, and the few regulars there. In those days we had to book Croydon flights with either Bish or Fitz who, it was rumoured, was once Norman's naval commander and like him had also served on minesweepers. To give an idea how disciplined the outlook was, here is a typical circular letter of Bish's.

Dear Member,   March '58

With the lengthening hours of daylight thoughts of all good TIGER CLUB members must turn to the coming season and the many enjoyable functions that it should bring. But these thoughts should also turn to the manner in which we hope to acquit ourselves at these displays, and what we must do in the meantime to see that we improve on our perfomances of last year.

In 1957 we started from scratch, and by the end of the season's flying had given several quite creditable displays and, we believe, gained a small reputation in so doing. This season we shall have to do BETTER THAN THIS; we must consolidate that reputation, and to do this we have got to start practising NOW.

Our aim is to have enough personnel trained in the art of formation flying, aerobatics (both solo and combined), glider-towing, racing, parachute dropping etc., to enable us to put up a fleet of ten aircraft at any one time TOGETHER WITH ADEQUATE RESERVES, as obviously the same bunch of members will not be able to attend all meetings. But to do this we must have your whole-hearted co-operation FROM NOW ON.

At our displays we hope that we shall have the use of some eight Tiger Moths, together with the Jackaroo, Arrow Active and Turbulent aircraft, but for training purposes we only have six Tiger Moths, three at Croydon and three at Fair Oaks. On Sundays two of these will be employed in glider-towing and/or parachute-dropping duties, so it follows that a great deal of our formation-flying and other practices will have to take place on Saturdays with — when the days are longer — evening flying at the two airfields. With over 30 possible 'contestants' for places in the team or its reserves, it is going to be very hard not to disappoint some at weekends and that is why I MUST know when you intend to fly.

As I have written before, we are not an ordinary flying club, and the majority of our flights are made in formation, as indeed they must be in order to get the necessary practice. And for the benefit of our newer members I would remind them that we often go away from our bases during the weekends to places which are more free from flying control than the London area; this being so it is even more important that I know when you are wishing to fly.

As far as possible there will from now on be regular formation flying practice from both Fair Oaks and Croydon Airport (or as often as 'control' at this latter airport allows). We want YOU to have a place in the Club Team, or be one of the immediate reserves, or, if a Passenger Member, a spare seat if available, and we hope from now on that you will be a regular visitor to Croydon or Fair Oaks.

In conclusion I must emphasise the fact that if we are to realise our ambitions for the coming season we shall require your unstinted support for the next few months. This means flying together as regularly as the weather and your purse will permit, although at our low rates, this latter should not worry you too much. It also means being at your base well before the time of take-off – for there are the aircraft to be pulled out and got ready for the day's work. TIGER CLUB members do not rely on ground staffs to do their pulling about! And as I said in the last News Bulletin, the Chairman rings me up at 06:30 hours each Sunday morning to discuss the day's programme, which is then finally arranged. If I do not know that you are coming along I cannot include you in the day's flying, should this be away from base . . .

All that business about aircraft having to be got ready was in earnest. We regularly washed and cleaned our mounts, and Bish was never backward in coming forward to tell us to get on with it. Fortunately my earlier Club experience had been catholic indeed, and so had prepared me for the unusual, no small thanks to an outfit that had got on with the job of self-help in a similar way. It was called the Brookside Flying Group, and I had started it.

In July of 1946 I joined the South Coast Flying Club. It was much the traditional sort of Club and based at Shoreham in Sussex. I was still in the RAF, but I lived nearby in Hove and on my leaves I would go to Shoreham and do the one thing the RAF wouldn't let me do: take my civilian friends flying. The Club fleet consisted of Tiger Moths, and the CFI was the most remarkable of men. Cecil Pashley, or 'Pash' as he was known far and wide, was a legend in his own lifetime, and about the most famous of all flying instructors. He'd been around a long while, too; he had built, and flown with his brother, his own aircraft before the first World War and in 1946 had around 18,000 hours instructing to his credit. Even with my current flying practice – and I was actually doing a refresher course on Tigers at Brough in Yorkshire – Pash insisted on showing me around the Tiger as though it was the first aircraft I'd ever seen. When I offered to swing the propeller for him he was horrified.

"No," he said firmly, "always leave things like that to qualified engineers, never do it yourself."

We climbed in and awaited the engineer. When no one turned up Pash began to fret. Impatiently he climbed out of the front cockpit, his long leathers flapping in the wind – I thought irreverently of Grumpy of the Seven Dwarfs for he was scarcely five feet tall – snorted around to the front and reached on tiptoe to grasp the propeller.

"Contact," he shouted.

The engine caught first swing and the Tiger nearly ran him over. He'd forgotten the chocks.

"Let that be a lesson to you, Benjamin," he barked as he disappeared back into the front cockpit. He was a great man and loved by everyone.

Flying was quite unrestricted immediately after the war. There were almost no recognisable regulations, and even getting an 'A' licence, as the private pilots' licence was then known, presented no problems. Eight hours solo was all the experience needed, then a simple oral exam plus a flying check which was observed from the ground. Civil flying officially began again on January 1 1946 and the first postwar licences were issued that very week: mine was amongst them. Since I was RAF-trained I was allowed to skip the flying test; all that was needed of me was to take the oral exam. I presented myself for this at the Royal Aero Club premises in Piccadilly on January 6 1946, in company with a fellow RAF pilot. The Secretary General had a bit of a cold that day, so his second-in-command, Colonel Preston, officiated.

We stood before 'Mossie's' desk like recalcitrant pupils before the Head. Needless to say we hadn't a clue what questions he was going to ask us. We'd swotted up on a prewar publication, and had an idea about the positioning of lights on a balloon cable, but little else.

He first turned to Dicky and snapped: "What's a Custom Carnet?"

Dicky was game for a try. "Isn't it something you need if you leave the country?"

Mossie growled and then turned to me. "And you, Benjamin?"

"I agree with Dicky," I said loyally.

He looked at both of us for a moment or two, gave an imperceptible shrug and a shadow of a smile appeared.

"I can see you two know bugger all about it. Here, give me the papers."

We were in and out in five minutes. We left behind a pound, I think it was, and came out with the prospect of a licence soon to be in the post, and clutching an aviator's certificate, which cost us five bob. I still have that little blue book with its behest in several languages that all who read this give the holder of this document every help. And all written in the most beautiful copperplate. It was worth five bob of anybody's money. An idiotically earnest boy looked out from the accompanying photograph.

I stayed with the South Coast Flying Club for over a year. They were a jolly lot and led by Duncan Davis, surely one of aviation's most irrepressible and cheerful stalwarts. Duncan was known as 'Drunken' Davis among the regulars. I expect if he knew his soubriquet, and he probably did, he'd have approved.

I remember one evening when Duncan was really drunken he decided to go flying with two pretty girls. The Club manager was in despair, and shot out ahead of him to urge the engineer to fix the Proctor so that Duncan couldn't fly. Anxious to help, I held up the cowlings with one eye on the Club doorway whilst the engineer, doing the best he could at short notice, hurriedly opened up something or other and inserted a piece of paper between two contacts.

"That'll never start," he muttered.

We had no sooner fixed the cowlings back when Duncan staggered out and pushed his giggling passengers into seats and clambered in after them. "Clear!" he shouted to the world at large, pressed the starter and the engine roared to life; before anyone could stop him – were that even possible – he rushed away and took off. White-faced, stunned, we watched him fly, tensed against the enormity of what could happen. The engine continued heartily and Duncan came back safe and sound, as good a pilot drunk as sober. Greatly shaken, the other two went inside, presumably to get as drunken as Duncan.

But I was restless with their slow and cautious approach to getting airborne, there seemed no room to progress to better things, and more important, there was the expense of it all. The more I thought about it the more convinced I became that the cheapest way to get flying was with an aeroplane of one's own; and a shared one seemed the only solution. I put the idea to Duncan.

"Excellent idea," he roared; "count me in to help!"

BROOKSIDE FLYING GROUP

So encouraged I began to scout around, but every avenue I explored had the same dead end. No money. That wasn't surprising. I had now left the RAF (May 1947) and had promptly spent the next six months sitting on a beach in a summer of brilliance such as one could only dream of. I got wonderfully brown, I swam, had parties, danced and made merry. I was nearly twenty-two. I had been in the RAF four years, and I wasn't going to do a thing until I was ready, and whilst I had some gratuity money left and parents who were glad to have me home again, I certainly wasn't ready. Two things finally made me think of work as autumn drew on. I'd run out of money, but worse, there was the threat of the then current Control of Engagement Order. It gave layabouts like me a choice of finding work smartly or being conscripted to the coal mines. I capitulated and went to work for a friend who had a toy wholesaling business. I was the office do-all, I tried to keep the books, collected and sold toys, but my mind was always out of gear. All I could think about was flying and owning my own aeroplane.

Then one night a brilliant idea came to me. What was wrong with a tiny share, I asked myself, as opposed to a larger one like a half or a quarter? There was no more sleep that night for me as I furiously extended my germ of an idea. I followed the idea up immediately. I put an advertisement in the local paper, the Sussex *Evening Argus*, announcing the first meeting of the Enthusiasts' Flying Club. Pay £10 a head, I declared, and given fifty members we would have enough for an aeroplane with a bit left over for luck and the insurance. It was quite a platform. The first meeting was a great success. But money, even at a tenner a time, was hard to come by. I'm not sure I believe in coincidences, but right on schedule my grandmother died, and with the few hundred pounds that came my way I bought, in quick succession, a big share in the aeroplane, an old open Armstrong Siddeley car of 1931 vintage, and a new BSA Bantam 125 cc motor bike.

The Club I founded late in 1947 at Shoreham eventually became known as the Brookside Flying Group, and we operated a Miles Magister which we bought from Rollasons for £325 complete with a year's Certificate of Airworthiness. We did everything ourselves, to the immense joy of the members and the alarm of others. We set up camp on the north side of the airfield and Duncan wasn't amused at all. When I reminded him of his offer of help he grumbled that he didn't think I meant it. But he eventually relented and proved a good friend. Incidentally it was the first community flying club in the South of England. We were beaten to being the first ever only by a short head when Jill Donnisthorpe started a similar club in Reading; neither knew of the other's existence at the time.

The fun we had is a story in itself, but a little background is important to get the feel of Club flying in the immediate postwar years. For instance, anyone could instruct and anyone did. Take me for instance. The insurance policy I negotiated was fully comprehensive, it covered any member under instruction or otherwise, and all for only an incredible £70 a year. That would take some beating today. It also listed me, a complete unknown, as the Club's Secretary, and one authorised to check out others. I did so, often. Even to putting on my most serious face when, as it once happened, I was called upon to give an A1 qualified Wing Commander instructor an initial check. If Wiggie ever reads this, I hope he'll forgive me the indignity of calling for another circuit because I wasn't satisfied with his first.

There was so much flying to be done – by this time we'd been loaned a DH Rapide and an Aeronca – that I offered my services as an instructor in spite of the fact that I'd never done any instructing before. No one was put off at being guinea pigs, and I blithely sent Jack Hamblett, my first pupil, off solo in the Magister after just three hours twenty minutes. Jack became a Tiger Club member many years later and none the worse for my youthful confidence. I still wonder if that wasn't some sort of postwar record. On reflection it couldn't have been a bad thing when tighter restrictions came into being – but oh, the fun of it all, and the freedom to be captain of one's own airborne destiny. Within three years the Club had folded, but the rot only set in when someone stole our beloved Maggie. Things like that happened in those days.

EARLY DISPLAYS

With singleminded enthusiasm I settled in with the Tiger Club to give my total support to their every venture. I yearned to join the elite at the air displays, flying with them all to every venue just in case someone fell sick and the opportunity to step in occured. For me it was a summer of formation flights, sometimes in a gaggle of ten aircraft down across the flat patchwork of Kent to Ramsgate, or go south perhaps above the undulating Hampshire countryside and over the misty Solent to land at Sandown on the Isle of Wight. Ever the bridesmaid, never the blushing bride – but not for long.

Bish's description of the Club's first displays best conjures up the easygoing garden party atmosphere of those early occasions. Fascinating too to reflect what happened to some of those who took part; several were still Club members twenty-five years later.

No 2 The Tiger Club Bulletin
The Spring Meeting, April 1957

Since the first issue of this newsletter appeared the Tiger Club have organised two flying meetings, both of which have been graced with fine weather. We may count ourselves very fortunate in this, and hope that our luck in this direction will continue throughout the coming season.

The first of these gatherings was held at Fair Oaks Aerodrome by kind permission of the owners, and took place on Sunday March 3rd 1957, the actual day on which the Tiger Moth aircraft completed twenty-five years flying as a fully certificated aircraft. The morning was brilliantly sunny, a fact which made hopes run high that we should get a great number of visiting aircraft. As things turned out the good weather had the effect of keeping a certain number of aircraft away from the Meeting as local Clubs found themselves besieged with sun-starved members all clamouring to fly, so their aircraft had to stay at base to satisfy this sudden craving. However, as the zero hour of 11.45 approached so did quite a number of Tigers, and by 1230 hours there were over twenty parked on the airfield.

A sealed time of arrival prize had been arranged and when this time was disclosed it was found that the winner was Capt. D.W. Phillips who had touched down in G-ANZZ within a few minutes of the appointed time. A 'Toast to the Tiger Moth' was called for at 1300 hours, and after an hour's general conversation amongst the pilots, aircraft left for their various bases, still in glorious sunshine.

The second meeting was held on Easter Monday at Sandown Airport, and can only be described as being an unqualfied success due in no small measure to the help and advice given to the Tiger Club by Maurice Imray of the Royal Aero Club, who was ably assisted by John Blake.

The Meeting commenced at 1100 hours with the briefing of all competitors by Mr Imray and at 1200 hours the first heat of the Tiger Moth Silver Jubilee Race, flown over three laps of a 4¼ mile course round the airport, was sent off. In this there were five competitors, the heat being won by the scratch man, C. Nepean Bishop, who was flying Norman Jones' G-AODR. Second place was taken by the limit man, Jack Harris in G-AOAA, Lt. Commander Overbury coming third in G-ANHI with J. Pothecary and Miss Rosemary Kirby following in that order and flying G-ANPL and G-AOXJ. The second heat resulted in a win for Dennis Hartas in G-AOAA with Margo McKellar a good second in G-ANZZ, third place being taken by Norman Jones in G-AODR. Desmond Norman flying G-AOXS took fourth place whilst Mike Odell, flying his first race, brought up in the rear with G-ANHI.

During the luncheon interval, members of the Isle of Wight Gliding Club kept the growing crowd of spectators interested with winch-launched circuits and landings in their machine. Unfortunately conditions did not permit of any soaring to be carried out.

1430 hours saw the resumption of racing, the third heat being won by Bill Bailey of Elstree, flying G-AODR, second place being taken by his Elstree chief, David Ogilvy, flying G-ANZZ. Tony Oldham brought G-AOXS into third place whilst Miss Audrey Windle, also from the Elstree instructional staff, came in fourth in G-AOAA, with Bev Snook in G-ANHI close behind her.

Aerobatics then took the place of racing, G-ANSH being put through her paces by Tiger Club C.F.I. C. Nepean Bishop; but then racing returned, with one confined to those lady competitors who were present. This was supposed to be of the same length as the others, but there was some uncertainty in feminine mental arithmetic and after two laps of the course Miss McKellar in G-ANZZ led in Miss Windle in G-AOAA with Miss Kirby third in G-ANHI.

Members of the Tiger Club then showed what they could do in the way of formation flying, Norman Jones (G-AOAA) leading 'Tony' Oldham (G-ANHI), Bish (G-ANZZ), 'Bev' Snook (G-AOAA) and 'Mike' Odell in G-AODR. Taking off in 'Vic,' the formation duly changed into 'Echelon Right' and from this to 'Line Astern,' finally finishing up with a stream landing, after which all aircraft turned to the left and drew up in a perfect 'Line Abreast,' a manoeuvre which appeared very neat.

Then came what must have been the pièce de resistance to the 1,500 spectators who were now present, this being a formation parachute descent by members of the British Parachute Club. These were Miss Sue Burges, Mr Peter Lang and Mr G. Bottomer, who were flown by Norman Jones, 'Bill' Bailey and 'Bish' in G-ANHI, G-ANPL and G-AOAA respectively. At a given signal from their leader, all parachutists jumped simultaneously and all landed within the airport precincts. Mr J. Basnett then ascended with 'Bill' Bailey in G-ANPL in order to make a delayed drop from 4,000 feet. But whilst the aircraft gained height for this Messrs Bishop (G-AOAA), Desmond Norman (G-ANSH) and Oldham (G-AODR) dealt summarily with gas-filled balloons which appeared from the east boundary of the airfield.

Height having been gained, Mr. Basnett then made a delayed drop of some 15 seconds before releasing his parachute. Like his companions he landed within the airport boundaries.

It was then time for the Final Heat of the race to be flown off, competitors consisting of the three heat winners plus the two fastest losers. As a result the first off was Dennis Hartas in G-ANHI, who maintained his lead to win a close race from the scratch man, Bailey, flying G-AODR, who in turn was hotly pursued by Bishop in G-AOXS. David Ogilvy finished fourth in G-ANZZ, whilst a gallant loser was Jack Harris in G-AOAA.

And so finished the first race meeting organised by the Tiger Club. The 'Basil Monk Trophy,' which had been specially presented to the club by Alderman Basil Monk, M.B.E., J.P. of Croydon to celebrate the Silver Jubilee of the Tiger Moth was, in his unavoidable absence, presented to Dennis Hartas by Mr Mark Woodnutt, Chairman of the Isle of Wight Conservative Association. He expressed the hope that the Tiger Club would make Tiger Moth races an annual event in the Isle of Wight. a sentiment with which the majority of those who had been lucky enough to be present heartily endorsed.

Many people deserve the thanks of the Tiger Club for their efforts to make the meeting the success it undoubtedly was, not the least of these being Mary Wilkins, Airport Manager at Sandown. Joe Taylor, who flew down specially to judge the racing, is another, as was David Ogilvy for his enlivening radio commentaries, whilst great help was given by Flight Lieut. Neville Jacob and the sergeants of the East Wight Squadron, Air Training Corps, who laid out and manned the turning points. There were very many more who deserve mention and if we have not given them their due, we proffer our apologies for an editorial bad memory . . .

I think Mary Wilkins deserves a special mention. Returning to Sandown some twenty years later I again ran into Mary. She was quietly washing up whilst around her in the adjoining Clubroom young pilots were busy reflying circuits. I couldn't help but remember that this lovely and most modest lady flew Spitfires and Mosquitos as an ATA pilot during the war. Knowing Mary I don't suppose she had ever bothered to mention it. Another name from that early Show is still closely associated with the Island: Des Norman went on to establish the successful firm of Britten Norman whose Islanders and Trislanders are in regular service all over the world.

During that summer I'd flown with everyone, often only as a passenger, but ever willing to swing propellers, hoping against hope that someone would fail to turn up so I could be called upon to take their place. Every display began with a mass flight over the local beaches. I remember when we were displaying at Ramsgate, we'd fly over neighbouring Margate and Broadstairs too drumming up business. What's more we paid for the privilege of flying for a paying gate, albeit it didn't amount to much at £1.50 an hour. By today's standards the display side was mild. Already there was a tied-together team, aerobatting, lots of formation flying, balloon bursting and parachute drops; it was all carried out in a leisurely comfortable manner that augured ill for no one. And expertise wasn't the first thing we thought of.

Apart from the display flying there was another field I wanted to get in on, but at the time it was something of a closed shop to the newcomer. It was one thing Bish authorising me as a suitable pilot for parachutists, it was another to get started as one. It was the catch 22 situation: OK, but have you dropped before? Then sorry, I'm afraid we can't use you till you have experience. The parachutists were a close-knit bunch with their own favourite and experienced pilots. The occasion to join them, however, came sooner than I expected.

OUR SUE AND THE SKY DIVING CLUB

I met Sue Burges at Croydon in 1958. I could hardly forget the occasion. An Auster had flown in and deposited first two huge ungainly valises which were shortly followed by a very pretty girl, who struggled out from between the awkwardly placed struts of that most awkward of aeroplanes. She paused only to look back and wave and then to turn towards me humping the two huge parcels in a most determined manner. My interest perked up and I rushed over to help.

When I reached her, her beautiful face was set in angry mien and her blue eyes flashed. I quailed beneath her scrutiny and contented myself to trailing behind with one of the chutes she'd imperiously dropped at my feet. Wordlessly we made for the hangar, the slim young amazon still muttering intensely under her breath. Not wishing to miss any of the coming battle, for she was working up a head of steam, I hung on, and in any case she was the prettiest thing I'd seen for ages. If the Club had any more like her, then this was going to be some Club.

For ten minutes in the office, this beautiful blue-overalled thing led off in a most alarming manner, and I hung back entranced at the entire performance, but no one seemed in the least concerned. She'd toss her head and her eyes would flash, and I hadn't a clue what she was going on about. Not that I cared for a moment, such was her entertainment value and command of fishwives' language. I was lost in admiration. She finished her tirade as suddenly as it began and smiled as though she had just arrived.

"Care for a lift into town?" I asked nervously, anxious to get my oar in first.

I suspect she was just about to drop me dead with a look, when she spotted the Auster pilot making for the office, and turned hastily and said: "You may, providing you leave now," and with that she strolled out, leaving me to stagger after her with her parachutes all tangled up with my own flying kit.

She was waiting impatiently at the bottom of the steps.

"Where is your car?"

I pointed as best I could, too breathless and in instant love to make more comment. She didn't say more than two words all the way into Earls Court, and the silence gave me time to rehearse my single sentence. I delivered it without a hitch after 40 minutes of shall I, dare I.

"Like a curry?"

"She gave me one withering look.

"Of course," she said.

Sue was, and still is, one of aviation's most remarkable characters.

At 23 Sue was then Britain's leading woman parachutist, had represented her country in the world championships, and was also a competent glider pilot. She had digs in one back room in one of those tall characterless houses adjoining London's mighty Exhibition Hall. It was a natural abode of hordes of London's nomad population. This particular narrow warren of rooms and stairs was the hangout of half London's Australian movement. I know, for no sooner had I found a shilling for the gas fire and settled down to put a match to it, than a thunder of noise shook the door, and cheery faces flung in a hallo as though to gain breath before their next assault on the stairs to the Gods.

"Don't you ever lock the door?" I asked in alarm.

"What for?" she said, and busied herself with coffee.

As evening fell and the claustrophobic brick wall that struck out in every direction from her window mellowed and faded with gloom, Sue brought down a Spanish guitar and, crouching down opposite me beside the fire, began to strum and sing gently. Mentally, I chalked one up for myself. I smiled encouragingly.

"You play the guitar?" she asked dreamingly.

I could no more stop what I was going to say than stop breathing.

29

"Yes, I love the instrument, especially the natural Spanish guitar. I studied under Segovia for three years."

I said it quietly and with a perfectly straight face. There has always been an irresistible clown in me waiting to drop me into trouble. I knew as I said it I'd never be forgiven for this one. Sue palled, got to her feet, and put the guitar back on top of the wardrobe. The room went cold. The only other word that passed between us and my exit was my "good night."

Even if our first meeting wasn't exactly idyllic, we became good friends. And it was through Sue that I became involved in parachuting. Notice I didn't say 'interested.' Nothing would have persuaded me to leap out of a servicable aircraft. I've always thought that anyone who did so wanted their heads examined, but of course I had no objection to them leaping out, as long as they left me in peace in my cockpit.

Sue's great friend and mentor was the late Mike Reilly. Mike was a sturdy ex-SAS man and as tough as they came. I sometimes think that he was the one man I knew who didn't know fear, and yet like many really tough men he was a quiet and gentle person. His passion in life was parachuting. Sue fitted into his picture perfectly. She was a complete perfectionist and utterly dedicated to this hairy sport.

By the time I met her she was already the British parachuting champion, and this was still in the very early days of the sport in this country. Parachuting was not new, but the art of free fall over here *was*. It is hard to believe, but in 1958 no one in Britain had dropped in free fall as long as a minute, and Mike and Sue planned to remedy this. Free fall of course can be defined as the time spent falling before one opens one's parachute. None of this "count to ten" business. As an active non-participant I can think of nothing more alarming than attempting to brave out the vision of earth coming up at around 120 mph, to count with mounting terror until you can contain your nerves no longer, and cry out with a shriek of panic and pull your ripcord, take a gulp of the good air, then look hopefully to see if you have beaten your previous time.

But it was nothing like that to Sue and Mike and the others of that intrepid band of the Sky Diving Club. They actually enjoyed that period of free fall. They began to live, to feel the meaning of life. Mark you, how anyone could meditate thus is beyond me. I'm assured it was not only true, but that there was a very real fear that the contemplation to savour every fleeting moment was so overwhelming that it was commonplace to delay opening that chute until it was practically too late. And if all the knowing looks and nods were correctly interpreted this deadly fascination was the cause of more than one premature encounter with Mother Earth. As a critical observer I had to admit that the effect of jumping into space had a remarkable effect on the parachutists. I have dropped many parachutists and from the relative security of the back seat of a Tiger Moth I can say that everyone, with the only exception of Mike Reilly, showed a nervousness that could denote fear – well, if not fear, it was an emotional high. It simply isn't possible to conceal emotion from one's pilot who is sitting only two feet away and is watching with a morbid interest the deliberation of someone about to launch themselves into space. Nevertheless, I didn't once witness a change of heart or see a parachutist hesitate when the moment came, such was their courage: or at least that's how *I* saw it – a staunch stayer-inner.

I believe too that my friendship and encouragement when the moment came meant a lot to them, and at this moment of truth too I never failed to sense a deep affiliation towards my companion. It was a sort of silent communion between pilot and a very lonely person out there in the slipstream. I've never mentioned this feeling before, but I now know that every jump I was in on left its mark on me too, but then I'd only dropped one person at a time. Today the vogue is *en masse*. It wasn't easy to be uninvolved when your friend was fast dwindling to disappear somewhere down there among that confusion of fields.

On the 10th of May 1959, Sue and Mike tried for that national free fall record. Four of us flew in the two Tigers from Croydon. Bish led with Mike as his passenger, and I in a brand new Tiger formated on him. We flew towards Stapleford Tawney, a grass airfield that snuggled away some miles north beyond the wide reach of the river Thames at Dagenham. It was a fine day, windy but clear and fresh, and I felt exhilarated and full of the joy of spring. Not so Sue. She was a difficult person before a jump, nervous, edgy and quite likely to leap down your throat with the least provocation. I understood, and had kept in the background as she and Mike dashed about collecting their gear together. They each had two parachutes, crash helmets, boots, gloves, stop watches and chest altimeters. It hadn't been easy to store all this paraphernalia within the confines of each machine, but we made it by removing the front control column and pushing all the stuff in the front cockpit along with our passenger.

My Tiger 'PRA was the very first machine to incorporate the little necessary modifications aimed at assisting a parachutist. 'PRA looked a bit clumsy with her padded front cockpit sill which was cut low to facilitate easy movement for a bulky occupant. There were two outsized handles on her cockpit side so positioned as to help the parachutist out into the fierce slipstream, and – strangest looking of all – the foot-square hole in the starboard wing's trailing edge through which, in theory anyway, the parachutist commanded a better view.

This was to be 'PRA's first operational run, and in honour of Sue's contribution to the parachuting sport the Tiger had *Sue Burges* written in bright orange across the front cowling. Only one other Tiger Club aircraft was named at that time and that was another fresh addition to the fleet, the single-seat aerobatic Tiger *The Bishop*. At Stapleford, Bish and I stoked up with tea, and watched Sue and Mike prepare their equipment. Around them stood the other members of the Ripcord Club helping wherever possible. It was already midday, and an air of urgency was abroad. The weather was getting into a marginal state for the attempt, the wind was rising and the then hitherto unbroken blue sky was fast building up with a host of cumulus puffs that threatened the necessary ten thousand feet clear space.

We took off in formation, Bish in the lead with me out on his port side some ten feet away where I could clearly see Mike's cheery face turn every now and then towards Sue and smile. Sue's edginess had increased. I could tell how the tensions were mounting by the way she sat crouched uncomfortably in the front cockpit, her silver crash-dome high above the windscreen.

We flew on, climbing slowly, and the higher we went the colder it got. The two aircraft were now suspended in the blue heavens. I shivered in the back and my heart went out to Sue enduring so much of the icy slipstream, for her bulky equipment prevented her from seeking the relative shelter lower in the cockpit. The extra weight and drag had slowed us up considerably; it took the labouring Tiger thirty-five minutes to get to our height and my altimeter was registering 10,500 feet when Mike indicated to Sue to get ready. Bish and I steadied on the run in, and together we reduced speed to a mere fifty knots. I could see Mike waving small variations in headings to Bish, and then suddenly he was ready. Mike and Sue began to get out of their cockpits and position themselves on the slim catwalk along the lower starboard wing.

Gently we further reduced speed until we were near hovering just above the point of stall so as to make things as easy as possible for them out on the wing. The unaccustomed drag and Sue's movement needed a great degree of concentration to keep the unstable craft steady. Mike nodded and Sue looked back at me and smiled. It was the first time in forty minutes I'd seen her face and then she had gone, falling away in that beautiful balanced manner of hers, face down, her arms and legs outstretched. She was flying, turning in great slow sweeps towards the ground far below. I watched them both weaving in unison as they swept space in complete happiness, a dwindling ballet in the sky to disappear from my shocked gaze. My blood froze and I shouted Sue's name out loud, and then rolled my mount onto her back and tore downwards, my eyes glued to the spot where I had seen them vanish. A short mile away I could see Bish coming down fast too, for neither of us had then experienced such a long free fall and simply weren't prepared for this disappearing act.

Like two birds we fell together seeking our young, and then far below a chute blossomed, and then another, a tiny cluster against the vast panorama of Essex that stretched in every direction for twenty miles. My relief was enormous. I flew nearer Bish and rocked my wings violently to attract his attention and then pointed downwards and, giving the thumbs up sign, he grinned and waved back and together we descended into the warmer air. Now the parachutes loomed large. It became immediately apparent that they were never going to make the airfield. Mike was dropping faster than Sue, no doubt due to his extra weight and standard chute, and from 1,000 ft I watched him touch down in a field just beyond the airfield boundary.

Sue swept on. I drew in closer to her and watched as she sailed across country. She had designed this chute herself. It was bigger than Mike's and the nylon panels were gaily coloured easy-to-see orange and white against the sunlit fields. Now we were alone. Bish still watched, but he stayed high leaving me to follow in Sue's path. They had obviously misjudged the windspeed, for now it seemed that Sue was moving not just downwards but even faster sideways. A busy road came up, and from above I was unable to judge exactly her height, so I held my breath, it seemed certain she was going to land across it. But she swept on, across fields and then with a sudden shock I saw the electric high-tension wires stretched right across her path. I let out an involuntary yell: "Look out Sue, the wires!" But my voice was dashed away by the wind, and I continued to watch from a safe 200 ft above her what seemed a certain catastrophe. I swear I willed her over them, but no sooner had I breathed a sigh of relief when my heart leapt again, and then I knew this time she was in trouble. Helpless, as only a hapless spectator can be, I watched Sue sail into the top of the biggest oak tree I ever saw. She crashed through the top branches, which broke her fall, but then, as though with a sudden change of mind, they clawed at her chute as well, and spilled the lifegiving lift from it. Sue plummeted to the ground, an unbroken fall of over 50 ft I circled desperately, looking for a field big enough to get down in, and passed as I did so over her inert body as she lay face down in the grass. Perhaps the sound of the engine got through, for she moved her hand just once. She was alive. I mentally marked the position, and at 50 ft. tore back to the airfield to get help, but others had seen her descent and help was already on the way.

She was rushed to the Epping General Hospital where they diagnosed a broken back. And what a fuss we all made of Sue just as soon as we were allowed to see her. The Tiger Club turned out in force during visiting hours, giving those kind and tolerant and very pretty nurses an awful time. The first occasion we were permitted to visit, no less than 27 of us, complete with standard get-well-soon kits, were cluttering up the passageways to that small hospital. There were flowers and boxes of chocolates and fruit and laughter and a couple of secreted bottles of champagne. And we all went in together, filling the small room with noise and people, overwhelming the staff as they busied around remonstrating at the number. They gave up the losing battle and tactfully turned elsewhere. Sue was to spend a long time on her back, before she again joined the gang, but she never jumped again.

1959

WE FOLLOW NORMAN, EARLY SYWELL AND MUSTAPHA

The Tiger Club was growing fast around me. From the 40 flying members in that thin 1958 Club Membership Book, the start of 1959 saw nearly 80, and with it a grand reputation for a Club that was different. Not since the prewar days of the big airshows at Hendon and the travelling circuses of Alan Cobham had the public seen much of light aircraft flying. Perhaps there was an occasional fly-in here and there among the more conventional flying clubs, but nowhere had there been real displays of the standard of those lush between-war years, when Britain led the world in the design and production of light club aircraft. The war years had soured the desire of many to fly. The political clime and the struggle to survive the immediate postwar years had left us a dulling existence. It was the final going of rationing and restrictions, that had only passed away a year or so before, that were the kindling factors in the recovery of the light aircraft movement.

By 1959 the public had eventually shed the last austerity, but it had taken a long time. The time was now ripe to enjoy life again, and Norman Jones' belief, that we should do everything possible to encourage the light aircraft movement, could not have been expressed at a more opportune moment. From those small displays at Sandown in the Isle of Wight and Fair Oaks in Surrey, to name a few during 1957 where pilots were asked whilst they were there to "do" something, everything was leading to bigger and better things in 1958. This really was the first year of planned displays, but even then no one quite realised how far Norman's dedicated belief would lead us. Bish was still the scribe on all things Tiger Club. An extract from the Bulletin No. 8 of the spring of 1959 indicated that Norman not only originated the "under the hoop" act but was prepared to practise what he preached.

For the first of our 1959 displays the clerk of the weather was kind to us and Easter Monday at Sywell was a sucess both financially and otherwise. The previous day had provided rain and still more rain, but the Monday morning dawned bright and for the rest of the day remained so.

First item on the programme was a formation of aircraft, eight in number, and at 2 pm sharp they swept over the aerodrome formed up into the letter 'T.' Items that followed included a tied together formation of three Tiger Moths led by "Bish" with "Benjy" Benjamin and Clive Elton on his flanks. This formation was airborne for some seven minutes, and landed and taxied in with their ribbons intact. Colin Labouchere made a formation parachute drop from 2,100 feet: a car was well and truly "bombed" by "Fitz": and "instructor" Charles Boddington demonstrated aerobatics to an apparently very dumb "pupil" who spun out of everything he attempted to do. Messrs Dennis Hartas, Ken O'Rourke and Bev Snook showed how to burst balloons with their aircraft and the proceedings continued with a demonstration race by four Turbulents in which Rosemary Kirby and three others showed how a close finish may be obtained.

Norman Jones and Margo MacKellar ably demonstrated two of our Turbulent aircraft, including flying "through the hoop" on two occasions.

Our best thanks are due to the Northamptonshire Aero Club and the proprietors of Sywell Aerodrome Ltd for co-operation with us in the organisation of this show, which has given us a good start to the 1959 season . . .

For the record: the first whole display put on by the Tiger Club – that is one promoted by and run by us – was in the previous year at Ramsgate on August 4th 1958. The organiser was the redoubtable Bill Chesson. My log book shows I flew both Tiger and Turbulent around the Bay and over neighbouring resorts drumming up business, but the actual programme remains something of a mystery. It certainly included what must have been our first Crazy Flying Act, for some unknown had later recorded: "We are pleased to welcome Flying Cadet Mustapha Shag, who put the fear of God in more people in five minutes than Billy Graham had done in five years."

Bish was ever quick to praise but then he was equally forthright on any occasion. In the same Bulletin he continues:

FORMATION TAXYING. It has been noticed that various members have different ideas in what constitutes the correct way to taxy out before a formation take-off. This is probably because this has not been ventilated in the Bulletin before, so will all interested parties please note that UNLESS OTHERWISE ARRANGED BEFORE A FLIGHT, or IF THE AIRCRAFT ARE TAXYING OUT TIED TOGETHER, all taxying will be carried out with a following machine TWO LENGTHS ASTERN OF THE ONE AHEAD OF IT AND SLIGHTLY TO THE RIGHT OF IT. This should in future be done at ALL TIMES, for if it is done in this manner it will then become a habit. This brings us to:

OH, I SAY THERE! After the Sywell display we were taken to task over the efforts of some of our members to land their Tigers as, sad to say, many were the 'wheel' landings seen on that day. Now we all know that if a formation landing is being made, or if there is a strong wind, it is better to land with the tail up, but on Easter Monday there was no wind to speak of and the landings noticed were not made in formation. Furthermore, we of the Tiger Club are generally supposed to be able to fly our aircraft more or less according to the book, and any who do not do so cause unfavourable comment to be made by those in the know, and our reputation suffers.

So it is suggested that certain members might well profit from an hour's circuit and bumps which it is no disgrace to be seen practising – and it's surprising how enjoyable this can be and also how much it will improve your flying.

THE TURBULENT, THE HOOP AND *THE BISHOP*

For a year I had practised, gone to every meeting and contrived to fly every aircraft the Club had, and it was also during 1958 that we first saw Roger Druine's little wonder, the Turbulent. My first encounter with this aircraft was ten hectic minutes at Sywell, a large hilly grass field to the east of Northampton during a lovely day in May. It was one of those weekends where everything was going on at the same time. And there I was taking it all in, when Norman walked up to me and abruptly said: "You will fly the Turbulent!" He was like this, and I for one needed no second invitation. I climbed in gingerly, and listened for a full minute as Norman briefed me. I can't remember his words, but it couldn't have consisted of more than two dozen, of which five were certainly: "Be careful, aircraft bite fools." He eventually had a plaque of those classic words installed in every subsequent Tiger Club machine.

With that warning and a meaningful look he swung the diminutive propeller, the engine fired and I was on my own. The Turbulent was then very much an exciting and new ultralight, as all very small and very light aircraft are known. As I moved forward I could feel the tail skid lifting in a rhythmic bump, bump, bump, indicating a nose heaviness I'd have to watch. It wasn't so much nose heavy as a very light airframe and the heaviest item aboard this 21 ft span low-wing gaily-coloured toy was probably me, closely followed by the VW 1100 cc engine up front. It was that small. Of instruments it was indecently nude. In front of me were the very basic: an airspeed indicator, altimeter, a rev counter and an oil pressure gauge. There were no brakes, no trimming device, just good old rudder pedals to rest my feet on and a control column. The throttle and a choke completed the cockpit check. Somewhere beneath the dash was a motorcycle 'push on' fuel switch, and wobbling in front of the windscreen where it pierced the fuel cap was a vertical length of wire attached to a cork that floated on the fuel in the tank. Simple and effective, the lower the level the less the wire showed. Clever. I tore off and was barely airborne when right at that crucial moment when anything untoward would put the wind up a better man than me, a dimwitted, short-sighted woman driver in a glider turned downwind in front of me, intent on landing the wrong way. She didn't see me and dashed by, peering intently forward, the whole fright passing no more than 20 ft away.

I loved the Turbulent. It was the nearest thing I had experienced up to then of having sprouted wings. Another ten minutes' experience came my way during the Ramsgate Show. Six months later I was at Fair Oaks for some reason or other, smooching around in a dreamy way, just happy to be near my beloved aeroplanes, when Norman spotted me and pushed me into his car.

"Come on Benjy," he said, "I want you to fly through the hoop."

We drove around to the other side of the airfield and there they had erected a hoop, at least that's what he called it. It was in fact two Dexion supports 30 ft apart, carrying between them a length of string some ten feet from the ground. In the middle of the string someone had tied a dirty white handkerchief.

"That's the middle," said Norman, proudly pointing to his hanky. "Go and fly under it."

He must think I've flown that thing a lot, I thought, but I got no further in pointing this out when he added: "Come on, get in; if I can do it you can."

I hadn't seen him do it, I hadn't seen anyone do it. But who was I to argue with the boss? So I did as I was told and got airborne.

As I came around after a quick circuit into the wind, all I could see ahead of me were a couple of the boys standing on either side of what must have presumably been the hoop. They were thoughtfully marking the contraption for me. I gripped the controls firmly, got the hoop lined up, muttered: "It's his bloody aeroplane," and tore in.

I aimed low, bounced heartily and shot through. Providing one aimed at the hanky, it was quite a trick.

"Good!" said Norman, when I had got down. "That will look fine at an air display!"

And having said that, he turned away, and got in his car and drove off. I got a lift back to the other side of the airfield with one of the boys.

Norman's idea of what was good for an air display was centred at the time on a new act he had worked out for himself. He called it 'Crossovers.' The idea was to position four aircraft at the points of the compass and somehow contrive to get them to cross over in unison at the field centre. Without radio or signals of any kind, it either proved too dull or was petrifying. From then on, whenever Norman came up and suggested pilots for Crossovers, we outdid ourselves with wild excuses. Eventually he gave up, but has been known from time to time to mention the act wistfully.

An important aircraft that was to have a profound effect on the Club's subsequent activities was first seen in '58. It was the single-seat Tiger, *The Bishop* 'PDZ. Aerobatics in this country had up to then been variables of the few basic manoeuvres. The RAF had taught us the classics, the loop and the rolls, both slow and barrel, and if we tried a flick manoeuvre it was strictly unofficial. It was so armed that the aerobatic enthusiasts in the Tiger Club entered the contests. It was soon blatantly obvious that the Continentals were going far beyond us in scope, and on machines against which our old Tigers were no match. This superiority was never more felt than in the 1957 Lockheed International Aerobatic Contests held, as in the previous two years, at Baginton near Coventry.

A LOOK BACK TO '57 LOCKHEED AND RACES AND A DINNER

From the Tiger Club Bulletin No. 3 for July 1957. Bish had bravely written:

THE BRITISH LOCKHEED INTERNATIONAL AEROBATIC COMPETITION was held concurrently with the racing at Baginton, and it is interesting to note that all but one of the seven British entries were members of the Tiger Club. As it turned out the Somers-Kendall SK.l had, unfortunately, to scratch owing to engine trouble so it was left to Messrs Bishop, Hartas, Langstone and Phillips (all flying G-ANSH which is now fitted with an inverted system), together with Charles Boddington (G-AHRC) and Squadron Leader E.S. Symondson M.C. (G-ANOR) to uphold the honour of Britain. Alas! Foreign competition in the shape of the Czechs, the French, the Belgians, the Spanish, the Swiss and the Israeli entries, all but the latter with specially built equipment, proved too strong for the home side, with the result that all the British entrants were eliminated before Saturday's finals when the Czech pilot V. Krysta won the competition, with last year's winner L. Biancotto of France taking second place. Third came le Chevalier d'Orgeix, also from France . . .

Our Club pilots had tried their best but were frustrated by the limits of their mounts. Now Norman came up with a very special Tiger. To better performance he did away with the second seat and buried the fuel tank there instead of in its high drag position between the upper wings. The machine was lightened using lightweight fabrics, and it had a slightly more powerful engine and a metal propeller, but the biggest single development was Tommy Thompson's (he was then Rollason's chief engineer) invention of an inverted system by which the engine could run upside down. Up to this time a Tiger had only to be turned onto its back for the engine to cough and peter out. The pilot also got an eyeful of fuel from the overflow in the filler cap for his pains. Now for the space of a few minutes we had power inverted (extended on one memorable occasion to some twenty minutes or so when Elwyn McAully flew *The Bishop* inverted across the Channel later in the year. If that feat isn't in the Guinness Book of Records it ought to be.).

The Tiger was never to prove the equal in performance to that brilliant Belgian-designed French-built Stampe, but it was the very first special postwar aircraft to be designed for aerobatics, in itself a portent of things to come. The single-seat Tiger was to be for many their introduction to one of the Club's most successful ventures, advanced aerobatics. But I wasn't much of an enthusiast for that sport. I had seen another and instantly set my heart on it.

I witnessed my first real air racing at Coventry in 1958. To me it seemed the greatest sport ever. I'd race if at all possible in 1959. Even a year earlier the National Air Races were dominated by Club Members. Bish had written:

No. 3   THE TIGER CLUB BULLETIN   July 1957

In the National Air Races of 1957 held at Baginton Airport, Coventry on Friday and Saturday July 12th and 13th last, the Tiger Club was represented by seven members who between them carried off four first, two second and two third prizes, all of which may be considered most satisfactory.

Dennis Hartas set the ball rolling in the Taxi-Tiger, G-AOXS, when he passed the post in the first heat of the race for the Goodyear Challenge Trophy well ahead of his nearest rival, and the good work was carried on some 30 minutes later when David Phillips in the veteran Tiger G-ACDC (which was built in 1933) scored a win in the first heat of the newly-instituted News Chronicle Trophy Race, he also being well ahead of his nearest rival, Tony Oldham, flying G-ANHI. In the second heat of this race, The Hon Peter Vanneck flying G-ANNK scored an even more decisive win, Tony Oldham being again in the running and coming in third on this occasion. In the third heat of the Goodyear Race Dennis Hartas came in third, whilst in the third and final race of the News Chronicle Trophy, our Chairman Norman Jones scored a runaway win in G-AODR, with Peter Vanneck second.

With one win and one second place Peter Vanneck held the highest score for the races and so won the actual Trophy.

Other members of the Tiger Club competing in the News Chronicle Race were Miss Audrey Windle flying G-AOAA, Miss Margo Mackellar in G-ANZZ, and Messrs J.M. Donald (G-ANZU), Jack Harris (G-AHVY) and John Pothecary (G-ADWO, another veteran aircraft in Tiger Moth history). In addition Jim Denyer, flying Auster J/IN G-AJEH, dead-heated with a Miles Monarch in the second heat of the Goodyear race and gained second place in the third heat, whilst Norman Jones flew the first Tiger Moth home in the King's Cup race although he was not quite fast enough to gain a place in this classic event . . .

40

Someone is going to ask what on earth the Taxi-Tiger was. Believe it or not, it had been designed for taxi work and for one passenger. It sported the added luxury of a neat coupé perspex hood which doubtlessly gave Dennis the extra speed he was always after. G-AOXS was written off some years later, a pity for it was a great idea.

From Flight, 31st October '58

The Piccadilly premises of the RAeC were shaken somewhat on Friday evening October 24 when members and guests of the Tiger Club celebrated with ferocious exuberance another year's successful flying. A list of the past season's events, thoughtfully inserted in the dinner menu, showed no fewer than 16 air displays at which the Club had participated.

Most of the after-dinner speeches were well nigh inaudible through a foreground uproar produced by euphonium, bugle, violin, harmonica and vocal cries of encouragement or criticism. The first speechmaker to enter this boisterous arena was the Chairman, Norman Jones. After thanking the Club secretary C. Nepean Bishop for his work during the year, and Bev Snook for his unique organization of the dinner, Mr Jones "forecast" all sorts of bright ideas for the next season, with the continued objective of encouraging flying for fun. The next speaker was Bish himself who welcomed the ladies (attending for the first time), reported a good year, exhorted everyone to get some practice flying time in, and said that the next forthcoming event would be a visit to Little Snoring. Also on the evening's programme was a brief appearance by a mysterious eastern gentleman who cocked a Snook, so to speak, at everyone . . .

BISH'S SPRING BULLETIN AND A CAPITAL TOUCH

Extracts from the Tiger Club Bulletin of the Winter 1958/59 began to show the rapid growth of the Club. Bish was now writing on every subject, doing all the secretarial work, and was about to get married. It must have been quite a decision for a man who had been a sturdy batchelor for some sixty years. We were young and at times unthinking and many the stories that were told. Bish, who loved martial music almost as much as his flying, thought he had found in his wife-to-be a kindred spirit. The moment they were married, though, poor Bish wasn't permitted to play his beloved gramophone records and Gladys never did go flying . . . My memory of her is of a wispy little lady with a firm idea of what should be done, a kindly manner and a dear husband who forever seemed in an other world in her presence.

AN AEROBATIC TRAINING WEEK

Our enthusiastic young member Colin Labouchere is at the moment busily occupied with the organisation of an Aerobatic Training Week; this to be held at Fakenham Aerodrome, Norfolk from April 5th to 12th inclusive. The meeting is being primarily arranged for those members of the Tiger Club who are intending to compete in the British Lockheed International Aerobatic Competition at Baginton in July next, and of course in the Tiger Club Aerobatic Competition in June. A number of our members have already been approached direct by Colin, but any others who may be interested are invited to get in touch with him at Sculthorpe Old Rectory, Fakenham, Norfolk as quickly as possible. In passing it may be stated that there is no better way to polish up one's aerobatic flying than to spend a week practising oneself, watching and criticising (helpfully) the efforts of others and generally getting together on the subject. It is hoped that *The Bishop* and *The Archbishop* will be available for this week and that it will be very well supported by our members.

THE AIRCRAFT POSITION

In recent months the Tiger Club has been fortunate in having the use of several more aircraft, all of which add interest to members' flying. The first of these arrived in the autumn, being the first British-registered Jodel D.117, and this has proved very popular with all who have so far flown the machine. This is registered G-APOZ, whilst the second addition to the fleet is a bright yellow Turbulent, G-APLZ. And talking of Turbulents, two more of these delightful little aircraft are now being erected and should be in service shortly. These, with 'PLZ and the first-built 'PBZ will provide very cheap flying for members during the coming season and, we hope, will be the highlight of a number of our displays.

Also taking shape is the Arrow Active G-ABVE which, when completed, will have a redesigned fin and rudder, experience having shown that this will enhance its flying characteristics; no doubt there will be many applications to fly this aircraft in the Nationals this year.

The Tiger fleet will consist of *The Bishop* G-APDZ, the newly converted *Archbishop* G-ANZZ, the dual-controlled G-ACDC and G-ANSH with our old trusties G-AOAA and G-AOXS. 'OXS, incidentally, is now at Sywell with the newly created Tiger Club branch which is being organised by Charles Boddington. Charles, incidentally, is the first of our members to start a branch of the Tiger Club away from the London area; it is hoped that his example will in due course be followed by others.

Our old friends, G-AODR and G-ANHI have now left us, the former as full-time glider tug to the Bristol Club at Nympsfield, whilst the latter now serves the newly-formed General Electric Company's flying club at Baginton. We shall look forward to seeing her when we visit that airfield for the Nationals in July.

Hornet-Moths G-AEWY, G-ADNB and G-AHBL are still with us, and the Jackaroo G-ANZT has recently been re-engined with a Gipsy Major 1C; with the extra horses provided by this motor she should be an even better aircraft than before.

NATIONAL AIR RACES

This brings us to the "Nationals" which this year are, as usual, being held at the Coventry Municipal Aerodrome, Baginton on Thursday, Friday and Saturday July 9th-11th 1959. The Tiger Club hope to have something in the neighbourhood of 14 aircraft available for the events, which of course include the British Lockheed International Aerobatic Competition. This year we hope to have in addition to *The Bishop* another aerobatic Tiger Moth, this being our old friend G-ANZZ which is at present in process of being converted to *Bishop* standards. In fact we hope that it will be an even better aircraft and it is to be known as *The Archbishop*.

The other aircraft available for racing this year will be Tiger Moths G-ACDC, G-AOXS, G-AOAA, G-ANSH, Hornet Moths G-AHBL, G-ADNB and G-AEWY, Jackaroo G-ANZT, Active G-ABVE, Turbulents G-APBZ, G-APLZ, G-APMZ and G-APNZ. Selected members will be able to fly these aircraft in the National Air Races, so if you are hoping to do this please let the CFI know without delay and at any rate not later than March 9th next, so that applications may be considered on their merits . . .

The naming of the single-seat Tigers provoked much amusement, with the ribald suggestion that the successor to *The Bishop* and *The Archbishop* should be called *The Actress*. Norman, sad to relate, was not amused and the third mount became known as *The Deacon*.

RACING, TWO CHIEFS AND ME

I asked for, and got, the mount of my choice for the 1959 National Air Races, Tiger Moth G-APRA, the *Sue Burges*. When I had presented myself at Baginton, Coventry, the venue for the races, I hadn't a clue about this racing business. I'd never flown a race in my life and my only qualification was a Competitor's Licence, which had been awarded for the asking. So I approached a most successful racing pilot and asked his advice. Dennis Hartas viewed me suspiciously, he always took racing seriously and saw me as a possible rival, which with my knowledge was laughable.

"Well," he said reluctantly, "what do you want to know?"

"I've got a new and unhandicapped Tiger," I replied. "It's faster than most, but I don't want to let on in the heats; I want to keep something in hand for the final race. What would you do, what would you suggest?"

"Don't hold back," said Dennis airily. "Go flat out all the way!

"Thank you," I said humbly, because he was very well-known and had been Air Racing Champion for two years. He must have seen me coming.

We had a day of practice circuits, as much to find our way as anything, and the next day the first race for real. I've never been so excited in my life. I won. Not by a head, not by yards, but by miles. I had been so determined that I had opened my throttle and had nearly bent the thing keeping it open. I didn't even think to look back and check where everyone else was. I got carried away. I was fêted. Cameras clicked, Press men crowded around my Tiger and the very next day all my friends and family learnt the great news – providing of course they read the *Guardian*, and I couldn't think of one who did. As it happened the Press photo which showed me grinning inanely over the sill of the cockpit at Bev with his Tiger Tim helmet on was the last of that occasion to reach an eager public. That evening the National Press went on strike.

There were two more rounds which I didn't win, not surprisingly since the handicappers, peeved at letting me slip through their fingers, clobbered me. Nothing though could detract from my fun. And I flew lower, I think, than anyone else. I went through gates and gaps in trees having a whale of a time. In my eyes I was the cat's whiskers. I loved every minute of every race. My every moment between races I spent either polishing my Tiger or trying one of a dozen different schemes I'd watched others do.

Someone said: "Put lots of air in your tyres; you get off quicker!"

I did so.

Another said: "Have you changed your plugs for a hard set?"

"What is a 'hard set'?" I asked.

"I don't know, but you can get a set fitted free – go over and ask them at the Lodge tent."

I asked and I got.

"What oil have you got in?" asked another lunatic.

"The usual," I said.

"Get it out quick! Esso have some real thin stuff. It's alright," he assured me when my face starred to show concern, "they'll flush out the old and put in the new all for nothing."

I tried that too. In fact everything was 'on the house.' The Shell tent was home to all of us with constant food and drink the whole weekend – even to those of us who were using free Esso products. My conscience wasn't that troubled.

At the Dunlop Caravan – I'd gone there to ask advice and get my tyres pumped up – I ran into my old Commanding Officer, Sqdn. Ldr. 'Wispy'

Turner. It was a great reunion and we repaired to the Shell tent to celebrate. Wispy had with him Dunlop's Chief Instructor who was dying to take a look at the circuit. I immediately agreed to take him, delighted to have an important chief instructor as my passenger.

I swept him away and into the Tiger. He was obviously unfamiliar on type for he tried to get into my cockpit and got all confused with the harness. Used to modern aircraft, I thought, and helped him. He even found the helmet a bit strange but I readily understood. Who flew these days in an open cockpit? I was so at peace with the world I'd have forgiven anyone. We flew off.

The course was now well-known to me, so I concentrated on impressing my passenger as to my flying ability. I did all the things thinking pilots do when they have another pilot at their mercy. I kept my top needle dead centre, my every turn was tight, full of 'g,' low and no climbing, and since I didn't have to worry as I would with a non-pilot I got even lower than before – whistling the wheels through the daisies and taking every short cut I could find. It was the most exhilarating trip I'd made to date. I was bubbling with joy when we taxied in and stopped.

My passenger sat low in his cockpit not moving. I leant in and clapped him on the shoulder.

"Like it?"

He didn't answer at once, he just sat there like a sack of potatoes.

"No," he whispered at length.

Wispy and I helped him out.

"Wispy," I said in a hoarse whisper: "what's the matter?"

"I don't know," replied Wispy irritably, "but he looks frightened to me!"

"A chief flying instructor?" I queried incredulously.

"Chief *driving* instructor," corrected Wispy.

I was getting on in years, at least that's how my family saw me, and I wasn't married – another black mark. I was still with Marks and Spencer and getting on fine as the Assistant Manager at their Tooting branch, but right at the back of my mind was the persistent thought that I'd be posted out of London to some better position, and that such a move would put in jeopardy both my flying and the fun of being a batchelor in London.

In that I had it made. To start with I had a great big flat all to myself in Putney High Street. It was a vast rambling establishment over Richard Henry's the hairdresser – alas, now no longer there. For a fiver a week I had all the hot water I could use, the salon's washing machine and driers in the basement which kept me in clean clothing, and a furnished pad that, although not luxurious, sported no less than three bedrooms, boxroom, sitting room and kitchen, and a passageway so long it was alternatively a shooting range or a bow & arrow gallery. I was always addicted to guns. The current weapons were air gun and air pistol, a bow and a quiver full of tatty arrows. I had the use of the garage, which was included in the fiver, and a succession of girls to help cook and so on, one of whom I was very fond of. She was a bit of a blue-stocking, Cheltenham, titled parents and perfect company.

I'd gone to Elizabeth's parents' flat one evening for dinner. Her father, a retired Air Chief Marshal, was a most charming man and an excellent listener, which was fine for me, an inveterate talker. On this occasion I was burning up with a crusade. Croydon's days were now officially numbered, a politician named Watkinson had said so, and I wanted everybody to rally to the cause to keep it open. I had already done all the things that one does do. I had written to my MP – a fat lot of good that did – and to the newspapers – ditto. And so that evening I made my target the one remaining organisation I had not started on, the Air League of the British Empire. In heated words I roundly condemned that patriotic piece of the Establishment for its failure to stand up and defend light aviation's need for such a historic place. My host listened attentively and made what I thought was a game and – for one who could have known little of the facts – a remarkably knowledgeable response, he added kindly: "You know, I do appreciate your point, but also that of the Air League; in fact I'm its Chairman."

At an opportune moment I hissed to his daughter: "You might have told me!

"You didn't ask," she replied sweetly.

TO PARIS BY LAWN MOWER

CROYDON AIRPORT

Whatever you may have heard on the radio or what you may have read in the newspapers it may be categorically stated that at the time of writing (summer '59) the Croydon Branch of the Tiger Club is still operating at Croydon Airport and hopes to do so for as long as flying is permitted from the site. It is quite true that all "pleasure" and instructional flying has now been banned there, but as the Tiger Club normally teaches no-one to fly and exists for the purpose of giving displays it does not come under the present ban, all its flights being of a business nature.

Flying rates in 1959 went up for the first time, although by today's standards they were still extraordinary low. For the first time – and the last – a differential was allowed between Full and Associate Membership. Lucky Full members now were asked to pay £6.25 an hour for the Jodel, which was then top of the range. Down 25p for the Jackaroo, £5.75 for the DH Hornet, and the Tiger came in at a round £5.50. It still only cost £1.50 to fly the Turbulent. Associate Members paid 50p an hour extra.

Duty flying remained at £1.50 and, since most of our flying was duty rate anyway, no one worried too much. The Club finances were decidedly thin. Every now and then Norman would write a Chairman's letter urging either prompt payment or more utilization in order to keep head-above-water. The Club was, I suspect, never to pay its way, and we the members were far too busy flying to pay much attention. I expect, if we thought about it at all, we could only have felt reassured by the knowledge that the Boss was then the head of a vast printing business, Samuel Jones, in those days very much a household name with their famous Butterfly brand on just about everything that one could write or stick on.

Not all our races were circuit bound, and it certainly wasn't the King's Cup that people wanted to know about in July '59. For there was another race just a week after the Nationals that had all of Britain on their toes with excitement. The Press Radio and the TV gave the Blériot Anniversary Race a degree of coverage that set new records.

The *Daily Mail* had offered £10,000 to the winner of the fastest time between London and Paris. It was later labelled the Race of the Century. It was. It must have been. The efforts of the challengers between the city centres were daring, sometimes funny, and often dramatic, and caught the imagination of the World. Their split-second adventures made headlines everywhere. The tense battles between crack service teams using jet fighters, helicopters and powerful motorcycles was followed by millions.

Somewhere in all this fuss and tension were several Tiger Club pilots. Quite what they did, and how they did it, is now hazy in my mind. I recall for instance that Norman flew a Turbulent. So did Joan Short. Jon Hutchinson flew a Proctor, but took a tiny motor scooter along with him and the journey took just under three hours. He said it only cost him £2. But I thought at the time, if you believed that you'd believe anything. Others were Ian Scott Hill, 'Mac' McAully and Ken O'Rourke. I know Janet Ferguson borrowed a cycle to finish the course, and I know beyond any shadow of doubt that I was a member of a team that went by lawnmower. Clem Pike, who was then CFI for de Havilland's at Hatfield and a Tiger Club member, phoned Bish and asked him if there was a member willing to fly in the coming Race. That's how I got in on the act. Hugh Tansley, who was then studying at the Hatfield Technical College, had got the sponsorship of Ransomes, the lawnmower people, with the offer of mowers for transport at each end of the course. I would fly Hugh over the Channel in the oldest Tiger 'CDC and so connect the two.

It took nearly four bone-shaking hours to trundle the motorised lawnmower from Marble Arch down to Croydon. Once there everyone seemed to be in the grip of a madness in their haste to get us airborne in the shortest possible time. We cleared Lympne down in Kent in an atmosphere of pure panic. A flashing green light from the tower urged me down ahead of a circling DC-3 scheduled flight which they held up above. A line of helpers led me at a fast taxying pace right up to the pumps, where Customs men were waiting to run with me to clear formalities. In vain did I plead that there wasn't any real hurry. They only knew we were in The Race, and no one was ever going to say that the boys at Lympne weren't helpful. We were airborne in minutes. It was unreal.

Over at Toussus, a small airfield near Paris, there was a huge contingent awaiting us along with a fresh lawnmower. We made the Arc de Triomphe in the remarkable total time of 10 hours 44 minutes. Crowds had lined the streets to cheer our slow, oh so slow, cavalcade of cars escorting one tired and collapsing mower averaging some 3½ mph. No one had considered the effect of the French *pavé*. Blériot undoubtedly crossed the Channel first fifty years earlier, and in doing so went a darn sight faster than many of us, but I bet he didn't enjoy it half as much.

A PARTY, RUM AND A LETTER FROM BISH

An idea was born that year that was later to transform the public image of the Club. It came suddenly to me to propose it at a very big and happy party I had given Sue Burges on her homecoming after ages in one hospital after another. Norman Jones had been preaching the need for new display ideas and new blood for ages. Whilst none of us liked the phrase "new blood" too much we did begin to hunt about for new acts. Whilst I was later to regret the impulsive idea, the scheme in the heady atmosphere of a party seemed fantastic. It was no less than "someone should stand up on top of a Tiger Moth in flight." Nor was I allowed to forget the project, but there was to be a longish period of beaurocratic humming and haahing before the off, but more of that later.

In the meantime the party took precedence. I had with a cheerful abandon invited the entire Tiger Club. All a hundred and ten of them. At the last count before all hell broke loose I'd got to over ninety. "Bring a bottle," I'd said, but just in case I had prepared a very special punch indeed. Some months earlier a friend had told me of a homemade rum that could be very potent. All I had to do, I was told, was to find a huge melon, cut off the top, scoop out the mush in the centre, fill with demerara sugar, replace the top and suspend in a dark spot for a couple of months. I did as I was told and put the lot under the stairs hanging in a net bag and promptly forgot about it. Perhaps its rediscovery some months later prompted the party, who knows, but the rum proved devastating.

I recall it needed only the slightest pressure on the melon's underside to release a torrent of richly coloured strong smelling "rum." I carefully decanted the stuff and in my innocence – I was completely teetotal –

48

thought it would form the basis for a punch. I spiced it with odd amounts of gin and whisky and anything else I could find to put in and, when all the normal drink had nearly gone, introduced the punch, thinking everyone would be so merry by then they'd never notice it. It was a great success for at least two. John Blake and the late Harry Cooper especially seemed to thrive on it. They were still holding the table up the next morning – from underneath.

Before 1959 was allowed to depart Bish wrote one of his best letters. His pride in the Club knew no bounds and it is only with hindsight that his organising genius and love of his task is really apparent. I can't recall at the time that he made anything of his dedication, but that he had the Club on his mind every waking hour is obvious now. His quiet drive and ever-positive presence was truly instrumental in welding this remarkable Club in its formative years, as indeed examination of the early documents show. Nor do I think the teamwork between the Founder, Norman Jones, and his henchman Bish has ever been recognised. Time had no meaning for either man. I know for a fact that Norman would ring Bish very early every weekend morning to plan the day. Nor was Norman, of whom we all stood in awe, adverse to phoning others at the same hour. I'd be dragged from my sleep around seven by the Boss, stifling a groan as I immediately prepared to jump to it at that unearthly hour. Bish wrote:

" . . . In the first paragraph of this letter I mentioned that the Club now boasted a membership of over 110, which is true enough, but I must now add that out of this number only a faithful couple of dozen or so have taken part in the events mentioned above. To these members I send the committee's congratulations and warmest thanks for all they have done on behalf of the Tiger Club and express the hope that they will be with us for many more seasons. And in doing this, I must not forget our "producer" Jack Piercy, our business manager "Bill" Chesson, and the one and only "Fitz" and his maintenance staff at Rollasons, without whose help we should find it far more difficult to do our shows.

Thank you again one and all.

This brings me to the reason of this letter. One of the primary aims of the Tiger Club is, as your booklet says, "To provide its members with good sporting flying at the *lowest possible cost!*" The only way we can do this is to make more money at our displays, and the only way that we can make more money at our displays is to have more of our 110 plus members taking part in them! BUT, and this is a big 'but,' display pilots are not made in a day and only by constant practice can one become proficient in this art. Likewise, if the same few take part each time, they tend to get stale; new ideas for display items are not forthcoming and towards the end of their season it becomes a little hard on the pocket!

Presumably you have joined the Tiger Club so that you can help to foster its success, and I sincerely hope that during the coming winter, I shall be seeing *you* making a start – if you have not already done so – at getting yourself in trim for 1960. To this end we are organising a "get-together" at Redhill Aerodrome during the weekend of October 24/25th next and we shall look forward to seeing all of you who are interested in helping the Tiger Club forge ahead during 1960 at this meeting. This is not to be a flying meeting as such – although we hope that there will be plenty on both days – but a meeting in which ideas may be exchanged on the best way to make a success of things during next summer. We shall be glad to get your ideas and from the response we get at this meeting we shall be able to judge who we have keen enough for us to coach for next year.

By this date we should be safely settled down in our new home at Redhill, and we shall be pleased to see you on Saturday from midday onwards – *and* on Sunday from 10 a.m.

To sum up, you have seen what the Tiger Club stands for and has done in 1959, and you have been told what we hope to do in 1960. Now, we want to know that we have members' full support for the future, and from those of you who come to Redhill, we shall learn who it will be giving us that support.

Although this letter comes to you via duplicator, I sincerely hope that you will take it as sent to you personally. I only wish that it were possible for me to write to all individually, but with a growing membership which is now over 110 this is manifestly impossible, so I hope that you will take the will for the deed.

Before I get down to the real reason for my writing I should like to let you know something of what the Tiger Club has done during the past few months. In fact, the Club has had a very successful season indeed, one which has noticeably increased our prestige in the light aeroplane world. We have given five full-scale displays – and by "full scale" I mean displays for which the general public has paid to come and see – these consisting of formation-flying, aerobatics, flour bombing, balloon-bursting, Turbulent racing, parachute dropping, aircraft demonstrations, pattern flying and, indeed, all the fun of the (f)air! Our *pièce de resistance* came on August Bank Holiday when we put on a 45-minute display for the Independent Television Authority which was voted "the tops" by all who saw it, "live" or on their screens. In addition to the above our members have ranged far and wide in their quest to enliven shows run by other organisations, and during the season they have been seen at Woburn Abbey, Lasham, Stapleford Tawney, Reading (two shows), Leavesden, Skegness, Barton, Elstree (again two shows), Exeter and Little Snoring.

In the spring of this year an aerobatic practice camp was held at Sywell, Northants where much good work was carried out, the results of which were patently obvious in the British Lockheed International Aerobatic Competition when this was held at Baginton in July last. No less than eight of the nine British competitors were Tiger Club members, one of these, Colin Labouchere, gaining a joint sixth place in the contest. In addition, M. Leon Biancotto, ·1958 winner, chose one of our specially adapted Tiger Moths as his mount for this year, gaining fourth place in the competition. On the following day we held our own Voltige competition at Sywell which was won by John Severne.

Fifteen of our members took part in the National Air Races, winning several hundreds of pounds in prize money, Dennis Hartas, flying G-ADNB, winning the Tiger Moth Trophy Race, whilst Beverley Snook won the prize for the fastest time recorded during the heats. He flew *The Archbishop* G-ANZZ.

On top of all this, there has been quite a lot of touring abroad both in Hornet Moths and Turbulent aircraft . . .

There was an agreement about prize monies. It was always shared down the middle with the Club. It was based on the not unreasonable concept that racing at full throttle drank extra petrol, and the post-racing rigging could cost a pretty penny too. Besides, the Club needed the money. We shared happily. 1959 had been a good year but it was the move to Redhill early in 1960 that was the impetus the Club needed.

TOP: Margo McKellar, Bish, Norman Jones and a delighted Peter Vanneck. Occasion: the National Air Races at Coventry in July 1957. Presumably that is the *News Chronicle* Trophy Peter won, although it is a very modest thing.

BOTTOM: Bish with a real Pot – the Basil Monk Trophy – in 1957. Venue believed Baginton. The photo comes from Bish's personal collection.

TOP: A wonderfully rare shot of Croydon Airport circa 1956/57. Over seventy Tigers are outside the Rollason hangar. Thank are due to Mavis Harriott for this photo.
BOTTOM: Sue Burges after parachute descent probably late summer '58. The Turb, I suspect 'PLZ, has airflow wool tufts around the cockpit. Venue was Sywell and the 2CV belonged to the author.

TOP: Just visible on the left is Norman Jones, then Tony Oldham clinging to 'OXS's strut. Nearest the camera are, L. to R.: Bish, Maurice Imray and John Blake. Probably it was Sandown on Easter Monday 1957 and at the Tiger Club's second meeting.
BOTTOM: An early formation in 1957. Includes G-ANSH, G-AOAA, G-AODR, and possibly G-ANLB and G-ANZZ.

TOP: Norman Jones, Margo McKellar, David Phillips, Mavis Harriott, Clive Compton, Bish, Mike O'Dell, 'Fitz' Fitzmaurice, Ken Smith and Bev Snook. Venue uncertain, but probably Fairoaks.
BOTTOM: Sandown in 1957. 'OAA is still a cooking Tiger. Bish is getting out of 'NSH, Dennis Hartas is coming round the tail. Norman looks on.

TOP: Evocative shot of a Tiger line-up outside Rollason's hangar at Croydon early in 1957. 'OBO still has its blind flying hood in place.
BOTTOM: Croydon Airport in the autumn of 1958. Our first Jodel, the 117 'POZ, is to the left of the picture. Some eight Tigers sit outside Rollason's hangar.

TOP: A youthful Clive Elton sits in the latest Turbulent from the Rollason stable at Croydon in the summer of '59. 'PNZ went on to win the King's Cup the following year. BOTTOM: 'CDC at Croydon at the start of its cross-Channel dash during the Blériot race in the summer of '59. Pilot, the author, with Hugh Tansley getting into the front cockpit, still shaking after his 4-hour lawnmower ride from Marble Arch.

TOP: A wonderful shot of Bish in his beloved *Bishop* 'PDZ. Sadly Elwyn McAully lost his life in her shortly after this photo was taken.
BOTTOM: Tiger 'PRA, the *Sue Burges*, glider-towing at Redhill in February 1960. The hefty handle alongside the cockpit and the square hole in the lower starboard wing for parachuting are just visible. Behind 'PRA is the Imperial College glider.

TOP: A lovely air-to-air of the Taxi-Tiger out of Croydon. The enclosed front cockpit can clearly be seen.
BOTTOM: An historic occasion for Tiger lovers was this, the very first meeting of the Tiger Club, at Fairoaks on March 3rd 1957 to celebrate the Tiger's 25th year of certification. 15 of the 20 Tigers that came along are visible in this picture.

1960

REDHILL, LONDON TO CARDIFF AND THE KING'S CUP

Croydon closed to flying late that autumn of '59, although the main Rollason team carried on there; a small detachment made the initial move to Redhill and the task was accomplished with the minimum of fuss. And so began the game for the last to land at Croydon. At the last count the game was still open in 1988. But more of that later . . .

The year 1960 was really the beginning of the Tiger Club as we know it today. By the spring we had taken Redhill airfield – then quite deserted – to our hearts. After the confines and relative officialdom of Croydon, the freedom of this unspoiled part of Surrey was like a breath of fresh air. Nostalgia for Croydon twenty odd years later is all very well, but at the time we were more aware of encroaching housing, long walks to clear air traffic and no Clubroom to congregate in.

The hangar, as today, housed us all. The upstairs Clubroom was decorated and furnished by the members amid much laughter and inept painting. Some of the original furniture was still to be seen 25 years later. If it was old and thrown out in 1959 its eventual state in the 1980s was something to behold. Yet it was cherished and enjoyed and even in its shabbiness had a dignity all its own.

Unlike any other flying club, probably the world over, the Club premises have always been "dry." Only once in our history did we ever consider a modest bar, and that was in early 1960 when Norman took over the big first-floor room in the control tower. It was really two rooms, one very small and in which we initially stocked crates of bottled beer in a sort of pilot scheme for a bar, but the drink side or it petered out and was eventually replaced by the inevitable kettle for endless cups of tea. The big room, though, was never used very much; it saw the odd film show and party, and the Club finally relinquished the tenancy in favour of the togetherness in the hangar. We have remained a "dry" Club ever since.

The solitary Newsletter that follows – the title was only used once – was undoubtedly the forerunner of the *Tiger Rag*. Bish had been under a lot of pressure during the summer of 1960 and I had offered to do some writing for him. I thought the word 'Bulletin' a bit formal so changed it. Bish remained Editor and his cryptic asides still delight. It is reproduced in full – call it personal nostalgia if you like – but the events portrayed had a *joie de vivre* all their own. By the way the London-Cardiff Race was a qualifier for the Big One – the King's Cup – later in the year.

LONDON-CARDIFF RACE NEWSLETTER, MIDSUMMER 1960

June opened in a blaze of sunshine and for the Club the beginning of the National Air Races. What a time to hold air races, smack over the Whitsun weekend, but hold it they did and eighteen of us booked in at White Waltham on the Thursday, nearly a day and a half before the race. Tiger Club members are nothing if not adaptable and in the absence of any refreshment facilities – yes, *any* – cars were commandeered to find local pubs for food. This lack of welcome at White Waltham showed the local Club up badly. Nearly forty aircraft had reported as directed by 1400 hrs and crews and passengers had to fend for themselves. One of the funnier sights that Thursday was half a dozen of our pilots led by the redoubtable Bish hitch-hiking back to the airfield. Still, the sun shone, and tempers were good.

Back on the Friday and airborne for Cardiff that evening. The visibility was good, at least as far as the Bristol Channnel, and at first the race seemed to be a procession. *The Deacon* spent its time following Bev Snook in *The Archbishop* who in turn was gradually overhauling Jack Piercy in his Hornet. It was as though the three of us were suspended in mid-air, and it wasn't until Dennis Hartas and Sue Burges overtook us in the Jodel, to the accompaniment of every conceivable kind of gesture, that the spirit of the race took over.

I don't think anyone found the Weston turning point difficult, for by the time we all arrived, aircraft were appearing from all over the place and a Tiger was actually seen turning towards North Devon. I remember grinning to myself and murmuring "John Donald." At the pylon "GB" (Golding Barrett) was waving furiously at us as we tore through the sky above his head. We later learned he wasn't pointing the way to Cardiff but voicelessly pleading to mind the HT cables no one had told us about. Several missed them by a matter of feet, Norman being the lowest. Poor Janet Ferguson didn't make the pylon, she force-landed just south of Bristol. After the race several of us tried to talk the Rescue Service chopper into popping over and picking her up. Dennis was briefed to take the Jodel over to collect her, but in the end Janet made her own way home.

The welcome at Cardiff was in complete contrast to that at White Waltham. The Glamorgan Club had laid on food and a coach to the Park Hotel, where spirits improved after dinner to such an extent that an imprompu party in the lounge brought the Management and a glittering chandelier down. One of our members paid up, but whether or not with a laugh wasn't recorded, anyway this recorder was himself trying to find a couple of taxis for the rest to tour Tiger Bay – or was it the following night? It was that sort of stay.

Race positions are now old meat. Dennis Hartas, John Severne, Clive Francis, Bish and Bev finished high up in their respective classes and earned themselves and the Club some prize monies, albeit there wasn't much going anyway. *(Our contributor seems too shy to mention the fact that he too qualified both for the prize money and the King's Cup race – Ed.)*

Most of us returned to Redhill on the Sunday. That was a mistake, it would have been better to have returned the previous evening. From all accounts, and believe me there were many, it was a low delight from the beginning to the end. Only poor Joan Short was eventually left at Cardiff and helpless with frustration – *Tallulah*, her Turbulent, just wouldn't start.

WHITE WALTHAM DISPLAY (Whit Monday)

Bill Chesson's idea of a display, at least as portrayed on his programme, has to be seen to be believed. There's a character hanging from a primitive parachute and absolutely surrounded by cavorting planes, plus a few bombs. Wren in the *Aeroplane* was later to regret not seeing such an incredible display. Lunchtime and no food ready for us. *(There was if he'd only troubled to look! – Ed.)* We all clambered into cars and went looking for a likely pub. At a guess I'd say Barry Griffith's car held the most. In the meantime a flock of Turbulents sallied forth to let the local population know of our presence, their gay colouring causing quite a bit of comment. Which reminds me of Clive Francis determinedly seeking some fluorescent paint back at Cardiff. 'PZZ proud in its coat of green blended far too well for safety's sake at low level, especially as a Prentice with four sets of eyes didn't see him at a distance of ten feet!

The actual display went well. The Turbs with James Baring, Clive Elton, John Severne and Sam d'Arcy·up enjoyed themselves hugely strafing certain falling paper rolls after doing some of the best formation seen yet. Flour bombing by the girls of the WJAC, and they'll forgive me for saying this, was sedately done. One bombing run in a Tiger began over Maidenhead! I think the crowd of several thousand found our male bombing a little later on more exciting. Jack Piercy, Director of Operations from Barry's open car, must have been well pleased with himself and timing was well adhered to. *(As usual – Ed.)* Oh yes, and Angela his lovely daughter did much to enhance the control point. Confess it I must, the tied together broke, the first time in the air for over two years..

MID-JUNE – ONE FOR THE BOOK

It's a choice line indeed. Barry Griffiths, returning one evening in company with James Baring from Woburn way, smelt burning and at the same time thought that he experienced a loss of power. With all sincerity he later recalled his instinctive action in the event of fire:

1. I immediately reached for my jacket pocket to check pipe was out.
2. Selected suitable field.

Incidentally the smell of burning came from the brickworks he was flying over, so in the end all was well.

The reference to the burning smell was a well-known local phenomenon. If the wind was in the right direction you could smell the London Brick Works miles away – as a navigational aid it had, and probably still has, few peers. An even more pungent one that we got to know well spent its time over Wandsworth in South West London. I can remember an early journey with Bish and Fitz, when, at a thousand feet in the Club's Jackaroo (flying over London non-radio in those days presented no problems) we first encountered a most familiar aroma. It was uncannily like Brand's HP Sauce. And so it turned out to be, for we were smack over their factory. All we needed to complete the meal was the sausage and chips.

JULY – AND THE KING'S CUP

The King's Cup was again held at Baginton. No less than ten Tiger Club members qualified. Surely the highest one-Club entry ever? Favourite to win was John Severne, and Bill Bailey's two-week old grin meant something to the knowing. Coventry weather was what was expected – alternate rain and sunshine. Enough has already been written about the race, but what of the personalities? Well there was Clive Elton in Tiger 'RAZ worrying himself over apparently large oil consumption – which in the race was to cost him power loss. Another worrier was yours truly, every time the Lockheed fellows clambered into 'OAA to cavort . . . one grows to care for one's mount. Bish and Sue Burges had teamed up again in 'CDC. Bev Snook was in 'OAA's rival 'NZZ, David Phillips flew solo in Pat Garland's Linnet, and of course John and Clive were Turbulent-mounted. The circuit wasn't the easiest and one pylon was nicely hidden in a clump of trees. Once again "GB" guarded a turning point and since it was the last before the aerodrome it got a considerable amount of attention on the final lap. Apart from the way-in-front Turbs the rest of the field went through in 40 seconds! Pat Peacocke, Sally and Ian Trethewey helped out and were they welcome – ask "GB."

Off the airfield spirits were as high as ever – the night before the race was the best. For instance seventeen of the gang invaded a Chinese restaurant *en masse.* To the consternation of the management, tables were pushed together, chopsticks were called for and seventeen prepared to eat and enjoy themselves. Traditional Chinese calm soon began to wilt under the pressure and delightful panic sent in. Bev's choice Indian seems to go down just as well in a far eastern setting. Heaven knows where all the energy came from, but several were later reported drilling outside Pat Garland's somewhat respectable hotel in the early hours.

I wonder if it was generally realised that the Tiger Club scooped the first four places? Apart from collecting the prize of prizes, John Severne, resplendent in his daughter's riding cap, also collared the Air Racing Championship. Clive Francis was second, followed by Bill Bailey and A.J. Spiller. From all accounts Charles Gardner in his TV commentary only mentioned the Tiger Club . . .

HRH, JOHN SEVERNE, THE LOCKHEED AND FAIR OAKS

John Severne was an equerry to the Duke of Edinburgh, in whose name the winning Turbulent had been entered, so his win was royally applauded. HRH had honoured the Tiger Club the year before by becoming a member and now he offered to fly with us. The photograph of HRH jammed into the winning single-seat Turbulent 'PNZ at White Waltham in the October was proof enough that HRH really did fly that day and flew well. What isn't generally known was that the little VW engine, which had been hotted up by Derringtons of Kingston for the races, failed on the subsequent flight.

It's idle to speculate all these years later, but at the time we fervently thanked the gods above that the engine didn't let HRH down, but instead put the wind up an unknown Tiger Club pilot who, glad to say, got it down in one piece. There is a postscript which isn't without a gentle irony. John wound up an Air Marshal and Captain of the Queen's Flight. I don't think we ever told John of his Boss's near miss; and it's a bit late now.

THE LOCKHEED EVENT

Of the five British competitors four were Club members. John Ayres led our team consisting of Charles Boddington, Mike Popoff and Peter Phillips. In the gently biased and honestly-held opinion of those of us who watched their aerobatics, the final could well have held them. The Tiger has never been displayed so superbly. The effortless flight of the Czech Zlin though was food for thought; given a like mount the finals would have been all British – I swear it.

After the big race, and 111 Squadron, a somewhat impromptu display followed which fell into a successful pattern, giving the crowd a best-ever and memorable show. Notable was Peter Phillips in *The Archbishop*; his slow rolls were a joy to watch and his inverted circuit ended an infectiously happy performance and brought the crowd to its feet with applause. Bish, Clive

Elton and Dennis Hartas in an immaculate tied-together, Clive Francis' and John Ayres' dogfight in their Turbs and a polished demonstration of the Linnet really gave this audience its money's worth. Then home to Redhill in heavy rain via the M1.

This was Norman's day, and he was entitled to feel proud. These major awards put the Turbulents really on the map. His Tiger Club was the talk of the day.

HANGAR TALK: It is widely rumoured around that the upper Tower room will soon be ours. Norman has suggested that it be used as a table-tennis room. Whilst on the subject of the Club rooms there's still plenty of decorating to do – sometime – and volunteers for paint slapping are aways welcome . . . obviously a subject for a rainy day. See a member of the House Committee if you feel like helping. H.C.? Its members are Margo MacKellar, Jack Piercy and Lewis Benjamin.

Sue Burges has two reasons to feel good with life. She has just passed her PPL tests and, secondly, after a short "op" in September she will again be as right as rain; yes, and cleared to jump.

Bish happily tells a true story of the pilot, who having watched him check a new member out recently, suggested that it wouldn't be a bad idea if long-established members got the odd check; in fact, he continued, he'd willingly submit himself to a test. With mounting enthusiasm this veteran of many years' flying taxied straightly and rapidly to take-off, out of wind, having got little if any of his "vitals" check in order. Cheerfully he gained height on his turns, hesitantly spun and stalled and he didn't look around once. He joined the circuit at the wrong height and in the wrong manner, throttled back downwind and got in nicely, still out of wind.

A BRICKBAT to the members who leave their dirty cups to the next visitors to enter the Clubroom and a big BOUQUET to Margo who regularly brings the cake and tea we get through at the weekend, and who in a sure feminine manner enhances the place with exotic potted plants.

FAIR OAKS – 31ST JULY

Seventeen aircraft stood smartly in line outside the Tiger Club hangar at Redhill early on the Sunday morning. It was a proud display, the weather was warm and sunny and we were all set for Fair Oaks, except perhaps Dennis Hartas, whose car had broken down on him.

Inevitably, or so it always seems when we give a display, the sky darkened threateningly on arrival at Fair Oaks and rain spattered ominously from the skirts of some magnificent cu nim. Over nearby Guildford sat a self-contained humdinger of a storm complete with lightning.

John Severne was on the marshalling line and taking over from Jack Piercy who was away fishing somewhere. John had obviously anticipated fine weather; he hadn't a coat and had further tempted fate by wearing a smart suit. He soon got wet. Over in the public enclosure, marquees and odd shaped tents were springing up, urgently being pulled into shape by whole families, one of whom would look up at the sky every now and then and get on with the job in hand with renewed enthusiasm. It was to one such haven that Bill Chesson led the pilots and where we were encouraged to eat all we wished – and all 'on the house.' But oh that it had been more than soft dull sandwiches and ersatz orange squash! It's not done to peer at gift horses and all that, but wouldn't it be fine – just once – to have a decent meal at one of these displays.

One by one, around 2.30, the aircraft took off towards Guildford, the rallying point for the initial Tiger "T" opening formation. This time 250 feet separation between types of aircraft was the order of the day – a wise move, for joining up can sometimes be quite a thing. Types? Well there was the Tiger Formation, a cluster of Turbs and a threesome of Jodel D.117, Mousquetaire and Garland Linnet. At 3 sharp three tidy formations swept over Fair Oaks. The crowd by now had swelled considerably, at a guess there were seven thousand, so something like fourteen thousand eyes constantly swivelling from black clouds to Mike Popoff who opened with some smooth aerobatics. Mike's landing run hadn't finished when three Tigers took off with the first three parachutists of the British Parachute Club in a loose gaggle and staggered to 1,500 ft. Pilots: Dennis Hartas, Clive Elton and self. This was the first of three frantic climbs for each aircraft. Three drops in ten minutes! Heaven knows what happened to the jumpers when they hit the airfield. We were later told of a contest to capture a flag or something – all we knew was that when we tried to lob in to take the next three up, the field was alive with running figures. It wouldn't have been so bad if they had all been running in the same direction. Full marks to the joyriding Austers – what brave men. How they managed to continue in such an imperturbable manner is beyond me. I should think they must have been beyond caring . . . or nearly petrified. The bombers disguised as Tigers had each five bombs to drop. "Let's do two steep dive-ins, then a couple at low level and finish up with another dive!" We did. In a tail chase of four – and all crewed up with clued-up bombardiers – we tried to plaster Bill Chesson who was only armed with a cricket bat; for all the damage we did he might have just as well had a snooze. But those Auster pilots, they deserved a VC apiece. And we weren't even trying for 'em.

The threateningly western sky grew darker, and against this awesome towering backdrop the tiny Turbs bucked in unison, ably led by Clive

Francis. As usual they put up a fine show, and their formation was as tight as ever. The rain fell gently at first as the balloon-bursters got under way. By the time the second Tiger was airborne, weaving and turning in the rising wind, the audience, already restless, began to seek shelter, slowly at first and then suddenly with a rush as the heavens opened.

For about half an hour the rain kept everyone clustered wet and miserable under cover and there we watched awhile the lonely, forlorn aircraft as they tugged at their pickets, and at least one pilot bemoaned a mislaid cockpit cover.

The passing storm left delightfully smooth air in its wake, just right for the tied-together beautifully led by Bish. Peter Phillips in 'NZZ benefited too, for his aerobatics were a delight to watch. Once again the controversial question of height arose – whether to be high and very safe but to do little for the paying public, or to come down to greet them, as he did and how they welcomed him, and rely on sheer competence and a dash of calculated risk to carry him through. *(All very nice but from now on the crowd has got to be satisfied with a 500ft minimum – Ed.)*

Then there were demonstrations of the Jackaroo and the Linnet, with Bish and David Phillips up, the two Jodels, the smaller one with Margo in control and Fitzmaurice in the new big one. If Fitz wore a grin on take-off it was nothing to the grin he sported on his return from paradise. He was like a cat with too much milk and not a little lipstick!

The combination of Mike Reilly, Dennis Hartas and David Phillips shook the crowd in the "instructor and pupil" act. Mike's superb drop from 'CDC and Dennis's slow spin to apparent destruction thrilled them all. Someone in the crowd, and right among the little boys, reported sounds like: "It's a swizz . . . it didn't really crash" and *real* unhappiness that there hadn't been a glorious prang. Whilst later Dennis, ever the perfectionist, bemoaned the lack of valleys to nip into and so disappear, spare a thought for Mike rolled up uncomfortably in the front cockpit and having to endure crazy flying under the cover!

What could surely be one of the most exciting items in our displays is the Turbulent race, yet it never really satisfies. Even the sight of Clive E. whipping his mount to go faster could hardly have convinced the punters that his gee gee hadn't been got at. The knowing of course could see he was pulling his mount! At one stage it nearly fell out of the sky. Why not a handicap race? The potential of each Turbulent is known pretty well, and handicap times could be published in the programme – and bingo – all the excitement of the race for competitor and spectator alike. Conspirators were Norman, Jon Hutchinson, Barry Griffiths, Peter Phillips and James Baring.

The finals of the parachute contest from a height of about 3,000 ft brought the display to a successful end. Among the flying visitors were the *Flight* Gemini, Sheila (soon to be a member) Scott's Jackaroo *Myth* and the Rollason Flying Group's all-black Tiger. Incidentally this Redhill-based machine must surely be the best kept Tiger ever; even the brass fuel feed from the tank is highly polished.

On a near miss, 6 miles and 3,000 ft separation: "I didn't see him but I could hear him" – a female passenger in a Tiger.

Overheard in the Clubroom: "I'll tell you this. I would rather go out by air than fly there."

CHARACTERS: REILLY AND BARRY AND JAMES

This was the first time we'd used the new Jodel 140, which had a very pointed fin and rudder. The modified and current Club model came over six years later. It was without question the most aerodynamically efficient aircraft of its day, and even now its performance would take some beating. It could with ease carry its own weight. In real terms that meant five occupants, some luggage and full tanks, cruise at 140 mph, and offer a range of 800 miles. All on seven gallons an hour. I can remember carrying nine souls on one effortless journey to a display at Panshanger, a grass airfield north of London. There were five adults, three small children on laps and a dog! It remains one of the Club's most popular aircraft.

I don't think anyone was ever fully aware of the late Mike Reilly's great skill and bravery, nor the difficulty he had in extracting himself from the front seat of the Tiger during one of his displays. The ploy was to leave one corner fastener of the fabric cockpit cover loose, and it was through this small hole that Mike at a given signal squeezed his hand to gradually undo the rest and to withdraw the cover, and all this whilst Dennis Hartas was turning 'CDC inside out. It was at Fair Oaks a year later, I think, that Mike embellished his act. His exit was never higher than 1,200 feet, but the first time I saw the new act I stood speechless although I knew what was going to happen. He got out, deployed a 'chute which he deliberately candled, discarded it, and then opened a reserve which scarcely had time to fully develop when Mike hit the ground in a cloud of dust. He lay still for a moment, got up, shook himself, and then went about gathering his 'chute. The fall would have broken bones in a lesser man. The trust that Mike had in his pilot was complete and always justified. Dennis had to position exactly, for Mike's drop was completely blind. It's an act that was alarmingly unique and I'm not sure I'd want to see it again. Nerves can only stand so much.

The mid-June 'one for the book' snippet was only part of the story. Barry Griffiths had actually been returning from Passenham Manor which was James Baring's mother's home. I know James will forgive me a brief description of that visit.

"Come back for the weekend," James had said. So I got into a single-seat Tiger, and Barry, who had also been invited, got into a Turbulent, and off we flew to follow James in his personal Turbulent. He led us northwards into Bedfordshire, and then by dint of playing 'follow my leader' at 100 feet up some winding river, we arrived at a long narrow strip into which James promptly disappeared. A quick circuit and we joined him on the ground, then taxied up to a little gate where a rather formally dressed man and a pretty maid respectfully greeted us. The butler, for that's who he was, led us across the lawns to the house. Neither Barry nor I had given any thought to what to wear or indeed take with us, and we exchanged uneasy glances. James, who had never been bothered with what he wore anyway, happened to be wearing a particularly worn out pair of shoes.

Over tea, formally served, his mother, a most elegant and beautiful woman, suddenly noticed.

"James," she said, "you've got a hole in your shoe" (knowing James he probably had one in the other as well).

"Yes," he replied unconcernedly.

His mother looked closer.

"James, it's through to your sock."

"Hm," muttered James.

"And it's dirty," she chided.

"I think it's my foot," corrected James.

It was an idyllic weekend. The following morning was one of great beauty. I left my bed and gazed out of the window at the sunshine that played over the lovely gardens. Without knocking, the butler entered; he seemed a bit put out to see me out of bed but quickly rallied.

"May I lay your clothes out, Sir?" he offered.

Knowing the state of my hastily-packed overnight bag I politely declined, but it was nothing to the shock that awaited him in Barry's room. Over breakfast Barry told me gleefully that the same thing had happened to him. The Turbulent doesn't have any room for luggage, so all Barry had taken with him was stuffed into a plastic shopping bag which during the journey had been in a tiny locker behind the pilots head.

"You should have seen his face," Barry said, "as he carefully laid out a pair of socks, a pair of briefs and crumpled shirt, and a toothbrush."

After the summer Newsletter I wasn't to be let off the hook. Since I was at the time on the House Committee my contribution got called House Notes for the first and only time.

HOUSE NOTES – AUTUMN 1960

BOWS AND ARROWS, "GB" AND THE I.C.G.C.

Table tennis and even darts are now established, if at the moment little-played games, in the upper Tower room. Through Margo's constant efforts, odd members have been seen, armed with pails etc., going up and down the Tower steps (Norman was responsible for the navy-style bound handrail) and the place is more than presentable. Whilst on the subject of the Tower, our lounge there is not only comfortably furnished, but for those who remember the chill of last winter, well heated. Yes, and there is TV up there too. The small room? It is now a bar. Members are welcome to use this bar, which is well stocked, but please don't forget to pay for your drinks, there's a price list and a cash box. How many know that there is a telephone for their convenience up there? It's behind the entrance door.

On the sports side the autumn report must be a quiet one. Bows and arrows, as we prefer to call our wild archery, have been seen three times. The target has up to now lacked stability in high winds – actually the ungainly contraption was originally intended for hangar use – and the last time it fell flat on its face it took several arrows with it. Perhaps there are members who have equipment spare to contribute . . . especially arrows – useage is high. Incidentally the latest target is a vast improvement – it's bigger!

It has been suggested we practise for a contest, strictly between ourselves of course. Our standard shouldn't deter newcomers, at thirty paces it's considered good form to hit the target – never mind where – with one arrow in twenty. So don't be put off by stalwarts all looking like Richard Greene looking like Robin Hood.

GB has given the Club a handsome ·22 Webley air pistol for target practice. The pistol lives for safety's sake in the sports locker along with the bows and arrows in the hangar, all are freely available. The key for this locker hangs in the hangar office. Shades of aircrew training, but wouldn't it be fun to have some clay-pigeon shooting too . . .?

That bit about sports proved something of a flash in the pan, but getting it all started though enlivened the year of 1960.

It all began with a chance remark. Older hands later learned to avoid them. Norman Jones had invited many of us to his home, the White House in Claygate, a small Surrey village north of Redhill. There on a sunny June afternoon we all had tea on the lawn. It wasn't long before I noticed an archery target in a corner.

"Got any arrows"? I asked.

Norman proved a good shot, and it was soon obvious that the rest of us weren't. I muttered under my breath that with a little practice we'd be just as good. Norman's hearing had never been at fault. His eyes gleamed behind his spectacles.

"And practice you shall, Benjamin. You are now Club Sports Captain." Me, the one member who disliked any active sports. Something told me not to argue. He wasn't joking about the practice either. In those days Samuel Jones Ltd had a fine sports ground at Greenwich, and since Norman was aware that I passed the place each day *en route* to my work at Woolwich, I got saddled with instructions to seek out the groundsman twice a week and get some archery in. And I know for a fact that he checked up to see that I did.

The Boss immediately presented the Club's new Sports Captain with several bows and lots of arrows, a target, a baseball bat, a couple of tired tennis rackets and the use of a locker labelled SPORTS LOCKER. Incidentally that wall of a target I'd built for use inside the hangar consisted of many cardboard cartoons heavily stuffed with newspaper and the lot lashed to a big wooden frame. It was designed to keep us busy and out of mischief on wet days. However even with a target area some twelve foot square no one, or thing, was safe. One day we couldn't find the target. The grins on the Rollasons' boys' faces gave us a clue. It had been fun.

Members with good club photos are invited to display them on the photoboards in the hangar. We are all fully aware of the cost of producing prints, and it makes it much easier to ask for copies if it is understood that payment is a "must" no matter how friendly the arrangement.

Big things are going on in the hangar Clubroom. After last year's upheaval in decorating (alright, so the dormitory looks great, but at what an *effort*, it took months. Who'll ever forget Angelo Sue painting the skirting boards?) the place is now being done up professionally. A new ceiling replaces the old droopy plastic one, and in goes strip lighting to complement the daylight panels. About that dormitory; there are comfortable beds and blankets and things. However if you want sheets you'll have to bring your own, and right next door are excellent cooking facilities. There is even an alarm clock and plenty of warmth from the latest in convector heaters, thanks to Ken Smith. The 2/6 asked per night is really little enough.

Margo and I have listed some of the items that would come in handy in our Clubrooms, and if any member can help out we'd be delighted. For instance, and starting with the most unlikely, a vacuum cleaner, coffee table and even a narrow hall table . . . and chairs, lots of 'em. For the fair sex Margo is seeking help with some needlework, any offers?

Jack Piercy has for some time found it difficult to cope in his limited spare time with the display organisation and his spot on the House Committee, and has been forced to leave the House side to just two, so we've personally co-opted another member to take the can with us. Welcome "GB" . . .

"GB" was short for Golding Barrett and his warm personality became more and more a part of the Club. At this time he hadn't been long with us, but he was, by our standards, somewhat senior. A retired Wing Commander, he was at one time reputed to have reached the rank of Air Commodore. He was both a modest and worldly person and nothing pleased him more than to be a trusted father figure to many of us. He would patiently hear out our problems and in his generous way try and guide us. He was a brilliant shot and had a mysterious past history of flying which he would promptly deny to all and sundry, but at the right moment he would go and let drop some tantalizing snippet that would hint at some great past adventures. The Club was attracting a lot of remarkable characters, and "GB" was undoubtedly one of them.

Going back just a little. It was during the spring of 1960 that Paul Minton and his friends in the Imperial College Gliding Club first brought along their glider to Redhill. Redhill airfield had had a long history as a successful gliding site, situated as it was close to the East-West ridge of the North Downs, so nothing was more logical or welcome. However their enthusiasm to get airborne knew no bounds, and prompted the following report in the very first issue of the *Tiger Rag* in November 1960/Jan 1961 of which I was now Editor.

NOVEMBER: The weather since the late summer became even worse during the period under review, if that's possible. Redhill lay under a pall of dripping dampness, the soggy field resisted movement and mud clung thickly to aircraft and crew alike. Inside the hangar things were brighter, the Clubrooms redecorated – let's change the tense – and are warm and ready for the dull cold weather to come. If all this sounds a bit gloomy you can blame it on the weather, but in reality spirits haven't been down, even if the flying hours have.

Medal of the Month undoubtedly goes to the Imperial College chaps under the tireless leadership of Paul Minton. As far as this awed observer can see they have spent most of their time assembling and dismantling their sailplane. Were this an easy thing to do one would understand, but it isn't. However they wisely don't commence assembling unless there is a possibility of flying that day. It is of interest to observe how they determine this.

1. That it is after 7 am and there is every sign that the sun will eventually rise; it is enough that it rises, no one expects to see it.
2. Visibility is such that a light can be seen. There is no minimum for this test.

Reassured by 1 and 2 nothing short of an Act of God will stop the sailplane's assembly. Rain, snow, fog, nil vis and mud are excluded from this Act. Joking apart, their constant good spirits and never-ending optimism makes their return to Redhill this winter all the more welcome.

QUOTE OF THE MONTH
Attributed to Peter Phillips on his return to this country after a long absence abroad.

Jested someone: "I expect all your girl friends were lining the runway waiting for you."

"Sure," replied Peter. "There were so many that I had to divert . . ."

A natural progression from tackling the House Notes had led to the suggestion from Nepean Bishop that I become Club reporter and in January 1961 appeared the first issue of the *Tiger Rag*. I've reproduced the remainder of that first issue. It conjures up, without embellishment, the spirit of the early '60s for it wasn't in just our Club that a joyous awareness of a brighter future had begun to manifest itself.

WE START THE *TIGER RAG* AND DANCE
AT THE PHOENIX
DECEMBER: All this dreadful weather – yes, it continued into December – did at least get some activity going on ground subjects, for the choice of a better phrase. For instance "GB" suddenly turned up one day with a ·22 repeater and got a somewhat earnest round of target practice under way. His biggest difficulty wasn't so much finding the best firing area but restricting it. Certain members were firmly reminded that it just wasn't done to pot at the odd gull.

Back in the hangar Bish had all members present that day on a DI check. This needs some explaining . . . It was presented to us thus:

Norman is at Fair Oaks and wants someone to go out and fetch him at once. *(Norman was actually in Australia and anyway the vis outside had dropped to 20 yd.)* You have ten minutes to inspect this aircraft and OK it for flight. Poor 'RAZ shrank a little further back into the hangar. We sensed the urgency of the matter and went to it – one at a time.

Phil Phillips had fixed the plane and five items had been got at. Most of us, in as close a scrutiny as we were capable of, found some unintended ones as well. The loose plug leads were easy to find (the cowling had been conveniently left undone). We even spotted the loose oil filler cap. But the lower inspection cover on the underside was only spotted by one. He crawled about on his back to find it. Good job it was only an exercise, methinks Norman would still be waiting.

CLUB DINNER AND DANCE: The writer is reminded of the touching cartoon of the little boy who, after gazing out of doors for days at the steady downpour reflected: "I know that into every life a little rain must fall, but this is ridiculous!" Well, that's how this writer felt when five days before the big event he and James Baring were asked to organise our Annual Dinner. Bev, it seemed, was nicely settled in Australia and couldn't get back in time to finalise things. Together we sought out Barry Griffiths probably on the assumption that three heads roll better than one.

"Can't be done," said Barry.

"Let's start dashing about," said I.

"Don't worry," said James. "It'll be alright on the night."

We drank on it.

Fortunately Bev got back in the nick of time, and were we glad to see him. The Dinner, held at the Phoenix in Cavendish Square, was an unqualified success, for most. Speaking as a member of the cabaret I go hot and cold every time I think of that performance (sic). The idea was great. We'd do a ballet scene, makeup, tights and all that. Act it straight, it's funnier that way. Trouble was we tried so hard that you the audience thought we were serious, and rather than embarrass us you just applauded politely. Oh that the ground could have opened up.

There were no speeches, but there was lots of dancing, drinking and nattering and we were very happy: and were turned out at midnight. It was a fine affair and our thanks go to Bev (90%) & James (10%) for his contribution of the Oirish Band of One, Two, Three, Four, Moind me haarap musicians . . .

QUOTE OF THE MONTH: "Someone has been pressing with their feet on the rudder bars in 'NZZ. They're not built for that sort of thing!" Norman, upon seeing the bent stirrups on The Archbishop.

1961

FILMS, JODELS AND CHECK RIDES

JANUARY: At the end of January the Number of Hours Flown board showed less than 100. That somehow summed up the weather for that month. It wasn't until late January that the airfield lost its waterlogged appearance and became just boggy. Whilst on the subject, several aircraft did bog themselves down and we learnt to give the highest ground the go-by. For some peculiar reason the one area that should be driest wasn't. Even Paul Minton couldn't fathom that out.

Ken Smith presented a film show in the Tower Room during the last weekend of the month. We were all grounded by the weather (yes, again) but we did manage to see the first showing of Barry Griffith's air to air film, and in its unedited form. There's nothing quite like the unexpected and Barry didn't let us down. For instance on one occasion he swopped cameras and lowered the ciné gently into the front cockpit – Tiger mounted. We know this because the camera was still running and recorded an instrumental impression – even if occasionally the dials were inverted. Just a thought: we often see ciné cameras at Redhill but whatever happens to the film? One never sees it. Here's a suggestion. Send or bring along any length of Tigerish film and then perhaps a member will volunteer to prepare and edit it. With proper credits we should be able to present a worthy and entertaining film.

QUOTE OF THE MONTH: Sue speaking. "Doesn't matter how far you go from the aerodrome, someone always sees you. Whilst I was doing rolls off the top over the Hogs Back, "GB" was watching from another cloud."

The French Jodel range of aircraft have been long associated with the Tiger Club. Rollasons began by introducing that wonderful little two-seater the D.117 into this country way back in 1958. The Jodels were designed by Joly and Delmontez and those we flew had all been professionally built by SAN in Bernay. Without question they were way ahead of their time. Even today their economy coupled with speed and range are well up with contemporaries. As load carriers they reign supreme. In 1958 there was little to be seen of the imminent invasion of American ware. At the time import restrictions prevailed. I use the term tinware in no derogatory way. Cessna and Piper build magnificent machines that have proved their worth the world over, but back in that year Europe gave little thought to tricycle undercarriages, and so the handling of those Jodels reflected the skills of pilots accustomed to making every landing a three-pointer – or at least trying to. The Jodels demanded and got a degree of skill that modern pilots taught on the near-foolproof nosewheel concept would scarcely credit.

The Jodels have always been what is called "a pilot's aeroplane." There is a degree of control response that would alarm – or delight – a pilot trained in modern machines and familiar with dampened, almost heavy, controls. The elevator is positively twitchy, the deep chord wings with their characteristic upswept outer panels cry aloud for a well-flared landing, which can be so short if need be as to make the aircraft seem STOL. A good touch was never more in demand than when landing in a stiff crosswind. A nosewheel in similar conditions can literally be plonked down firmly and steered. A Jodel in a crosswind can be a handful with a ready swing off centre if unexpected. But then to those familiar with her ways it was all part of the game. A lady with character will always be affectionately respected, and she was and is. The key word here is 'skill.' Perhaps without being aware of it, Norman was laying down one of the Club's unwritten beliefs, that an aircraft that demands that much more from its pilot would in turn be that much more rewarding. Who knows? Is it not likely that this subconscious thought has been the reason the Club has always flown tailwheel aircraft? It isn't that we haven't introduced the odd nosewheel aircraft from time to time, but they have never been popular and have, without exception, had to be withdrawn.

The ability to fly a taildragger well – a blunt but not unattractive Americanism – is still the dominant factor for Tiger Club pilots. In an age when all things are made easier for us, from synchromesh and auto-change on our road transport, to every conceivable electronic help in our business and home lives, there will always remain the purist who relishes using skills that others bypass. Like the cook who rejects convenience foods and takes pride in presenting whatever fresh foods are in season, so a great number of pilots the world over take enormous pride in the art of airmanship. It is not uncommon to see an experienced Redhill pilot spend an hour just doing circuits. The joy of a perfectly timed three-point landing is something to savour as you walk back to the hangar. It puts a spring in your step. If the landing is south, and the touchdown is right in front of the hangar there's the added *kudos* of others appreciating your efforts as well. But of course if you hit the ridge that every airfield has when spectators are around, then hard luck. The mythical ridge just out there beyond the hangar has caused more red faces than I can recall; if you'll forgive the play on words, it's a great leveller.

For years I was a check pilot sitting in the front cockpit of a Tiger whilst new members essayed their initial check. Without fail I would, as they completed the forty-minute flight, say: "I have control," and do one final circuit. I shudder at my confidence today, but then it seemed the proper thing to do to cement a relationship that up till then had been very one-sided. Now there was a chance for the observed to observe, to relax and try and spot the mistake that solid-head in front might make. My circuit was a swift one – a demonstration precautionary I'd insist, should anyone have questioned me. Arrow straight take off, hold it down to some two feet until a good flying speed had firmed up all the controls, and then a sweeping left-handed climb to downwind at never more than 500 feet. The needle dead centre. The grass threshold passes hard by the lower port wing, a firm but gradual reduction of throttle back to idle and a steady but positive turning descent to finals. A real bootful of rudder for a flamboyant nose-high sideslip, followed by a neat three-pointer just inside the peritrack. A turn left at that precise speed when one felt the turn would be comfortable and without dipping the starboard wing – a glance back to the gap of a hundred yards or so to the peritrack. Satisfied, I'd say: "OK, you have control; let's go back to the hangar."

Trouble was, it wasn't always like that. I reckon I got away with it 9 times out of 10, but I could bet my bottom dollar that if I was going to muck it up it would be with one of that rare breed – the 'natural.' My logbook doesn't identify the first occasion I got egg on my face but my memory isn't so forgiving. The young pilot had presented his logbook and licences for perusal. His meagre Tiger hours spelt nothing, except that he was unfamiliar on type. I would have to be that much more relaxed to encourage him to do his best, and for him not to feel that this was too formal an occasion. From the moment we taxied out I sensed that here was no ordinary pilot. In the air, after a few minutes of settling down, he flew every exercise in a smooth and decisive manner that could only be the flying of a very good pilot indeed. His approaches and landings were impeccable.

"I have control," I said after he'd finally landed. He acknowledged, and I swung back onto the grass runway and into wind. From then on everything I did was less than perfect. It was as though the gods had decided to mischievously play a game. I swung imperceptibly on take-off. A lesser pilot might not have noticed, but I knew and, worse, I knew that he knew. The needle moved across before settling centre, the airspeed varied. I wiggled into my seat and was aware I wasn't comfortable, my goggles were loose and my straps weren't tight enough. That short flight was definitely not perfect. The final humiliation was the landing. I was slightly late in kicking off the slip, settled heavily and at a slight tangent.

"S***," I said loudly and felt a bit better; but not much.

LANCELYN

Not far from Redhill airfield, north of it and only a mile or so away was, and probably still is, the Lancelyn Club. It was here that we would gather some Sunday evenings during the summer of 1960 after flying, to have dinner cooked to perfection and served by a cheery Scots lady we knew as

Mrs Mac. The Club's owner, John Dade, had done a lot of flying in his time, and it was during a bit of mutual reminiscing that he happened to mention that there was possibly enough room in his grounds to fly from. Over the following weekend we took a look, and just to make sure I paced the field. There was certainly 300 yards, and with the confidence of youth we all rushed back to Redhill to find suitable mounts to fly in with.

I left Redhill first in a single-seat Tiger, closely followed by the Super Cub flown by Barry Griffiths, then Carl Hampshire and Bill Holland in Carl's BA Swallow, and last, but not least, James Baring in his own Turbulent which he'd been given a couple of years earlier for a 21st birthday present. (Please understand if I've thought it proper to change some names).

The landing area lay just over the village cricket green which was skirted by a 20 foot overhead power cable. The strip ended in a line of trees. I did a precautionary run and began to regret my impetuous decision but, armed as I was with a very lightweight Tiger, I was confident I could make it. A sideslip over the wires and with much swishing of the rudder side to side I got in – just, and taxied quickly out of the way of Barry in the Cub. With full flaps he crept in with ease, and James did likewise, but it was certainly a tight fit. Bill, who was flying the Swallow for the first time, came over the wires at a snail's pace and made a short but very heavy landing. We cheerfully retired to the bar to celebrate with sandwiches and soft drinks, for by now it was lunchtime. Bill, though, was uneasy. He remained quiet and wouldn't be drawn, and when we began to discuss the return trip Bill suddenly said he didn't want to go. We tried to jolly him out of his strange mood, but whilst he eventually agreed to leave he insisted on Carl doing the flying. We sent James off first so that we could help him get the maximum run. Of all the aircraft his would take the longest. With his rudder hard in the hedge and with us holding back the wings, James half jokingly made the sign of the cross, and then opened up his tiny 1,300 cc engine fully. When it seemed to be going flat out he nodded his head and we let go. He gathered speed slowly and finally tottered off over the trees. I breathed a sigh of relief, the worst was over, the rest of us could get out easily. Someone swung my propeller and I soared away. Above, I watched first Barry leave and then the Swallow cleared the trees and begin a turn. I waited no longer, satisfied all was well. I went off to do some aerobatics and when that mood was out of my system I flew home.

Bish came running out to meet me.

"You have killed them!" he shouted. "They have crashed!"

Alarmed, Barry and I rushed off to where they were reported down. The Swallow had hit a cottage in Merstham and the two had been rushed to hospital. Sad to relate Bill died and Carl was badly hurt.

It was a terrible tragedy, and we sought to find the reason for that inexplicable crash. When we examined John's landing strip we found an aileron mass balance lying in the grass alongside the wheel marks of that heavy landing. With a broken aileron Carl had been unable to lift the wing to stop the turn he had initiated, had continued to roll and at that height a crash became inevitable.

Four practised pilots had watched that heavy landing and not one of us had thought to suggest the obvious – a heavy landing check. Years later the field disappeared under the invasion of earth moving giants as the local quarries extended their ravages of the landscape, but to this day whenever I pass the Lancelyn I remember Bill who had a premonition and didn't want to fly.

GATWICK WELCOMES THE BOSS

Redhill lies very near London Gatwick. That busiest of international airfields is only a matter of a few miles away, yet the two airfields have lived together in harmony for over twenty-five years. Albeit there has been the odd occasion of infringement, but never anything serious, but then Gatwick wasn't always that busy.

The big airfield was still little used and far from finished in the January of 1961, and so to encourage movements they opened their vast runway and all their facilities to General Aviation, and all was free. The date I first took advantage of that offer is still vividly in my memory. In my logbook it's an entry for New Years Day 1961, a date I suspect was their official opening to the flying world. I was unaware of this on that clear cold morning down at Redhill. All I knew was that Norman bore down on me and in his abrupt Naval manner said: "Get in," and pointed to the Jodel Ambassadeur – 'RFT.

"We are going to Gatwick."

"Yes, sir," I said, and got aboard.

He settled into the left seat, started the engine, and without any further ado or another word taxied out and took off down the long west runway. We climbed briefly to around 500 feet, and still at full chat turned left towards Gatwick. I began to feel uneasy when the Boss showed no inclination to climb any higher. We sped on at 500 feet.

I couldn't very well just say to the Chairman: "Hey, Norman, you're approaching a huge unknown, what about getting at least to circuit height?"

So I reverted to subterfuge and, leaning forward, tapped at the altimeter as though the needle had stuck. Norman never ever missed a thing.

"What's the matter, Benjamin?"

"Do you not think we are a bit low, sir?"

"Hm," he grunted, and went up another 100 feet.

Over our nose appeared the massive ramifications of a big complex beyond which the vast new runway loomed alarmingly. We tore on at 600 feet. My eyes were everywhere, all we needed now was someone on approach, and worse, what on earth were they thinking of us down there? I squirmed in my seat. I suddenly remembered: the radio of course. I leant forward and switched it on and said as calmly as I could: "Perhaps they are calling us."

Norman put on earphones and looked to me expectantly. I didn't know what to say but something to be said and quickly.

I said: "Say 'Gatwick, this is Jodel Foxtrot Tango – permission to land please.'"

My radio procedure was pretty well zero in those days. We'd seldom if ever used it in the RAF and for the last several years I'd lived, breathed and enjoyed the peace and true responsibility of radio-less aircraft.

Norman spoke firmly into the swing microphone. "Gatwick, this is Norman Jones, we are coming in for tea!"

He turned and smiled at me with pleasure. After all these years I must be forgiven if I don't recall the exact words, but please believe me when I say I'm not far out. Conversations like this are all too priceless to be forgotten.

Gatwick Air Traffic were imperturbable. They came back smoothly like the top professionals they are, gave instructions to let down over South base and to call finals.

"There!" said Norman triumphantly, and he nodded his head to indicate he understood.

"Norman," I hissed urgently, "tell them. Say: 'Roger, will call finals.'"

If he heard me he made no sign. We tore over the new terminal still going south at 600 feet. The term "South base" was new to me but whilst I was still grappling with the unknown, Norman swung sharply left and then left again.

"Call finals" I cried in alarm.

But the Boss had the bit between his teeth and in a flash we were lined up with the greatest runway I'd ever seen . . . it seemed to disappear over the horizon.

Norman tore towards it happily. As we approached, ATC turned on all the runway lights. I burst out laughing. It was a wickedly delightful gesture. Norman beamed. His face was a picture of achievement.

"There," he exclaimed; "they are welcoming us!"

And of course so they were, but the welcome wasn't to the aircraft but to one of the most remarkable men in aviation – the Boss.

TURBS, FARMERS, A RETRIEVE AND RUSSIANS

TURBULENT MODS   *Tiger Rag*, February '61

The latest Turbulent from the Croydon stable to join its Redhill mates is 'RGZ. It looks the same but nevertheless this tiny plane hides an interesting feature, its six-channel radio. Installation is excellent, it is neat and unobtrusive and the aerial tucks within the fin. The only external indication is the small blister beneath the fuselage that conceals the battery. This particular Turb carried Norman into Gatwick recently, surely the smallest aircraft ever to cross that vast runway threshold. Yet another big improvement was seen for the first time. Across 'RGZ's front cowling are the words: DANGER – IMPULSE STARTER. It's a most efficient unit and imparts a ripe kick to the propeller. Michael Jones will show his bruised knuckles on request. The engine starts incredibly easily with the ratchet starter even when hot . . .

The radio in 'RGZ had been specifically installed to get it into Gatwick and beyond for a flight to Australia by Brian McAllister. Norman enthusiastically gave approval but unfortunately Brian, *en route* for Cairo, only got as far as Deauville! On the bright side we gained a radio Turb but poor Brian must have been a bit fed up. It would have been a great trip.

The ratchet starter was a lever deep in the cockpit on the right hand side which when given a pull turned the prop. It didn't work that well, and was soon discarded. An electric starter was tried too, but the combination of starter and battery proved too heavy. Today, as twenty-five years ago, we swing them by hand.

THE FRIENDLY FARMER SCHEME

On the left wall of the hangar is an extremely well-hung map of England. It's quite huge, the scale is no less than two miles to the inch. Across its vast sprawling area of greens and brown is a rash of white spots, or rather flat headed pins. They pinpoint suitable fields or strips that are scattered throughout the country where a landing won't be met by an angry farmer, but instead with friendliness and help. The data on each strip is carefully filed and the file is alongside the map. Members are invited to extend this welcome service by contributing field locations . . .

The map is still there to this day but sad to relate we no longer use it as a guide. We use a Bob Pooleys instead.

ONE OF OUR A/C WAS NEARLY MISSING

David Phillips and I went down early this month to a tiny strip at Bognor in the new Ambassadeur. We stayed ten minutes and then clambered aboard and attempted to start. The check list said: 'Pump the throttle until the fuel pump stops.' We agreed it sounded the wrong thing to do, but there it was in black and white, so pump we did. She wouldn't start. We exchanged a glance that said: "I told you so." The engine was obviously too rich. I got out to turn the engine back. As I pulled the propeller through I was puzzled by what seemed to be copious exhaust smoke billowing from the cowling. I arrived at the obvious conclusion at the same time as the flames, which spread around the cowling with devastating swiftness.

"Out, David!" I yelled. "It's on fire."

David acted with incredible promptness, 'offed' switches and fuel, didn't wait to open his side of the canopy, but leapt over the adjacent seat and was clear in one mighty bound. I spared a moment to be most impressed. The grass beneath the aircraft was now well alight, so we pushed her backwards and out of wind, and then, mindful of the flame-licked fuel tank, we hastily rummaged in the cockpit for the extinguisher but looked in vain. Fortunately help arrived in the nick of time. Ian Trethewey and Roy Heath came up at the double with the extinguisher from the smaller Jodel and successfully killed the fire. Cause? An intake fire caused by our rich engine.

There must be a moral somewhere, not that we can see it, but the only aircraft in the whole Tiger fleet without an extinguisher at that time was the Ambassadeur. Fortunately only superficial damage was done. Yes, there is an extinguisher in there now, and the check list has been altered.

A little known piece of background was how Roy Heath – he'll forgive me if I reveal he is now the Managing Director of a big airline – came to be rescued, for that is why we'd gone down to Bognor. Roy at the time was very much a new member and very conscious of his responsibilities to both Club and aircraft. He had landed at the LEC strip, fog had descended, and he was unable to get away. Rather than leave his aircraft – the Jodel 117 – unattended, he stayed with it despite bitterly cold weather. I seem to remember he stayed in the field two nights. He had of course informed the police and they in turn had kept us informed. A friendly farmer kept him in food.

It was to this background that David Phillips, the late Ian Trethewey and I decided to rescue him. By hugging the ground and flying as slowly as we dared, we crept through the fog with three pairs of eyes map-reading. LEC was still fogged in when, a little later and after the fire panic, we left with Ian keeping Roy company in the 117 which followed us. The return journey was every bit as bad as the outgoing one, but feeling like a pair of Sir Galahads helped.

QUOTE OF THE MONTH: Sue (no watch) on estimating the length of an aerobatic trip: "What? As long as an hour? It couldn't have been; I'd have felt queasy if it had been THAT long!"

BARRY AND THE RUSSIANS

Early this month – April – Barry Griffiths got himself into the news. Some time ago he secured a remarkable photograph of the Turbulent team in a brilliantly accurate stepped-up formation; those who received or sent a Tiger Club Christmas card will remember the picture. Then a few weeks ago *Flight* published it, and in no time at all everyone wanted to be in on the act. It soon transpired what that was to be. The *Daily Express* were first off the mark and the following morning a tiny photo and a misquoted report appeared on Barry and the elusive Russians. . . . Obviously someone had discovered that Barry had hoped to lead a band of Turbulents to Moscow during the Trade Fair there in May. The Russians had said "No" and a good old fashioned "No" from the East is always news.

The BBC, not wishing to be outdone, informed Barry at breakfast the following morning that they would like to send an outside broadcast unit to Redhill, and in no time at all representatives from the Russian Embassy were expected too. What was rapidly developing into a good old intrigue blew away on Sunday morning as rapidly as it got under way – much to everyone's disappointment . . .

The late Barry Griffiths was a clinical observer of human nature, most articulate and in his suave, rather cynical manner, a most delightful raconteur. He was a regular member of the Turbulent team at the time, and was a talented photographer recording much of the Club's activities.

Barry was by profession a solicitor and he handled all his friends' business, and since most of his friends were in the Tiger Club, all appreciated and enjoyed his company.

SEEING THE JODELS

A vigorous sales tour began mid-March for the latest two members of the Jodel family. This two-week tour took the Ambassadeur and the Mousquetaire right around the country. Everywhere the two aircraft were shown, people flocked to see them. Farmers urged – and were given – short field demonstrations, often on their own fields. Civil dignitaries came in their official capacities to have a look and of course to fly. Executives, would-be and private owners, all flew them and commented in enthusiastic terms.

An interesting, and for Michael Jones who was in charge of the tour, an encouraging point, was that the Jodels followed closely on the heels of a sales tour by some well-known American light types, and the customer thus had the perfect opportunity to assess their various merits. On nearly every count the Jodels were way out in front. Top feature was the incredibly good visibility for crew, unlike the high-wing jobs flown earlier . . .

We sold one too. It went to a member of Wills the tobacco family.

Aware of the many characters within our Club there now began a series of thumbnail sketches. They were written by Barry Griffiths who called himself Arthur Non. And easily identified was Mike Reilly, the master.

CHARACTER REFLECTIONS I

Clutching a camera, I lay on the floor of the Rapide among seven pairs of Army boots. Their owners clustered around my position by the open door, a group of tough, resolute characters, clumsy as deep sea divers with their thick boots and two parachutes apiece over their bulky clothing.

The slipstream and the racket of the port engine came unchecked through the door and buffeted around inside the fuselage. Looking down there seemed to be a very great deal of water and remarkably little dry land. It was miserably cold.

The leader of the group had one foot inside the aircraft, the rest of his person being out on the wing root; he maintained his precarious position by clinging on with one hand, holding with the other a microphone into which he shouted directions to the pilot. Suddenly he threw the mike back into the aircraft and vanished as suddenly as if he had been extinguished. Instantly the rest of the group followed, jostling over my recumbent form as I leaned out after them.

It was a dramatic moment. The world was filled with the roar of the engines, the rushing air was a blind force, stopping breath in the throat and blinding the eyes with tears. It struggled for possession of the camera as, with blurred vision, I peered through the viewfinder after the swiftly-diminishing figures. They fell whirling, whipped away behind the aircraft like black birds, helpless in a gale beyond their strength. They turned and fell, faster and faster, growing smaller and fainter until they melted into the pattern of the fields.

I craned my head round to see if they had all gone, and there was the master himself, trundling imperturbably towards me like an elderly and portly commuter about to miss his station. He stumbled over my legs, stopped, bent down and said: "I'm so sorry!" He straightened up, paused in the doorway for a moment and plunged into twelve thousand feet of space. As he went, I just caught the words: "Excuse me."

CHARING AND A BONANZA THAT WASN'T
EASTER DISPLAY (OR 8/8 CLOUD AND ZERO VIS)

It says a lot for our enthusiasm to see so many members out at Redhill that morning. Dreary low cloud and a curtain of rain enclosed the field and stretched its wet folds just short of our feet. The owners of the feet stood in a long line in the shelter of the hangar and just watched. We began with a brew-up of tea, heard the call for briefing at 11.45 then went off to find some amusement. That didn't take long. Some of us discovered a new version of table tennis, four-handed with only two bats . . . it's a game to be recommended.

The briefing was hilarious. Outside conditions seemed if anything worse. It all depended now on the weather clearing. Down on the farm, Snoad Street Farm, Charing Hill, Kent, to be precise, Norman waited along with Phil and the service van.

Norman phoned. "Are you coming?"

Back at Redhill John Severne and Jack Piercy went up in a Hornet to see, and couldn't. Norman rang again . . . now the cars were bogged down. It was obvious the display would never be.

CFI'S NOTES: THE CHARING DISPLAY

I am very glad to report that after the disappointment of Easter Monday when the projected display at Charing Hill had to be postponed owing to impossible weather conditions, we had another go on Sunday April 23rd, and this time all went very well indeed. Despite a doubtful start, there was no rain after midday – in contrast to the home base where it poured most of the time – and everything went according to plan. Benjy's formation team led by Pee Wee Judge with Dennis Hartas and Clive Elton on his flanks performed wonders in quite bumpy conditions before (purposely) breaking their connecting tapes before landing. Clive Francis's Turbulent team did their stuff in an exemplary manner, the performers in this case being James Baring, Peter Phillips, Derek Dempster, Ian Trethewey and James Gilbert. Formations, paper cutting and air racing were the order of the day and the crowd of some 2,000 certainly had their money's worth. Bish aerobatted to good effect whilst Sue Burges excelled herself as a bomb aimer by producing the only direct hit of the afternoon with Pee Wee Judge at the controls. Pee Wee also excelled himself in the balloon bursting as did Bev Snook, whilst the members of the British Parachute Club led by George Bottomer also performed enthusiastically.

All in all, it was a good start to the season, and a good augury of things to come. BUT – and I underline this BUT – the same old few members provided the show. Giving public displays is one of the chief aims of the Tiger Club and I cannot understand why more of our members do not come forward and compete for places in our various teams. Presumably they joined the Club knowing what it stands for and I DO ask them to take more interest in our display side . . . The Turbulent training is under the aegis of Sqdn. Ldr. Clive Francis, whilst Tiger Moth formation flying is presided over most efficiently by Lewis Benjamin when he can tear himself away from his new 'bonanza' in Colindale! But we MUST have new blood for these displays as it is not possible for each of the 'Regulars' to take part in each and every show . . .

Bish's letters to us were always a collection of demands in capital letters. His enthusiasm comes out from every line.

The Tiger Club by now had me by the throat. My days with Marks and Spencer were about to end. The ever-present threat to promote me out of London grew with every day I remained in the capital. The crunch came when I exploded at some silly thing or other whilst I was Assistant Manager at their Woolwich branch and I decided to leave. After fourteen years with that great firm it was going to be some wrench. With an understanding that did them credit, my employers repositioned me back to Putney for the last few months.

My younger brother had started a menswear shop in Uxbridge, and I watched the operation with unconcealed fascination. He simply didn't a have a clue, I decided. All he needed was my expertise, so I moved in as an unpaid helper, intent on not only putting his business to rights (he was indeed patient with me, for not only was he making lots of money, but in retrospect I realize now that he was very efficient too) but to get him to immediately expand so that I too could run a shop. The Gods this time had a good laugh and indulgently let me make a fool of myself without too much harm being done. I rented a shop in a new parade in Colindale – the 'bonanza' Bish mentioned – and with stock borrowed from my brother, opened with great expectation. Aware that all the money M and S had finally parted with – around £700 – wasn't going to do more than particularly fit out the shop, much less stock it, I had also borrowed another £800 from my mother with which to finish it. Money was so short that I decided to live on a fiver a week – all in!

Dear Bish, 'bonanza' it never was, call it an inspired and colourful failure, and when I sold it some two years later I was back to square one and broke, but I had learned quite a bit.

THE CLUB BRANCHES OUT AND AUBREY

Several innovations were put into being at Redhill during the summer of 1961. One that was to prove both practical and important was the suggestion that in future we have a rota of Duty Pilots over the weekends. Until then the onus of responsibility for the flying was with any

Committee member who happened to be present. Bish was quick to recognise the need to get more members involved. The authority of the Duty Pilot was firmly established when, quite early on, the Committee was called upon to uphold a grounding decision made by a Duty Pilot. It was unanimously given, and the Committee has been unwavering in their support ever since. The first entry in the new airfield log – made by Pee Wee Judge – was a sighting of a donkey on the field. It took Pee Wee a long time to live that one down although he always swore he did see it.

Another decision was the one made in May to buy a Stampe biplane. How big an influence that initial purchase was is little evident in the one-line Committee minute. It read: *"We agree to buy a Stampe if reasonable."*

Incidentally the first to arrive was called *The Curé* but the name didn't catch on. After that we gave up naming newcomers to the fleet, and reverted to the time-honoured nomenclature of registration letters.

By now there were two other UK branches of the Tiger Club, each run by a local member. Sywell in Northants was run by Charles Boddington who, although he had only just officially become a member, had been associated with the Club for two years, primarily through aerobatics. The other was of course at Fair Oaks. In each case they had a couple of aircraft for which they were responsible and a certain number of annual flying hours were expected. 150 was the target, but never reached. Other branches were proposed, among them Syerston, Cranwell, Little Snoring and Blackbushe. A few became operational but in every case were shortlived.

The Fair Oaks unit was then being looked after by Aubrey Offen. He was a friendly and most generous character. He seemed to collect "things": aeroplanes, boats, anything, and all seemingly a bit run down and invariably "one-offs." He owned an aged Aeronca for a while and most generously let Club members have a go. It really was a menace; it flew at just one speed, the same for take-off, cruise and landing. Just getting into it through the birdcage of wires was a feat. Another aircraft he happily let anyone fly was an old Miles Gemini.

One day he offered it to me. He never ever asked questions about experience, being only too happy to see our faces light up at the opportunity. His parting shot as Juanita, my wife-to-be, and I climbed eagerly aboard was: "I shouldn't worry about the undercarriage – I'd leave it down if I were you."

He didn't say it, but I suspect the unit didn't work too well, if at all.

He quit flying a short time later. We never discovered why. It may have been on medical grounds, for he was no longer a young man in years, but I suspect that, with much affection, he ever remained young at heart. I met him again in strange circumstances some years later. It was during the summer of '69 when with my small family I was cruising on the Thames with our first boat, an ancient motorcruiser called *Purple Broom*. We had moved over close to the bank to make way for a huge barge. It made a remarkable sight for it must have been well over 80 ft long and looked nearly as wide. As it slowly steamed by, a great shout came from the helmsman who, with no more ado, drifted the great thing into the bank. A girl got out with a rope and made fast forward and the helmsman did likewise astern. Then he turned to wave. It was Aubrey. It was a wonderful reunion, and he proudly showed us over his floating palace and insisted on us staying for a drink. Aboard were many happy American visitors who were not in the least put out by an unscheduled stop to say hullo to friends, for that was how Aubrey and his paying guests preferred to explore the river, they stopped wherever they felt like it. We continued to see him on the river during the following summer, then we heard to our deep sadness that the barge had been retired. He used to operate it himself with just one other hand who doubled as cook/hostess. His was a remarkable feat of rivermanship.

THE CONDOR, A PICNIC AND CLUB NEWS

CLUB NEWS – JUNE '61

Next time you're on the Redhill circuit take a look in a south-easterly direction about one and a half miles from the airfield. There, on a small rise, is a windmill that still turns, grinding out grain as it has done for hundreds of years. Its owner, an old farmer, still sells his produce at the mill door. I suspect there can't be more than a couple of other windmills still working in the whole of the country. To catch a glimpse of the great white wooden blades turning over slowly in the sunshine is a breathtaking sight.

Whilst most of the club aircraft were busy looking for Berck on the 18th, Margo and "GB" stayed behind to fly members of the St. Martin-in-the-Fields Air Guides in 'CDC, a kindly act that was much appreciated.

The new Druine Condor has blossomed out in its dashing new coat, looking very French in yellow, blue and white. Another stranger to join the Club is the more soberly painted D.117 G-ARNY. She looks in fine fettle and differs from 'POZ by virtue (or not) of being without airbrakes. Other differences are mere detail; she has a landing light and her ignition switches will take some fathoming out . . .

The switches were soon changed for a more conventional pattern after Dennis Hartas had a combined incipient forced landing and heart attack whilst over France. You pulled the switch out for live and then could turn it to position one, two or both. Dennis had unwittingly pushed it in whilst rummaging for a map and the engine had died. Only a lot of quick thinking saved the day.

"GB"-ISM: Peter Masefield brought his new Beagle Airedale into Redhill one weekend. It was covered with tufts of cotton wool – not just the wing but fuselage as well. Obviously someone was taking this airflow business seriously.

"GB" took all this in for a moment, and then asked reasonably enough: "When are you going to knit another one, Peter?"

BILL CHESSON'S AFTERNOON PICNIC PARTY
(from June *Tiger Rag*)

For those members who like to enjoy something a little different, Bill is laying on a get-together "fly-in," "sail-in," "drop-in," "drive-in" picnic party on Sunday afternoon, 16th July. He has found one of his special fields, and if you know Bill Chesson you know that he has fields and fields dotted about all over the country – whenever I am flying with him and we pass over some remote little hamlet or other Bill says: "Oh yes, there's so and so. I've got friends down there, let's drop in for tea!"

Anyway this particular field is about the same size as Charing but it is right by the sea, and as the tide will be up on this particular afternoon, Bill has invited along a number of his boating friends. They will be bringing along their speedboats and water skiing outfits so that any of the Tiger Club members who fancy their chance can have a go. Music, tea and refreshments will be laid on for free, and you are asked to arrive as near 2 pm as possible. Bring your swimsuits. A runway will be marked and a 'T' shown. Should be good fun.

BILL CHESSON'S PARTY, 16TH JULY,
SOMEWHERE, THAMES ESTUARY

It was all Bill said it would be. A pair of good landing strips right on the estuary, a cluster of speedboats bobbing at the water's edge, lots of cheerful people, a marquee with food and drink and a cool jazz group that were absolutely 'with it.' As we stepped from the Ambassadeur the sound of music drifted a greeting from over the rise. The party began for us from that moment. Then two Turbs joined us, but no others, the overcast weather had deterred them from coming. When the sun broke through over that corner of Kent our day was made . . .

THIS PLACE IS A MUST. Quiet, miles from anywhere, and the owner, a charming and friendly man, even offered to improve the landing run. All congratulations to Bill and our appreciation too, for without this sort of gesture we'd miss so much of the fun that light plane flying can bring . . .

So many years later the true picture – that of the early '60s – begins to fall into place. At the time, of course, it was simply how we wanted to fly, and more important, were allowed to. There was a freedom of thought that soared in its imagination. Nothing was impossible and the Tiger Club was the perfect vehicle for such thrusting spirits.

The *Tiger Rag* immediately became the focal point; it gathered in the events that mattered so much to us all, and with an equal enthusiasm reported them. Now from a distance the true verve of that period becomes apparent. The Tiger Club flew a banner for light flying, a banner to which so many remarkable people flocked. The Club unhesitatingly took the lead in every aspect of the sport – to aviation's common good. The freshness of those early days, as expressed by the introductions each month to the *Tiger Rag* CLUB NEWS, remains today.

CLUB NEWS, JULY 1961

It's been a crowded month – the hours have shot up to 2,000, no doubt aided and abetted by some long European trips. For instance the Ambassadeur, with Barry Purcell driving, visited Greece, and many others sunned themselves, or may still be doing so, in Holland, France, Germany and Spain. The end of July saw the International Business and Touring Aircraft Competition at Kidlington. If the two aircraft entered by the Club didn't make the prizes, the pilots and crews put in some excellent work. Norman in the new Druine Condor flew for seven hours, his only food two oranges and a bar of chocolate.

James Baring, whilst handing coffee around, raised one cup near the fresh air vent and for a brief spell they were all on IF. Clive Francis pulled off a magnificent short landing in the ensuing contest, beating the field – no mean task in the Jodel 1050 with a stalling speed way above many of the other competitors.

I hear the Turbulents will be at Farnborough this year, and although I haven't been able to get details, I understand that John Lemon recently led a "Round Britain" flight of Turbulents . . .

OF AIRMANSHIP, COBHAM AND LEYSDOWN

I'm not an historian, I have always prefered to observe and report and to leave the history to others. But as I reflect back to those early displays I can now clearly see a developing pattern – the presentation and standard of flying were becoming more professional. We were learning.

The Tiger Club had unwittingly become an advanced school. Already there were emerging cliques of pilots devoted to their own disciplines. And as they flew those early shows, they not only gained a growing following that would one day recognise them, almost as household names, but the competitive nature of these outstanding pilots ensured a progressive excellence of quality for the rest of us to live up to.

And it was as a participating observer that I recorded those early events and within these reports began to trace the growth of the postwar scene.

Incidentally it is not unrealistic to compare the Club's showing with that of the prewar Alan Cobham shows. They were certainly the leaders then, but arguably the Tiger Club had probably, even by the early 60s, become their equal in scope and unquestionably they were later to do better. The Cobham Shows had laid great emphasis on joyriding, because it was financially essential to do so, but in doing so they laid an inflexible arm on a broader presentation. Not so within the Tiger Club displays which, unencumbered with the need to fly passengers, enjoyed the freedom to express ourselves in an unrestricted sky, which in turn led to a style and polish unequalled in Europe.

We had of course tried to mix joy-flying in with the display proper, but quickly learned they didn't go together on safety grounds. Purists will protest that the Cobham shows were professional, and the pilots so practised as to be head and shoulders above the so-called non-professional. True, and there were some legendary figures to support the claim. But the postwar pilots were far from lightweights; practically all of them were RAF trained – several still serving – and the others, with the odd outstanding exception, were professional men from the airlines. It wasn't exceptional to find that a typical team's average hours in the region of 3-4,000, sometimes more.

And of course it was this expertise and flying *elan* that drew so many fine pilots together in the first place to our Club. Interesting to note that several of Alan Cobham's "greats" supported the Club's ideals in a practical way. They were amongst our earliest members. We'd always pull the crowds, but then we were always adventuring into new places.

FULL DISPLAY, LEYSDOWN, ISLE OF SHEPPEY, 9TH JULY

Chesson does pick 'em. Leysdown had the roughest surface we've encountered for ages, yet it was ideal in every way. Flat unobstructed approaches, right by the sea and hallowed ground into the bargain . . . AND licensed. Why this and not Charing I shall never know. It's a little-known fact that Leysdown was Britain's first airfield. A certain Colonel made the first flight in the country from here in 1908 in an aircraft made to his order by the world's first aircraft factory, also right here. The firm was Shorts and the intrepid aviator was granted the RAeC licence No 1. No prizes for correct identification.

No grumbles this time about the lack of food. Bill treated us to a four-course lunch at the Country Club. I didn't exactly choke when I saw the crowd awaiting the show on our return to the field, but I felt Bill wasn't likely to even recoup the cost of the coffee from the round dozen eager purses of the spectators.

Bish began his briefing. "First item is the taxi-past of the crowd." "Wouldn't it be simpler," said Pee Wee, "if the crowd walked past us?"

Amid laughter the taxi-past was cancelled . . .

Dennis Hartas got in the first really new act. For some reason the programme proclaimed it a "first solo". John Blake, who incidentally did an incredibly good job on the commentary, reckoned Dennis was about to do some crazy flying. I reckon he was right. It was a brilliant act, hair-raising, breath-taking and all the other shocks attributed to the human frame. But all safely. I thought Norman looked torn between a desire either to stop the act or to applaud it. I sympathised. It's probably like watching someone else backing one's car out of the garage; it had the crowd gasping and laughing alternately.

Parachuting was much more entertaining than on previous occasions. Possibly because two of the competitors landed in the crowd. Unfortunately one broke an ankle.

George Bottomer had a second outing with his Col. Crackshot. I must say George cuts a dashing figure in his Legionnaire uniform as he stood on the wing of Tiger 'PRA, with tails streaming in the wind. Glad to relate that his marksmanship is as deadly as ever – even if one of his bullets chose to travel rather slowly!

We flew homewards across the estuary, a huddle of Tigers and Turbs, to tea at base, all organised as ever by Marie Hargreaves and helped by Mrs Lovell . . .

QUOTES: "The trouble with winter is that it gets late so ruddy early."
"It is difficult – I tried to think about it once."
Both quotes attributed to Tom Storey.

COL. CRACKSHOT, AEROS, RACES AND PAT

ONEUPMANSHIP: In the quiet of the evening after Leysdown members relaxed out on the grass ahead of the long shadow of the hangar and talked. One of the group looked around him and almost sniffed the air.

In an apologetic manner he arose and said: "Just to 1,500 feet and down again."

Then someone suggested: "And make it a spot landing in front of us – from 1,500 ft."

With mounting interest the group watched as one pilot after another entered what was now a spot-landing contest. All were eager to have a go. Eight good and experienced pilots tried, but no one quite made it. One to be sure did scrape over the imaginary hedge, but only just, it was no clear-cut victory. Rollason engineer John the Twin (Brother Jim), overalled and on duty, hesitantly asked if he too could try.

The black Rollason Tiger cut a sharp silhouette against the sky – the last rays of the sun glinted golden on John's goggles as he turned above – tighter to the field than any of us, the bumble of his idling engine and the sweet rush of the wind in the rigging the only lovely sound. A short sideslip above the imaginary hedge, a clean three-pointer – and John put down exactly in the middle of the green, a faultless performance. He taxied in to a standing ovation. Then John became John again and organised the hangar for the night and shut the doors . . .

It was around this time that the Rollason team got no less than 34 aircraft into the hangar – a record that was never repeated or attempted.

The Col. Crackshot act was very much George Bottomer's. A long-time parachutist, he seemed to have no fear of heights, and would cling to the Tiger with one hand as he waved a big revolver in the other. He stood on the inboard lower wing disregarding the slipstream with an aplomb that never failed to delight the crowd. The act was superseded the following year by the introduction of the more spectacular, yet far less dangerous, act of standing on the top wing. Almost needless to relate, no one ever volunteered to take his place as Col. Crackshot.

We had by then devised a method of remotely exploding strategically placed hydrogen filled balloons. A pair of bare wires were close-Sellotaped to the balloon, the wires then led to a concealed observer who short circuited his two ends across a 12-volt car battery to burst the balloon, and the hydrogen would go off with a bang. If he didn't synchronise the shorting with the flash of the exploding blank the bullet would seem to have either travelled too slowly or too quickly – like before the gun was fired. Either way the act always mystified, always them, sometimes us.

THE BRITISH LOCKHEED INTERNATIONAL AEROBATIC COMPETITION, 14TH JULY

Nick Pocock reporting. The United Kingdom was represented by Club members John Ayres (leader), Charles Boddington, Nick Pocock and *The Archbishop*: unfortunately Michael Popoff couldn't make it, and Frank Price from the States was unable to get his special Great Lakes biplane over here in time.

We arrived at Baginton on the Wednesday in company with cold, wet and windy weather which was to last for the rest of the week. The consumption of coffee was almost as heavy as the rainfall. Still we were able to get a bit of practice in before the eliminating heats on the Thursday afternoon, which were held in very windy conditions although the cloud base lifted considerably. Unfortunately none of the Tiger entries were chosen for the finals, but we enjoyed ourselves nevertheless.

In the evening the weather improved and Francis Liardon indulged in a very spirited (in more ways than one) practice session, starting with a flick roll on take-off in his Jungmeister and finishing with a rather unsteady stroll back to the Esso caravan. The final on Friday was postponed until the evening when we all enjoyed watching some beautiful flying by the first three: Blaha (Zlin), Verette (Stampe) and Trebaticky (Zlin). These three gave another unrestricted exhibition of their artistry during the display on Saturday.

The Zlins were certainly completing some elaborate manoeuvres – I didn't know who must have devoted the most time to practising, the Czech pilots or the band who played their national anthem during the prize-winning.

It was certainly a fine effort by the Czechs, but Verette has shown that they must not forget the Stampe!

The following day Brian Iles won the Kings Cup in his one-off Miles M18. (Brian was a serving RAF officer and at the time a Squadron Leader.) His passenger was Pat Peacocke. Wg. Cdr. McIntosh came second in a Cessna just nine seconds ahead of T. Knox in a Proctor. The next four aircraft were sparated by only 2½ seconds in a wonderfully close finish, with Dennis Hartas in the Active just being pipped at the post by Vivian Bellamy in the Spitfire. Only 1 second behind Dennis was Sid Aarons, the new Air Racing Champion, who beat The Archbishop (the world's fastest Tiger?) by just half a second.

Pat had joined the club recently, having had a chequered career riding racing horses and, after another accident, had found herself in the same hospital as Sue Burges. A more hilarious pair would have been hard to find. She was later to marry Brian.

Pat could when she wished put on a very upper crust voice. I remember once phoning her shortly after she had married Brian, whose father I recall, was a very high-ranking RAF officer. Her upper crust voice answered the phone.

"Lady Iles?" I asked in a polite voice

"Yes," she replied.

I burst out laughing.

"Come on, you silly old cow, it's me, Benjy."
"I beg your pardon?" said the voice this time much colder.
A sudden fear struck me.
"It is Pat, isn't it?"
The voice softened a little bit.
"No, it's her mother-in-law."
"Oh my gawd!" I said and apologised.
I swear I heard a gentle laugh the other end. To this day I don't know who I spoke to.

THE TURBULENT TOUR, CEZANNE AND COGNAC

The following tale from the *Rag* of September '61 was a classic of its kind. The Turbulent boys were a wild lot but all were hugely experienced above-average pilots, and it showed. That none of that regular team came to a sticky end is a fact that must, in view of their antics, be regarded as simply fortuitous.

James himself became relatively serious around 1970 when he went and bought himself a vineyard in Avignon down in France where he claimed he would teach the French a thing or two. And he did too. Today his wines and olive oil are highly regarded. I love best the story of the first wine he bottled. It was a modest and rather plonkish wine of which there was but 3,000 bottles. He is reputed to have given away or sold 2,000 of them . . . he claims he drank the rest.

THE TURBULENT TOUR OF FRANCE – AS RELATED BY JAMES BARING

The Tiger Club *Tour de France* was delayed at the outset by a gale which kept us on the ground at Berck for a whole day; the same gale that, unbeknown to us, brought disaster to a plane full of Croydon school children on the jagged coast of Norway.

However, at the time we knew nothing of this grim tragedy and our spirits were high. The next day we went swooping down to La Rochelle, stopping at Laval for a delicious lunch. At La Rochelle Dr Forestiere and the local flying club members entertained us in grand manner. We were presented to the Mayor, who made a speech of welcome. In reply, I spilled my champagne, and Chris Carver knocked over a flower pot. (Fr.: – 'pot de fleurs.')

Leaving the Mayor and Corporation to clear up the mess, we bade farewell to Dr Forestiere and, full of lobster and *vin du pays*, we staggered off to Cognac, where aspiring French pilots grapple with Harvards. After 25 minutes taxying round the peritrack behind a jeep, we arrived at the flying

Club, tucked away in a corner of the airfield as far away from the military as possible. During this manoeuvre, one of the Turbulents got lost.

Chairman of the Club was M. Briand. He was a director of Hennessey's, and here again, as at La Rochelle, we were shown the most lavish hospitality. The first evening we drank with M. Briand and members of the Club. The restaurant was situated on an island in the river, and we sat at a long table beneath the trees. A never-ending supply of Cognac loosened our tongues; I managed to knock over an enormous flower pot. *(Fr.: 'grand pot de fleurs.')* A truly memorable evening.

The next day we were shown the vineyards and distilleries, and were entertained at lunch by M. le Comte de Pracantal, another director of Hennessey's (more cognac). We were by now saturated with alcohol and becoming extremely funny.

On Saturday morning I departed for Spain for three days to sober up. In fact, I had nearly made it when Geoffrey Hancock turned up in San Sebastian with the rest of the troops, as I was halfway through lunch on Sunday, and recommended some wine or other, which got me right back again. Tuesday morning I decided to leave Spain before I was arrested, and six o'clock that evening I joined the others in Aix en Provence. They seemed none the worse for their experiences, but apparently John Thomson had arrived without his aeroplane. I never did discover how he did this. When we left two days later, he still didn't have his aeroplane and, of course, he got left miles behind.

At Aix we were once more magnificently looked after by the members of the Club. We were delayed an extra day because of the *mistral* (a word about that later), and this gave us time to have a go at a few more flower pots. About this time a large number of paintings disappeared from Cezanne's exhibition at Aix. It was rumoured that John Thomson used the canvas to patch up a rent in the fabric of 'RCZ. When the *mistral* is blowing you have to take off at sunrise and fly all day in order to be in the same place when you land at sunset.

Of course you are going to tell me the same thing can be achieved much more simply by not taking to the air at all, and you would be perfectly right, but this seldom occurs to one in the heat of the moment.

Tired and hungry, we arrived at Nevers but soon recuperated 'chez de les Gomcuffs,' who wined and dined us till we were quite our former selves. Late the following afternoon, we flew off to Epernay, where we were joined again by Geoffrey and John, who this time brought his Turbulent, repaired with Cezanne's canvasses. M. Vazart filled us with champagne for two days, and gave us a bottle each to bring home.

You know the rest. With the aid of stomach pumps and Alcoholics Anonymous we returned to a normal life within a few weeks, and even a bit of weekend flying. Congratulations to the two Cranwell boys, Hoppy Granville-White and John Thomson, for really excellent airmanship on their first trip of this kind, and once again many thanks to Geoffrey Hancock for making the whole thing possible.

OF FAIR OAKS AND ROAST LAMB

OUR ANNUAL FULL DISPLAY, FAIR OAKS, 7th AUGUST

I sat for five minutes rejecting opening sentences; what I wanted to say came over dull – and it shouldn't have. After all, what's dull about the sight of seven gaily coloured Tigers bright and youthfully alert in the sunshine? Add to it a dozen other light aircraft and a glorious day, and you have something to relish. That was Redhill that Bank Holiday morn.

I counted 18 club aircraft at Fair Oaks, a couple of course belonging to members, but it was the year's best turnout before the year's best crowd. A guess would put the numbers at 8-10,000. Undoubtedly it was also the year's best display.

At 15.00 precisely the two formations of Tigers and Turbulents arrived from different directions to slide one beneath the other in a pretty display of precision and timing. The Tigers broke over the boundary and as they landed in rapid succession, Nick Pocock was climbing to begin his aerobatics. He introduced a new manoeuvre called the "knife edge." It looked for all the world like a hesitation roll that had got stuck. It looked spectacular. As he landed the Turbs flew in to give of their antics. Clive Francis led Peter Phillips, James B. and Julian Zuromsky. They were to do a lot of flying that day . . .

Dunlop did us a good turn by producing a pair of fluorescent bright posts for the Turb boys to fly between and Bish and "GB" to fight over. Add a round dozen photographers, several parachutists, their markers (female and resplendent in fluorescent jackets), throw in the odd wheeled transport, plus three joyriding Austers and an odd act or two, and you have a strip of airfield vying with the Strand. The three parachuting Tigers flown by Jacko, Bill Laslett and Jack Piercy did well to get down at all and, on reflection, to even make the necessary 1,500 feet.

Dive-bombing really brought the crowd to its feet, figuratively; once immersed in a cup of tea, nothing will bring a British family to its feet.

From out of the hat a new act. It was one no one honestly thought would steal the show, but it did. It started as a short take-off contest between two, nay three, elder members of the Club. One was armed with a Piper Cub ("GB" up) and *The Archbishop* (Bish) with Norman dying to have a

89

go in a Turbulent. Add John Blake's hilarious commentary and we found we had a winner on our hands. The crowds loved it.

"GB"s tail-lifting antics and near-vertical take-offs really got them going. Incidentally it's interesting to note that the first take-off in the Cub was without flap and in much the same distance as 'NZZ! When Bish finally flew through the tapes (the act was cheerfully rigged) the crowd cheered. Norman in the Turb then began to taxi around and around in angry circles, furious that he had been deprived of a chance to have a go. With much fist waving the tapes were hastily repaired and Norman, obviously having a whale of a time, promptly flew straight through it all, scattering tape and flags all over the place. The act was home and dry. The crowd roared their approval. "GB" the winner was besieged for his autograph. Well almost. A little girl went up to him and asked: "Please, old man, may I have your autograph?"

By 5.30 it was all over, and no one wanted to go, least of all the crowd, many of whom stayed to see us on our way.

Brief extracts perhaps from a longer report in the *Tiger Rag* but enough to saviour the atmosphere of the last show of the season about which there seemed a garden party spirit that lingered long after we had flown home.

A letter from "GB" was always worthwhile. I had been leading him back from somewhere in the West Country. That much I remember. I was in a Tiger and "GB" in the Super Cub and the weather was certainly awful, that I remember too, but I was unable to find the flight recorded in my logbook. Every now and then one got away.

"My Dear Benjy,

So great is my admiration for your airmanship that I would follow you anywhere, well almost anywhere, except into 100 ft cloud base, in mist and rain towards hills and adjacent to two control zones, in an aircraft without radio or B/F panel. But nice of you to waggle your wings invitingly, nay, enticing me into a combination of all these hazards.

Having already allowed myself to be lured above a layer of broken clouds to 1,500 feet-- and watched the holes begin to fill up – I was in no mood for further experiments. Earlier on, before I sighted you, and after the radio-equipt Condor had done a 360, and I probably a 390 turn, I lost visual contact and all became very bleak. I carried out some interesting tests.

a). I proved that, trimmed out on half throttle, half flap, hands off, 'RAM will descend through 200/300 ft of cloud/mist/rain with intermittent visual contact quite splendidly and be instantly manageable on emerging underneath.

b). That in rain and mist, nothing whatever can be seen ahead – and damn little if you manage to get your head far enough back to peer out of the side window.

c). That once you deviate from the straight and level, the compass instantly starts rotating at about 8 revs per minute.

d). That it is a superb machine for a treasure hunt – the treasure being a field – despite the fact that when you bank suddenly, the wing blots out the field, so one must always have a spare field or two in hand.

When I sighted you in the rain below, I was deeply engrossed in attempting by a steady turn (rate 1 on the oil gauges), to catch up with the compass and trying to assess the pleasure and advantages of flying, if any: my brief attempt to follow you until you disappeared under a gate into the muck satisfied me that there were none. So, with a smart 180 calculated round a road/railway, I returned to square one, an area of splendid fields full of HT cables, stock, roots and straw bales. Two or three houses were sighted fleetingly, but I was attracted by a well-kept pink house with orderly gardens and grounds, outhouses and a telephone. The smoke issuing from the chimney, smelling of roast lamb decided me (I chanced the mint sauce), and a nearby 10 acre stubble field seemed a likely spot, so I lobbed in and was vastly relieved when a nearby tractor driver spoke English.

The owner was at church and Mabel, the maid, was suspicious of an unlikely tale, but on his return he could not have been kinder. After lunch (there was roast lamb [and mint sauce], cocktails, wine, apple fritters, liqueurs and coffee) our host retired to rest, John Blake had a zizz and I examined the changing weather through alternating windows.

Telephone calls to Odiham, Gatwick and Redhill convinced me that nothing whatever is known about weather reporting or forecasting. But at 3.30 it had stopped raining and a bright patch due North suggested I have a bash at Lasham, Fair Oaks and possibly base. So I roused all from their sleep and after a short, muddy walk, took a fond farewell from our new friends, and set sail, only to find I was well and truly in it again at 100 ft with no future.

In ten minutes I had located and landed again in the same old field, and tied the Cub to a tree. No time for tea – pity – but host drove us to Guildford Station (did I mention there was a Rolls Royce too?). The road over the Hogs Back and the rail going to Redhill were mostly in mist and cloud, all of which proved what I believe C.G.G. said years ago: "that presence of mind is better than absence of body" – or something like that. But please, Benjy, don't hesitate ever to waggle your wings whenever we meet in the air. It might be a fine day, and then, unless there is a good lunch locally, I might follow you, or try to.

Yours, GB."

FARNBOROUGH, NIGHT FLYING THEN AND EARLIER

CLUB NEWS, SEPT 1961

Last time I looked at the notice board, the total hours flown had topped 2,600. September must have been responsible for quite a bit. Farnborough was a tremendous success. Clive Francis received a warmly congratulatory letter from the Chairman of the SBAC Flying Control Committee, a well deserved accolade for a fine performance.

Of the many stories to come out of Farnborough this year, James claims the most original. Asked by an attractive woman if he often came to Farnborough, he replied: "Oh yes, but only in the formating season."

This *Rag*, on behalf of all the TC members, offers sincere congratulations to Sue Burges and Peter Phillips on their engagement. After several rumours, the *Evening News* came out with the news in a big splash.

The invitation to Farnborough was a very considerable accolade. We flew a nine-plane formation on the three public days. One of the acts was very much a new one. Clive Francis led four of us in at around 800 feet in line astern, and then with a raised arm Clive indicated the paper drop. Over the side went the toilet rolls and in a hairy 180 degree diving turn Clive led us back on our tracks to get in among the streaming lines of paper. We cut them into as many pieces as possible before they fell to the ground. It was nothing if not spectacular, with the tiny Turbulents tearing in and out of the long streams in a vigorous dog chase. A pilot quickly learnt not to follow the paper too low in spite of the temptation. The first time this act was tried out in public at Farnborough, one of the Turbs suffered engine failure as paper got into the air intake. It was the biggest forced landing on record, for three other aircraft landed in sympathy. The following day the act was modified. The wing was used to cut instead of the propeller.

Night flying has a hold on everyone. Just how much can one use a Night Rating with normal resources in this country? Nevertheless, the question on many lips is: "Are you having a go?" I've been asked so many times that I feel positively guilty when I reply "No." It helps to add: "As yet . . ."

No one has yet got their fingers on the Cosmic Wind, the new racer that Norman has bought for the Club. This low sleek potent aircraft – not unlike a scaled-down Mustang to look at – has a tremendous rate of roll and a reputed top speed of over 200 mph, all on 85 hp.

If there's a crowd outside the hangar any weekend chanting numbers, it's probably someone going solo on the Pogo Stick. 12 hops gets you an 'A' licence, 36 for a 'P' and 72 for a full Commercial! The Master Pilot's rating demands a triangular cross country and set figures. The only Master Pilot to date is Paul. I think he's twelve . . .

Night flying at Redhill, with flares to light our way, became very popular. The air was usually still and the gentle warmth of an autumn evening lingered. Then too there was the prospect of an Indian curry down in Reigate later that night. It made many reluctant to go home.

Back in the summer of 1948 when I was flying with the Brookside Flying Group I was asked by Danny Taylor, who suddenly felt like visiting his friends and family in Scotland, if I'd fly him up there, and would yesterday be too soon? Danny was a tiny man who ran an amusement arcade in Brighton and he, and his sister-in-law Eileen, were firm supporters of our small Club. As usual it was a case of no sooner said than done.

We flew north in our open two-seat Miles Magister, and after stops for fuel at Sywell and Yeadon we pressed on into the gathering dusk above Yorkshire. By now I'd flown off the south of England map. I hadn't been able to find a north of England map before we left, but Danny's logic that you couldn't miss the Firth appealed to me, and we left without one.

Darkness closed gently about us. There was a full moon and the evening was beautifully still. The land beneath us was ghostly in its pale whiteness, and our Maggie flew herself and her contented passengers into a dreamy state. Sure enough some two hours after leaving Yorkshire we saw the Firth of Forth in the moon's reflected light, found the bridge, and turned westwards to Grangemouth, our destination.

I had reckoned to arrive in the early evening, but we'd stopped for a chicken supper at Yeadon and it had put our timing back a bit. It was dark over the airfield, but I could just discern the even darker triangle of runways below, but as I dropped lower, I saw too the big white crosses painted on the ends of them. Unserviceable.

Just after the war airfield runways were often used to store munitions, bombs and the like, so no way was I going to land blind on one of them. I eased the throttle and set up an approach on the runway up moon, aiming to land on the grass alongside. The Maggie sank softly below the tree line, and the moon, low on the horizon, vanished. It left us in stygian blackness. The grass couldn't have been 80 feet beneath us, so I closed the throttle and eased the stick into first a glide, and then, when I thought the moment was right, eased the stick further back . . . and back, and finally right back.

Nothing happened. I could see nothing, there was no instrument lighting, nothing. All I was aware of was the rhythmic bark of the engine up front ticking over. I held the stick fully back and waited. Still nothing happened. Perplexed, I shut off the engine. The black stillness of the night embraced us.

A voice from the back said: "Are we down?"

"I don't know," I said.

We sat there a bit longer and the voice said: "I'll climb out and see."
I said: "Be careful."
There was a sound of Danny undoing his harness and fumbling around.
"I think we are down," he said. "I'm going to jump."
I waited with bated breath. A hand tapped on the fuselage. "We're down," said a voice from below me. He was only a little bloke, even shorter than me, and the wheat we'd landed in came up to his chest.

From afar came voices and flaming torches as Danny's friends and family ploughed their way to our rescue. I slept soundly that night in a showman's caravan, woken only once when someone implored me to stop Danny, who couldn't fly, from going for another flight. The full moon was overhead now and probably affecting Danny as much as the whisky.

NORMAN, THE LAW AND TIGERAMA

REDHILL HOMER – OCTOBER

Ken Smith was recently demonstrating his tiny VHF transistor radio when he picked up on the Biggin frequency a call to the Tower for Redhill's frequency. It was late afternoon and the visibility was extremely poor, and quite obviously the aircraft, a Proctor, was going to have its work cut out finding Redhill. The Tower's reply was of course negative and the Proctor notified them of their intention to call Gatwick. A quick switch to Gatwick earned the information that the Proctor was going to attempt to land at Redhill and, if unsuccessful, would make Gatwick. Gatwick acknowledged and Ken organised a reception.

An Aldis lamp was quickly brought out and very soon they heard the sound of the Proctor's engine. It wasn't until the aircraft was overhead that it was seen and Ken let off a couple of yellow Verys, and then a 'green' from the lamp encouraged the Proctor in. This bit of quick thinking was much appreciated by the anxious visitors.

The Legal Fund was founded in December. The original idea was for a confidential fund available to assist members who fell foul of the law. It was supposed to be confidential so that members wouldn't just assume we'd pay their fines and fly with more abandon than usual.

It wasn't that there was any feeling against the Law as such, but bitter experiences had shown that the Law could be an ass over flying matters. We were only following the Boy Scouts' motto: "Be Prepared."

Norman Jones, who had suffered the Law's ignorance some years earlier, provided the first donation of £248. His case became something of a *cause celebre* at the time and over the years something of a legend too. I like the legend version best. Norman had landed his Tiger at a disused airfield down in Hampshire. He had been on his way to play golf and a change of heart or plan necessitated a phone call.

He was over Beaulieu so landed there to look for a telephone. A Ministry policeman eventually arrived on the scene, and in the ensuing exchange the copper was firmly told by the Boss to stand to attention when addressing an officer. That Norman was in civvys – and probably scruffy ones at that, for he cared little for things sartorial – is by the by.

When the policeman began to splutter Norman cut in with: "And get your hair cut!"

Knowing Norman Jones it's quite on the cards that he helped himself to a slice of that unreasonable fine of £200 with £48 costs with his less than tactful manner, but the injustice of the case attracted much comment and was widely reported. The wisdom of starting this Fund was highlighted some two years later in tragic circumstance.

In the autumn we sent a wreath to Leon Biancotto's funeral. He had died whilst practising for the Czechoslovakian World Aerobatic Championship at Bratislava. Leon had been a magnificent aerobatic pilot, and during the previous summer of 1960, and by then a member of the Club, had brilliantly flown one of our single-seat Tigers in the Lockheed Contest to that aircraft's highest ever position in that prestigious competition.

Generally speaking no one ever mentioned death. It happened: we mourned briefly, went to the funeral, and then got on with our thing. In some strange manner, a hangover from the war years perhaps, it wasn't considered the done thing to mention the sadness again. The Club was to lose many fine pilots and dear friends in the coming years, but apart from the odd commemorative trophy and a brief obituary, their passing was scarcely mentioned: but all without exception were remembered, and many with great fondness.

Towards the end of 1961 flying dropped off considerably and there was more hangar flying than usual. Bish had organised a photographic display in the hangar called Tigerama. It was well received, and Bish was to be seen beaming proudly whenever someone stopped to look at the record of thirty years of the Tiger.

It was around this time too that an aged Monospar came to Redhill. This tired Gipsy-powered twin had been flown all the way from Australia by an outback flying doctor member of the Club, John Morris. He and Bruce Harrison had shared an incredible journey, and we had welcomed them with some pride. The Monospar disappeared soon afterwards in the direction of Ireland, but not before we had clambered all over it making noises of ownership to Norman, who for a change didn't seem to hear us. One memory of that old bird stays with me. Attached to a piece of string and hanging in the cockpit was a 15 inch piece of pencil-thin wood with a metal hook at its end. It took a long while before we were able to fathom

95

out its use. When strapped in, it proved impossible to reach the altimeter and the device was used to adjust it!

Norman had not done us badly with new aircraft that year, what with the big Jodel, the Condor and Super Cub, and that beautiful new toy, the Cosmic Wind *Ballerina*. We had first seen her demonstrated late in the September at Eastleigh, by a tall lanky Texan by the name of Milton Blair. Its performance had left us breathless. We weren't to get our hands on her though till the New Year.

Another aircraft that came on stream late that year was the Arrow Active. Although the Club had owned this historic and unique biplane for some time, it had had a chequered career and been pranged twice. The most spectacular occasion was Clive Elton's start in the National Races back in '59. He had pushed on full power too quickly and VE gracefully, and so very slowly she went over onto her back. Since then it had been modified a few times, and now the Committee felt it could safely be let out again providing it was flown by approved pilots only. Some of us were to fall in love with her.

1962

STANDING ON WING AND PANSHANGER

1962 opened sadly with the death of the much loved Mike Reilly. Mike had been a remarkable and brave parachutist and, such was his closeness to all of us, his loss hit us particularly hard. He had been working with Sue Burges on the film *The War Lover* and they had parachuted from a B-17 Flying Fortress into the Channel. It had started as a straightforward drop but he had become tangled with his parachute shrouds on entering the water, and although the safety boat got there in minutes they were unable to save him. His book *Alone in the Sky* was published shortly after his death with a sad preface by Lord Brabazon of Tara.

My log book for February 1962 records a first flight in the Cosmic Wind and a check flight with a new pilot, Neil Williams. In the remarks column I wrote: "Formation check – very good." That comment was to prove something of an understatement in the months to come. On March 4th my logbook records: "Standing on the Wing – live trials. Dennis Hartas."

In 1959, after a season of air displays that could have been better, the cry went up for new ideas to make the coming season more successful and exciting. It was at a party I gave for Sue Burges, to celebrate her return from a long spell in hospital, that the Standing on the Wing idea was born. On the night in question the conversation inevitably got around to "shop" and new display acts in particular. Heaven knows what made me say it, but before I could stop myself I had suggested that someone should climb up onto the top of a Tiger and stand there. I knew the moment I had said it I was not going to get off this hook.

I presented the idea to our Chairman. He got three bits of paper pinned together, one of which portrayed someone crouching wildly above the fuel tank of a Tiger. He was hanging on grimly to a reins-like arrangement strung back from the leading edge of the wing. The foot holds were ski-like and designed to prevent the rider going up when the aeroplane didn't.

Not in the least put out by the proposition, and obviously approving of it, Norman Jones handed the idea over to Rollason's Chief Engineer. It didn't meet with much enthusiasm and Adrian Deverell did his best to forget its existence. Not without reason, for he was far too busy rigging and preparing lots of aircraft for the coming National Air Races to take such a mad idea seriously. Eventually he came around to it, produced a working set of drawings which he wisely had independently stress-checked, and then presented the lot to the proper authorities, the Air Registration Board.

If making the rig was not without its moments on our side of the fence, at least we had the same conductor. Norman had done the right thing, and in 1960 had got the approval of the Ministry of Aviation with certain provisos. There is no simple "Yes" in the Ministry. The ARB got to work on the drawings submitted and approved them. They treated the matter in a pleasant manner, were stringent in their demands, and once satisfied stayed that way. The Ministry of Aviation obviously didn't know what to make of it; and didn't. To this day I don't believe they thought we were serious. The ARB had demanded that the first trials be conducted with a life-size dummy. Dev and his team produced Brother Ben, a substantial 150 lb stand-in, an overalled mass complete with a painted face, flying helmet and a pair of Dev's old shoes on his metal feet.

In February, over two years after the idea had originated, one chilly Monday afternoon, I began the first test before ARB officials – a series of taxying manoeuvres followed by a straight run or two and finally a brief hop skip and a jump. I conferred with Dev, David Phillips and Dennis Hartas, both experienced pilots, and then taxied out to complete a first circuit.

The Tiger Moth has had some incredible things done to her in a long and versatile life, but a heavy figure perched above the top wing must surely represent her strangest assignment. Tiger G-ARAZ managed like the tolerant creature she is. I have never seen Adrian Deverell so happy. His face reflected all the love he felt for Tigers and he was just bursting with pride.

Several more circuits were made that day with David and Dennis also at the controls and all reported the Tiger fully controllable and straightforward to fly – within, of course, the limitations that so much drag must present. A test report was made out and accepted, and the stage was set for the first live run. On March 4th the 'guinea pig,' me, was fussed over and generally said goodbye to by the entire Club. Layer above layer of clothing was put on, an oxygen mask so that I could breathe – it was generally believed that the wind would make normal breathing impossible – and someone even suggested a body layer of fat, channel swimmer-style.

There was snow on the ground and it was bitterly cold. Dennis was the pilot and David flew escort in the Piper Super Cub with Barry Griffiths as photographer.

It worked, I lived, and in the process discovered a delightful new way to fly. Barry had a go and came down as intoxicated with the experience as I had been. Within a few minutes of landing the phones began to ring. Was it true that people were reporting a man standing on an aeroplane? Barry, who was in charge of PR, and had anyway been urged by Norman to try and sell the story to recoup some of the project's research and development, was cagey indeed. He had promptly sold the exclusivity to the *Daily Express* for a fair sum, but I suspect poor Norman never did get back much from his investment. We tried Norman, honest we did.

The public first got a glimpse of the new act at Panshanger some eight weeks later. The time in between was well spent in promoting the forthcoming show. It was to be the first time there, but so effective were Barry's endeavours at publicity that it turned out to be a great success.

It was there too that Neil Williams' potential as an aerobatic pilot was first appreciated – then by the few: his international recognition was still some years ahead.

PANSHANGER: FIRST FULL DISPLAY

Weather was good, an occasionally elusive sun and cool easterly wind blowing soundly down the main runway was as much as we could wish for. And the crowds. From 12 onwards there was a steady flow of cars until at 2 pm there was a solid jam down the lane and along the main road. An estimate put the number of cars at 2,000 and from the air it looked one of our biggest crowds; flying in downwind on the flypast aroused thoughts of Farnborough – so said several pilots.

The noisy opener was a low affair with 17 aircraft all up and down in six minutes. Let's go through the programme in roughly the right order. And talking of programmes, this was a vast improvement on last year's. I'm talking of the one shilling variety. This year there were numerous photographs of the "glamour boys," as Bill Chesson calls our humble flying members.

Bish opened with classic aerobatics in his incomparable style and James Baring led the Turbulators: Shaun de Salis, Ian Trethewey and Barry Griffiths. Couldn't help noticing how nicely coloured the streaming paper was. Changing the subject slightly, it seems that a firm specialising in toilet paper has written a letter to the Club in which it writes flowingly of its products.

Methinks Pee Wee Judge picked a loser in flying the Piper Cub for balloon bursting – the high wing must have made life impossible, especially since the balloons were a shadow of their former glory in size; and as he was trying, Peter Phillips flew the Cosmic Wind unobtrusively away to suddenly return when the balloon bursting was over to give a shatteringly fine performance.

We saw the Wind twice that afternoon in a pair of displays that were a joy to behold. These were displays of memorable brilliance. Strangely enough, both performances were utterly different in character. Peter, for instance, flew with a diamond-sharp precision and his 8-point rolls were the finest the writer has ever seen, and yet Neil Williams' verve and showmanship went over big and in a way that delighted pilot and layman alike; perhaps this will become a friendly rivalry that will enhance our displays and delight us all in the summer to come.

Something went wrong with the 'Challenge' – too few tapes to burst but the crowd enjoyed the spectacle of three of our elders hopping about in aeroplanes, even if they must have wondered what on earth it was all about. About this time the sun got lost behind a frontal covering of cirrus, but the spectators would scarcely have noticed this, what with their "Ooh"s and "Aah"s at Dennis Hartas's crazy flying. What a blessing John Blake takes on this job of commentating, for a more suitable commentator would be impossible to find.

The SOW (Standing on Wing) project came of age with some nice flying by Dennis and with Benjy on top. This act was certainly a high spot, capturing something of a spontaneous enthusiasm that made spectators and passenger wave happily to each other. A new innovation by the way, was to fly under the tapes with the rider endeavouring to burst a balloon en route and on the second pass, succeeding in taking the tapes with him.

This was a display that owed much to the many and not, as in the past, to a few. A good display, and if the number of autograph hunters is any indication, played to a younger generation increasingly more flying-minded than its predecessor. It's nice to think we in the Tiger Club are playing some part in this . . .

The 'SOW' act, as the Standing on Wing became known (we ruefully accepted the inevitable), was still in its infancy, and as the year progressed its shortcomings were to be revealed, but not before some well-publicised flights had entertained the media and public, and on occasion, frightened the lights out of the airborne team.

I was ever a collector of remarks. I used to rummage around for the odd backs of envelopes whenever I heard something for the collection, and the *Tiger Rag* was ever the place to pass on the fun.

"I've given up smoking – unless I want to think – and that's very rare." Attributed to a thoughtful Sue.

The *Rag* too welcomed letters. One to Bish read:

"I was most interested to read in the current issue of the *Tiger Rag* about the Club's 'Standing on the Wing' idea.

As you know, John Holmes (brother of Fred Holmes of Tiltman and Langley) and myself were the first to 'walk on the wings' in this country, which we did many hundreds of times on a 504 during the 1919-1923 period. That was many years ago, and it was not so spectacular as standing on the top wing, but, nevertheless, quite exciting for the performers, ever with the thought of a possible engine cut.

It is rather amusing how we came to do it in the first place. Business was bad during a visit to Taunton, and one evening we were chatting with the Editor of the local paper on ways and means of drawing the crowds, when he said: "Why not try walking on the wings, as they are doing in America?" After a few rounds of the local brew, we agreed that perhaps it was a good idea, but did not really consider the suggestion seriously. The next morning, when walking through the town to our flying field, we met half a dozen sandwichmen carrying posters announcing to all and sundry that an attempt – the first ever – would be made to walk on the wings of an aeroplane at 4 o'clock the following Sunday. Our first reaction was: "I wonder who those silly so-and-sos are?", and then we realised it was us!

There was no getting out of it, for on the Sunday morning the police informed us that special coaches were on the way from all over Somerset, and they were expecting a large crowd. Sure enough, we had a crowd of over 7,000 people and a gate of over £100, and at 4 pm we 'walked the wings' for the first time.

It was such a success that we repeated the performance whenever the crowd was large enough. I shall look forward to seeing the Tiger Club's version at one of your many flying meetings.

Yours sincerely,
Joe Taylor"

With "Standing on Wing" in mind, a charming young French girl recently wrote:

"My dear Mr Benjamin,
I should like to take this opportunity to request that this summer I be permitted to perform the aerobatic exercise of flying flat on top of the plane, and also the exercise of lying on the bottom wing while the pilot is performing.

Yours sincerely,
Paulette"

INSTANT RESPECT AND THE EATING OUT SOCIETY

The popular Duty Rate of 30/- an hour (£1.50) was withdrawn in March. We'd enjoyed five years of subsidised flying at a price unequalled since the prewar days of the Civil Air Guard. If we were surprised at all, it wasn't at the withdrawal, but that Norman had let us get away with it for so long. In its place we now were asked to submit our duty hours flown, and hoped the proportion of the gate monies set aside for the pilot's expenses was high enough to meet them. It was often a case of swings and roundabouts. If the gate was good we got it all back. I can ruefully remember times when we went without.

Around March too, a long-range Turbulent came on stream and immediately Norman Jones began to think of ways of promoting this new aircraft. The first I realised what was up was when Norman buttonholed me and suggested I took the new Turbulent down to Cape Town.

"You don't weigh much – you're just the fellow!"

I thought so too for a time but had to cry off. My tiny business was a one-man affair, and anyway I had no money.

The Turbulent in question was fitted with a 4-gallon auxiliary belly tank extending the range to some 400 miles which, at around a windy noisy 80 mph, would have been more than enough.

Naturally, we do not all see Redhill through the same eyes, but recently the images have become truly Alice-like. For instance: let's reflect on Robin d'Erlanger's introduction to the airfield. He arrived there for the first time seeking his new Turbulent the very morning of Sue's wedding, not that he was to know, poor fellow. Everyone was hurrying and scurrying about including a couple of gentlemen wearing full morning dress. One of these dignified gentlemen was detailed to show Robin around. He immediately thrust him into the Piper Cub and, with tails caught in the door and ends flapping, his top hat at a jaunty angle, did a three minute circuit, burbling about zones and instant respect. If this made Robin catch his breath, the sight of another top hat, firmly clamped down, riding a Turbulent must have choked him . . .

The two gentlemen were "GB" Golding Barrett and Norman Jones who had indeed jammed top hat and all into a Turbulent. Robin had, when he was young, a bit of a stutter. There's a delightful story told of this very popular Club member's visit to Shoreham, where he was introduced to the Beagle Airedale. The Airedale was a variant of the range of latter-day Austers which were then being built there.

The salesman, aware that Robin's father was Sir Gerald d'Erlanger, the then Chairman of BEA, was obviously anxious to impress.

"What do you think of it?" he asked Robin, referring to the Airedale.

Robin, probably at a loss for words anyway, for the Airedale was never much of a machine, began to stutter.

The salesman misunderstood and hurried on. "Yes," he admitted; "it isn't up to much."

The Club had a Beagle Husky for a while and although it was used quite a lot, mainly for glider towing, it was never popular, being both noisier and slower than the lower-powered Jodels.

QUOTES: Said John Blake during a curry dinner: "Bring on the dancing girls."

The Indian waiter was most apologetic: "So sorry, dancing girls not on menu."

And Robin during the same meal: "What a hell of a place to make a forced landing," said he, looking hard at his dish of curry, and he added: "You couldn't possibly get down on that."

I hear that a successful Turbulent tow was recently completed down at Farnborough, and that Arthur Humphreys, during the ten days of the National Championships, got in over a hundred tows . . . and he had a very sunburnt face to show for it.

Presumably Arthur used a Tiger for this towing. Although the Turb did tow a glider off, it only once, to my knowledge, repeated the performance. At the time it was said that it was the lowest-powered aircraft ever to tow a glider off the ground.

The Tiger Club was ever noted for its characters. It attracted men and women who in any other organisation would have been square pegs in round holes. They all fitted in our Club. Such a character was Arthur. Arthur was the most loveable of men. An Australian, he had come to this country to fly with the Club. He was very small, and no matter what the weather, never ever took his coat off. In fact we suspect he wore several, the outer one of which trailed near the floor for all the world like Disney's Dopey. Around his neck was wound a vast woolly scarf.

No one ever saw Arthur without a smile on his face and he helped everyone. He rode a huge motorcycle everywhere and no doubt was as short of money as the rest of us. After about a year he returned to his homeland where to his good fortune he had two loves – his new bride, Joan, and an old Tiger Moth. Arthur and Joan were later to present the Club with a magnificent reproduction of Joan's father's log-book. He was the legendary Capt. Hinchliffe, who was lost in March 1928 attempting to cross the Atlantic from east to west in company with the heiress Elsie McKay.

The Stampe is back with us, resplendent in yellow and red, not unlike the gay colouring of the original *Bishop*. A Gipsy Major replaces the heavier Renault unit and, according to those who have flown it, is a vast improvement. A special word of appreciation is due to Dev and his associates for making such a beautiful job of this aircraft.

It was "GB" who once lamented that there wasn't enough respect going around, and promptly earned himself a tin labelled "Instant Respect." Now

John Blake has thought up a new game and already there's a growing list of "Instants."

To list a few:

For Instant Blake just add nausea.
For Instant "GB" just administrate.
For instant Nav just adrift.

Some of the better ones aren't really suitable for publication.

Members with growing families will welcome a new junior membership subscription of 10/6 (age limit 14), and news of another Club within our Club – the newly formed Eating Out Society. This most exclusive of Clubs is at the moment restricted to just four members; it's impossible to give their names for fear of them being called hogs. The sole aim of the TCEOS is succinctly summed up in one word: nourishment . . .

I recently came across the original rules. The Society may not have lasted for long, but whilst it did we had some great evenings out. In revealing all I ask the other members' indulgence in breaking Rule 16.

First General Meeting held at Brooks', 14th May 1962
THE TIGER CLUB EATING OUT SOCIETY

Present: J. Baring, L. Benjamin, R. d'Erlanger and John Blake. Rules
Object of the Society: Nourishment.
Membership: Founder Members – see above.
Ordinary Members – see above.
Associate Members – see above.
Passenger Members – see above.
Honorary Members – see above.

1. There shall be not more than one dinner per fortnight, organised by the duty Member, who shall, on that occasion, appoint the Dining Member next for duty.
2. There shall not be less than one such dinner per month.
3. The place and style of the dinners shall be entirely at the discretion of the convening Member.
4. On the unanimous approval of a quorum of Members (4), an extraordinary general dinner may be consumed.
5. Guests: Scale of guests – one per Member. One honoured guest per fortnightly dinner is the entitlement of the convening Member.
6. No respect for "GB."
7. No fiddling without the connivance of the other Members.
8. Robin is usually wrong.
9. Benjy is always wrong.

10. Once every year each Member shall dine the other Members abroad, preferably by Mousquetaire.
11. Benjy must not, on Society occasions, mention the Newsletter (one member dissenting).
12. No assets.
13. Dinners shall be held on alternate Mondays.
14. No excuses.
15. The next meeting shall be at the convening Member's convenience.
16. No non-member shall be privy to this.
24. Robin shall keep the Society's copy of *Eskimo Nell*.

There were, to my knowledge, only two other Clubs within the Club and they came somewhat later. One was the Tiger Shooting Club, and such was the enthusiasm members showed with either bow and arrows and an air rifle that others, alarmed at the goings on, disarmed us! The other met with Norman's profound disapproval. It came into being some years later and gathered to itself all those who had pranged a Club aircraft. Just for the record it was called the Black Cat Club – although for the life of me I can no longer remember why.

The summer of 1962 was now upon us, and for some extraordinary reason, people still thought that 'SOW' was news and we gained some good TV spots, but undoubtedly the most momentous was the unforgettable *Tonight* programme. That hilarious ten-minute spot, during which scripts were forgotten and one windswept passenger, me, who was past caring, sang *(sic)* the closing signature tune, to the delight of the production team and the amazement of 8 million viewers.

There was a wry postscript. James Baring later gave us fifty recordings of the occasion for a wedding present. (Guinness Book of Records for originality?). In an attempt to get rid of some of them I sent one to Cliff Michelmore. I got back a warning about copyright for my pains, and a legal threat if I didn't destroy them all. Over twenty years later the BBC got their wish; I can no longer lay my hands on one. The Pathé Pictorial colour feature was also now being seen all over the country, adding its weight to numerous newspaper photos and features the world over.

OPERATION 'SOW' – JUST

It had long been the aim to put a woman on top – apart from the advantagous weight factor it would mean yet more good publicity. Already two female Club members had flown up there and enjoyed it. It was originally agreed to let Sue Burges (soon to become Sue Phillips) and Juanita Jover (later to become my wife) alternate appearances at the remaining displays. Sue's turn was at Fair Oaks, but it was washed out the first time, and thus it fell to Juanita – by now nicknamed Lolita (I suspect it had something to do with our age gap) – to make the first appearance at Shoreham. Whilst a man on a wing had been seen before, it was certainly the first time for a girl.

But if we were all smiling faces for the cameras and the public, all was not well with those in the know. An unknown jinx plagued us and, when it made itself felt, taxed the pilot's skill to the limit, and left the anxious passenger up there with more to think about than was good for him. For in spite of full throttle, there were times when, near the ground, the Tiger wouldn't go fast enough. High on success no one stopped to reason it out.

We had flown up to Rearsby in May for a full display. It was a small airfield north of Leicester, and 'SOW' was to be the big feature. My pilot was David Phillips. Came the big moment and we took off, but instead of climbing to around 100 feet or so David flew straight on at about 15 feet. From up on high I was able to see clearly down into his office. If I had expected a reassuring grin, I didn't get it. He was staring rigidly forward, tense and alert, his knuckles white with the strain of willing even more power from a throttle already wide open.

By now we were passing the Clubhouse, which stood on a slight rise, and was if anything slightly above us. We headed out into the valley still at some 15 feet. What was wrong was painfully clear to me for the first time. We had full power all right, but we were well and truly on the wrong side of the drag curve, and poised between sky and earth at a whisker above the stall, unable to climb or turn. Things were getting interesting.

Ahead was a garden with washing on a line flapping in the breeze. We missed the washing and flew between a couple of trees. All the while David was inching to his left around a tiny hill intent on regaining the airfield. I'd planned for moments like this. Originally I had decided that, if things ever got beyond a joke, I'd risk the unsecured slither down over the trailing edge of the wing to drop into the vacant front cockpit. In theory a great idea, but impossible this time for our balance was so finely drawn that any movement of the centre of gravity would be fatal. I waited and made myself as small as possible.

Still edging to his left, David contrived to encircle the rise, and then with relief we saw the airfield boundary coming up. In the slight turn, though, we had lost altitude – if that's the right word for anything so near the ground. We were now heading for the wire fence. David, aware of the danger, pulled back at the last moment, and in that final flare both contrived to land and take the wire with us at the same time. A hasty unhooking, and we taxied back to cheering crowds who had barely seen us airborne before we'd disappeared.

We had seen the light. Immediately we ensured that in future we'd always take a longer run, and so be sure of sufficient forward speed before we climbed out; agreed to fit a fine-pitch propeller; to not fill the fuel tank; and to seek lighter loads. That's where the girls scored. I soldiered on until the autumn, appearing at Sywell and Bill Chesson's race track, Lydden Circuit, near Canterbury in Kent.

At Lydden I appeared dressed as a French Legionnaire complete with a beard and firing off blanks from a huge ·45 revolver. (I think that Legionnaire outfit was Bill Chesson's only disguise – it certainly went the rounds). The wind was strong on the day and as Dennis Hartas ploughed slowly eastwards from Hawkinge where we'd landed so I could get dressed up, we overflew a cricket match. One by one the players stopped to look up in amazement as we slowly went by. I looked back as we left the boundary. They were still gathered in groups: speechless.

One more dubious excitement remained for me before the lightweight girls took over for good. The occasion was again inspired by an idea for a new act for the following season. Over tea in the Clubroom we reasoned that if someone could stand on top of a Tiger, what was there to prevent an extension of the theme – to transfer to another aeroplane whilst in flight? The most suitable aircraft to accept the weight of the standee was the Super Cub – it stood just outside the hangar – and from it someone could lower a rope ladder. With the Tiger pilot doing the formation from below the transfer could be effected at the precise moment of passing in front of the crowd. It was a great idea.

We couldn't wait to go out and try it. We laughingly decided to mount the operation step by step. Firstly, we wanted to see if the Tiger pilot could clearly see the lowered ladder and so ensure its safe arrival in front of the passenger up there on the wing. We couldn't find a rope ladder, so we settled for a length of rope weighted down by a bucket . . . and since the bucket was not only a weight but also a container, couldn't we also effect a transfer of something or other? Excellent idea, everyone agreed, full of enthusiasm. A young lad was recruited (Paul Conyers, who was then about twelve) to do the bucket lowering, and he was asked if he would put something into the bucket so I could reach in and take it out whilst in flight.

I climbed up onto Tiger G-ARAZ and with Dennis Hartas as my pilot we flew off to await the arrival of David Phillips and young Paul in the Super Cub. Below us Club members stood in front of the hangar, having been briefed to watch proceedings and to give opinions as to the act's audience potential. We took up station below and behind the Cub, and together we curved left over the southern boundary at Redhill to straighten out in a slight dive at 500 feet. We were now going north towards the hangar aiming to arrive some 50 feet up in front of the small gathering.

David already had the starboard doors of the Cub locked open, and I could see Paul lowering his bucket. When he had about 12 feet of rope out he gave a big grin and a thumbs up. Dennis moved upwards and forward to position the bucket in front of my face. He was extremely precise. I fumbled in the swaying bucket and my fingers felt rope which unthinkingly I tugged out. It came out alright, along with the heavy metal picketing anchor tied to its end. The metal, assisted by a 60-knot wind, smartly hit me on the head and knocked me out.

This was even better than the crowd expected and they applauded wildly. David though, at once aware that something was wrong, moved to one side and indicated to Dennis to have a look. He couldn't have been reassured. I was unconscious and slumped in my harness, blood on my face. I came to as Dennis completed the smoothest-ever landing, running on his wheels straight towards the help awaiting us at the hangar.

"We'll have to think of something else," said Dennis when I stumbled down.

I agreed.

TURB ROCKETS AND DOG FIGHTS

The Turbulent in its own way was becoming almost as versatile as its big sister in the Club, the Tiger. The Turb had appeared with wheel spats on 'Sunday best' occasions, but were usually left off, for in muddy conditions they gathered mud like it was going out of fashion. Clear plastic cockpit canopies were popular for a while, but they too fell out of favour for one of the charms of the little Turb was the sweet fresh air. Unlike the Tiger, the Turbulent had a fairly draught-free cockpit, and it wasn't really necessary to wear either helmet or goggles. The delight of just getting in and spending ten carefree minutes alone in the sky blowing the cobwebs away was, and still is, one of the better moments in life.

She flew in winter on skis, and the Club still put them on as soon as there is enough snow about. She flew, and eventually sank, with floats, and once without the benefit of floats, she floated long enough for her salvage and the rescue of Robin d'Erlanger. He later said after his wet forced landing that he didn't even get his feet wet. There's a photograph of this incident in the Clubroom to this day.

Some of the funniest stories about the Turbulent and her pilots were current around the early sixties. There always seemed to be a ready preoccupation among the members with the idea of producing new acts to entertain our growing public. One such idea occured to James Baring. He wanted, no less, to fit a pair of rockets to his Turb.

Nearby was a famous firework factory so James went visiting. No trouble, they assured him. We could easily provide the rockets, and would you like some electrical igniters? In no time at all Baring was in the air to test-fire his rockets. He tore across the airfield, touched them off, and with a spectacular whoosh they rushed on ahead, a delight in smoke and fire. I can't remember why he abandoned the idea, it looked great to me. I think it might have been something caught fire.

James featured in another escapade during that summer of '62. Somehow or other he contrived to fly his Turb into some local power cables. His description was a classic of fact.

"There was an almighty bang and we stopped."

He landed safely, presumably the shortest landing on record, only the prop got broken, and a shaken James reported in. Operation 'Protect James' went into gear. I was instructed by "GB" to take him away and hide him. With an inspiration worthy of the moment, I took James to a cinema in Redhill, left him to enjoy the film and instructed him not to reappear for two hours.

Meanwhile the Law visited the airfield. It turned out the policeman was staunchly Irish (as was young James) which must have helped, for before he left us, satisfied no one was to blame, he was heard to say in a rich Irish brogue:

"Those power cables are a bloody menace to pilots."

And we heard no more about it.

One event that would have put the icing on the Turbulents popularity everywhere, had it come off, was the Navy's invitation for some Turbs to land on a Carrier and for the pilots to be their guests over a weekend. The Admiralty unfortunately got to hear of the plan and vetoed it.

CLUB NEWS, SEPT '62: Those at Redhill these last few weekends have seen nine Turbs formating with a rare skill . . . and not without raising an occasional laugh. To illustrate the point, eight pilots on foot were lately seen trotting about in formations of four with arms outstretched and burbling like motors as they played "aeroplanes" in front of the hangar. Simulated training, they called it; those who watched curled up and found another name for it.

Robin climbed to 12,005 feet in a Turbulent on the 7th October. At least one other pilot has since attempted to better this and given up. Thus to Robin d'Erlanger goes the Turbulent Altitude Record . . .

ON THE SUBJECT OF RECORDS: John Severne wrote: "I also read in the *Rag* that Robin climbed to 12,005 feet in a Turbulent on Oct 7th. This may be a misprint for 12,500! However, if I read it correctly, he's got another 456 to go to beat my own best height.

On 24th June '61, on my way back from the Bristol Air Races, I climbed 'PNZ to 12,500 ft, reaching that height just south of Reading (it's all in my log-book!). She would have gone higher if I'd tried. When nearing the ceiling, every pound of weight is critical and I had about 4 gallons left. If Robin likes to take the fastest Turbulent up on a nice cold day, and climb it till he runs out of fuel, preferably near somewhere he can do a decent forced landing, he'll get a lot higher than 12,000!"

As it happens, 'PNZ has just had a powerful new engine fitted, 1500 cc of "go" which when flown by Pee Wee Judge on the 2nd December reached 700 feet over the airfield boundary in a climb from take-off. Should prove the ideal mount . . .

SHOREHAM FULL DISPLAY, AUG '62. Another winner was Lolita. She stood on the wing for the first time in public, and bravely fired a huge ·45 revolver held most determinedly in both small hands, and what's more, got the balloon first time under the hoop. Her voice too was heard describing her experiences; all very cool, calm and collected. A fascinating new technique was seen in the flour bombing. To Dennis Hartas goes the credit of performing a sensational and highly accurate LABS. Yet another newcomer to the scene was the Dawn Patrol 1917 variety. Strictly speaking this is the first *new* act since 'SOW,' but somehow it never really got going. Both aircraft were out of phase and the sound effects were ineffective, but with some practice, and the blank-firing machine guns Dev is building, it should eventually prove a winner.

LABS was quite a sight to behold. It was based on the then current technique of getting rid of an atomic bomb, and retiring as quickly as possible. Dennis dived on the target, dropped his flour bag and then pulled back sharply into a loop and rolled off the top to dive out of the way in the opposite direction. The Dawn Patrol may not have been much to watch on this, its first showing, but it was hard work for the pilots and not without its dangers. Two Tigers flew the patrol, and the scenario called for the wing man, Bill Laslett, to be bounced by the Active boldly disguised as the Hun by the addition of big black crosses on fuselage and wings. Pilot Neil Williams. Neil flew out of the sun in a steep dive, and inspite of the crowd shouting: "Look behind you, Bill!" Bill got the chop. He streamed smoke, whipped into a spin and made himself scarce. Then I joined battle with a single-seat Tiger.

We had rehearsed the dog fight. The general theme was clear – that for good patriotic reasons I should win – and then triumphantly do a victory roll. That was all very well to decide in cold blood, but anyone who knew Neil also knew that it wasn't Neil's style to give up on anything, especially on anything to do with flying. What began in fun soon began to get a bit earnest. The final sequence called for Neil to pull up and stall turn to the right and so present me with a chance to shoot him down. By this time I thought Neil had thrown away the script, and so when he went into the final climb my blood was up too, and I ruthlessly followed Neil upwards only I forgot to keep slightly to port. He winged over on schedule and we literally came face to face. For a moment he just hung there, a few feet away, and then he was gone. The old adage, "a miss is as good as a mile," doesn't say it all.

Dev's machine guns were never a winner, but they were an entertaining interlude. The sounds of battle up to then was provided over the PA system, an inadequate method that was very hit and miss – mostly miss. The guns were an ingenious device. They looked real enough mounted as they were on the fuselage ahead of the pilots, and the drum of ·22 blanks was revolved and fired by pulling a handle in the cockpit. The pilots though, only had two hands, and in a scrap we had to relinguish the throttle lever to pull the gun handle . . . not a good time to lose power response, when at any moment, a good burst of power, or the lack of it, was essential to maintain position or to move out of the way in a hurry. Then we discovered the guns couldn't be heard above 100 feet, and only then if we closed the throttle as well. We gave them back to Dev.

THE CLUB, PETER'S PLACE AND MARRIAGE

CLUB NEWS, NOVEMBER '62: Of late, members have been jumping out of their skins every time Neil Williams barks. No, Neil isn't, but he has the extraordinary urge to bark. Just how loudly and startling is the yap can best be judged by the uncanny (forgive me) effect of a bark when heard from the Stampe five hundred feet over the hangars; yes, it was Neil barking from on high – one day someone is going to bite him . . .

Talking about hearing from above led at one time to a series of experiments to see if one could talk to one's neighbour in a formation. It all started when, late one summer's evening, Dave Allan, a Tiger Club besotted Australian, dived his Tiger gently over the hangar at around one hundred feet, closed his throttle and bellowed something rude. He was clearly heard. In no time at all the Turbulent pilots were shouting to each other, but it only worked if the throttle was eased at the same time.

But since the throttle could only be eased momentarily or position wouldn't be maintained, the yell was strictly monosyllabic. Nor was there ever time to yell back: "What?" It is possible though to hear a good ground-based PA from the air. On one memorable flight in a low and tight box of four at Farnborough, we all clearly heard John Blake's booming commentary.

Rochester Airfield first came under Norman's wing in the June of '62. Only twenty minutes away from Redhill, it promised to be a very popular rendezvous. It was officially opened as Rochester Airport by the Mayor on September 29th, and at the same time in another part of the world a new branch was formed. Frank Price, the American acrobatic member, had returned to his native Waco in Texas after a summer with the Club, there to open his aerobatic school and local Tiger Club.

It was also during September that Bish was awarded the Paul Tissandier Diploma in recognition of his work in reviving interest in the art of aerobatics. Incidentally he was the second member to be awarded this prestigious diploma – Norman received it the previous year. Unsung was Peter Phillips' remarkable showing in the Lockheed Contests where he took third place flying a Stampe. It was then, and at the time of writing still is, the highest ever British placing.

CLUB NEWS, OCTOBER: September was an eventful month, with plenty of flying, a fine display and many new credits to mark up to TC members. One such event came as a complete surprise to all of us, for those who saw the Turbulent formation take-off at Fair Oaks gasped with astonishment as the No. 4 stayed in place in box, and the four were tied together! It is now possible to reveal that James Baring carried out no less than 22 experimental take-offs with Peter Phillips to establish the correct procedure, only to eventually discover that the best way was the perfectly normal TO.

CLUB NEWS, NOVEMBER: October, early mists and the long, golden brown of autumn sunshine; Redhill has never looked lovelier. A gentle wind of change must have swept over the flying, and left a more leisurely field and members content to just amble and sit around enjoying the last of the warm Indian summer. Unwound, relaxed, and all rather nice, but now October has left . . .

CLUB NEWS, DECEMBER: Just across the airfield from the hangar at Redhill can be seen a little pump-house. It snuggles down amid some trees right on the edge of the N-S runway, clearly visible but seldom seen, even though everyone taxies by but yards away. Yet right outside the little place is an apple tree and it was recently spotted. The tree yields a fine crop of Worcesters, as so many discovered to their delight this year . . .

Alas, neither the pump-house or trees remain.

It was whilst I was spending my last days with Marks and Spencer at their Putney store that I had became aware of a good-looking receptionist that my landlord was beginning to use in his hairdressing salon below my flat.

Juanita was dark, petite, and gifted with a warm infectious smile. She came from a long established circus family – the Jovers – and claimed she was the sixth generation of that great European family, who were still very much stage people.

It wasn't long before I was taking her flying, and it wasn't long before I was being invited back to tea, and no doubt a good vetting.

We can't all be perfect, and one of my failings was that I wasn't very romantic. I'd always felt a bit silly holding hands, and never did get around to writing poems to loved ones, or even do the Valentine routine properly. If once in a blue moon I sent flowers, it was usually as an expression of apology for having forgotten a date. Juanita must have been sadly resigned to my shortcomings, for when I eventually proposed to her, I found myself saying it between mouthfuls of a hot Indian curry. She gave me a little smile and raised her glass. It had taken me nigh on two years to get around to something everyone else had expected during the first six months.

We got married on Fireworks Day, 1962, at a North London Registry Office. The Tiger Club were reasonably in the know, but only just. Norman wrote briefly – he never wasted a word:

"Am delighted to hear that you are getting married on Monday, although this is rather sudden.
All the best,
Yours,
Norman."

Twenty words said it all.

"GB" had rallied a small contingent of members to support me: I could hear their ribald remarks as the ceremony got under way. The groom, overwhelmed by the entire proceedings, and heaven knows they didn't amount to much, was heard to mutter as the final words were said: "Now let's go and get a cup of tea!"

The run up to the big day was well in line with my romantic track record. I gave Juanita all the money I had – £13 – and told her to go out and buy a ring. I was still continuing to take no more from the struggling business than a fiver a week. Juanita, who was now a receptionist at a swish London hairdressing salon, earned little more than enough to keep us in food. What we hadn't got we did without, and were blissfully happy.

It was to this O'Henry background that the Tiger Club came to our rescue. We hadn't asked, for in our happiness we didn't need, but the Club was preparing behind our backs. Quite unknown to us they had booked us into a Kensington hotel for the Wedding Night. Sue and Peter Phillips opened their huge Cadogan Square flat for a party in our honour, and had invited nearly everyone in the Club. We were shocked when we learnt of these kindnesses and deeply touched. Our old Citroen 2CV had a door missing, so my brother, who was in on the secret, offered us the use of his car for, unknown to us, even our honeymoon had been taken care of, and transport would be needed. Pat and Brian Iles had lent us their home in deepest Gloucester and, so that we could be alone, had temporarily moved into quarters at Little Rissington where Brian was taking an Instructor's course. Faced by such a united front of friendship, we capitulated and happily departed.

1963

SKIS, JOHN AND VITAL STATISTICS

The winter of '62/'63 was one of classic beauty, and crisp clear skies brought the white landscape into a sharp and breathtaking focus. I wrote at the time:

There must be a mystic quality about Redhill, there has to be, for who in their right minds would have ventured into that white wilderness for any material reason? Yet members did get down there, struggling and slipping through snow and ice just to foregather and talk aeroplanes. For the whole month of January the airfield lay under a mantle of snow – the temperature never rose above freezing point and was invariably several degrees below. Until the introduction of skis in the middle of the month, there was no flying. The aircraft huddled together in a hangar so cold that even to open the doors needed chains and the Land Rover . . .

It was early in the new year that the Turbulents followed the Super Cub onto skis. To romp amid this pristine splendor was blissful. Both the Super Cub and the Turbs were absolutely straightforward to fly providing of course you kept moving, for the skis would freeze to the snow if you didn't. If anything it was easier to land on snow providing one didn't misjudge the height, something that was all too easy to do.

The prototype installation was made on 'PNZ, which seemed to be the guinea pig for most of the mods on the Turbs at that time. Skis on 'PZZ and 'RRZ quickly followed.

SKI-FLYING

Michael and the writer were ambling through the Boat Show recently when Michael suddenly changed the subject. I looked too. At the time we were passing an attractive shape tightly clad in leopard skin ski trousers and obviously part and parcel of a stand featuring skis.

Said Michael: "Must buy some skis for the Piper Cub," and before I could stop him, he stepped forward and politely asked if they had something suitable for an aeroplane.

'Ski-pants' gave a tired, resigned look and moved away.

Michael looked bewildered. "What did I say wrong?" he asked.

The next person he spoke to showed more understanding. And that's how skis came to the Tiger Club. Of course I could be wrong.

I flew over to John Wright's field one Sunday in the ski-equipped Cub. John had a precarious strip near Cranleigh, which overlooked Guildford, and which seemed to attract accidents as jam attracts wasps. On this day though, all his fields were levelled to one big airfield by the deep snow with an inviting profusion of choice of landing direction.

And there was John with a broad grin on his face to welcome us. John, a staunch ex-Navy pilot, happily saw life as a cross between high humour and a pink gin. He had an unenviable wartime reputation of having had to ditch into the sea several times, and his survival stories were hair-raising. I should think by the time I'd met him he'd used up eight of his lives. He got through some more without effort whilst I knew him, and he is still going strong – I hope.

I remember once we arranged to fly to Baden-Baden in the Jodel 117 for a weekend rally.

"Pick me up in the Super Cub," he urged, and added cryptically, "We may have to get away in a hurry!"

His tiny strip, roughly east-west, lay just beyond a line of trees and in a slight dip above which his farmhouse stood some 200 yards away. It was bounded by fencing and was bisected by the road to the house. Beyond the road in those days was a little but rough overshoot, so it was considered *infra dig* to finish one's landing run beyond the road. I think he claimed 300 yards including the overshoot, and that was generous.

It was a sunny day to begin an adventure. I set up a steep descent with full flap, and as I dropped over the trees I saw John running down the road towards the landing strip lugging a huge suitcase which was bumping clumsily against him with every step. He was in a terrible hurry as though someone was after him. I looked back up the road behind him and there was. His wife. She was closing the gap at a rate of knots. He fell breathlessly against the Cub, gathered what strength he had left, threw in the heavy case and clambered in as best he could.

"Take off," he yelled, and with him still half in, I opened the throttle and with the help of 150 hp we were airborne in yards. I looked down with interest as we turned above. The lady was literally bouncing up and down with fury and was waving her fist.

"Cor!" said John. "That was close."

No one had seriously got away with formation aerobatics until the spring of '63, when for the first time the three single-seat Tigers came on stream, 'NMZ, 'NZZ and 'OAA. The earliest attempts had been back in '58 and every once in a while the idea had been dragged out and tried – Clive Elton and I had a fling in '61 – but all attempts had been vetoed by Norman. "Too dangerous," he had said. No one argued. We had of course used the 'cooking Tigers,' a Club reference to the basic two-seater.

The first attempts with the three new single-seaters with the benefit of less weight and more power was in March. Pilots, Neil Williams, John Ayres and I. Then in quick succession Nick Pocock and James Baring joined in.

In an interview with Charles Greville of the *Daily Mail*, Neil had said: "It was a bit hairy to begin with. You see, it's a matter of handling your power just right at the top of the loop and the bottom."

That was typical Williams understatement. The old RFC adage: "There was I, upside down, with nothing on the clock but the maker's name," comes to mind.

And upside down with nothing on the clock – for 'clock' read 'Air Speed Indicator' – was no place to be with someone just feet from you. An aircraft at the point of stall is an unpredictable creature.

At one remarkable practice session James Baring had been flying to the left of Neil, who was leading the formation. Neil had indicated a loop and they were upside down at the top when James could feel he was running out of speed – fast – but at that stage there were no options left, so he just clung on with fingers crossed. The Tiger suddenly gave up the unequal battle, stalled, then flicked and rolled around a startled Neil in the lead aircraft, to wind up in perfect formation on the other side of an equally aghast Number 2. They pulled out of the loop in a perfect echelon to starboard.

"A little more speed on top next time, if you please, Neil," said James.

The fine new heading that graced the *Tiger Rag* in March '63 was by that superb aviation artist and Founder, Chris Wren. It was he who had designed our Club emblem and this, his latest contribution, contrived to trace our progress to date. It showed Bish wearing a mitre, flying as he was so often seen, upside down, and Norman Jones, with deerstalker, leading his team of Turbs. The Esso windsock may have been in deference to their generous sponsorship, and to the fact they had just given Chris a job.

As usual, the Chairman was the first to fly the latest Club acquisition, a 1931 DH Puss Moth. He literally got out of his sick bed to fly it to Redhill from Fair Oaks on the 24th February. A point of interest this, "NJ" has always been the first to fly every new Club machine, not excluding the prototypes, Condor and the original Turbs, and the "hot jobs" like the Active and the *Ballerina*. The Puss Moth G-AHLO is a high-wing monoplane armed with a Gipsy Major engine, a delightful vintage two-seater with fine hand-worked leather upholstery and polished woodwork. She was once the personal mount of the American Air Attaché in prewar days.

Flying practice began with a rush just as soon as sufficient snow had melted away. The Turbulents have been tearing about in close proximity and the Tigers have essayed their formation practices in more dignified mien. James Baring has had a wicked-looking hook fitted to his wingtip and has been practising picking up hankies with a considerable degree of success, every bit as spectacular a performance as his rocket firing episode – if that's possible . . .

MAE WEST'S VITAL STATISTICS
(from a letter from Dickie Reid):
"My very good friend Pee Wee gave me a Mae West two or three years ago, ex-Luftwaffe I fancy. I always considered it a very necessary piece of equipment for crossing the Channel to France etc. and I used to either wear it or keep it in the locker of the old Tiger Moth. It has always given me great confidence. About three months ago a friend of mine asked me if I possessed a Mae West for use in the Flinwell Drama Club as they had to dress up one of the members as a fat woman. I said I thought this would be admirable, so I lent it to them with a strict instruction that it must be returned as soon as the production was over as it was a very vital and necessary piece of my flying equipment.

About three or four days later I got this rather charming little stanza back, but no Mae West:

'To help us swell our drama group
You lent a Mae West, mate,
But I've got something that I must say:
"The darn thing won't inflate."
We puffed and puffed and puffed quite hard
Till someone said: he is a card,
It won't stay up – it just goes down.
Don't think that I'm ungrateful dear,
For this kind deed you do,
But tell me when you use the thing
Does it inflate for you?'

Dickie Reid was yet another of life's characters, one of so many who have threaded their way through the fabric of the Tiger Club. He operated his really ancient and decidedly tatty Tiger out of a very tiny strip on his farm in the heart of Sussex. It was respectfully noted for the obstacle course on the final approach. I doubt whether his particular Tiger had ever been cared for in the conventional sense. It flew, and Dickie obviously cherished it, warts and all. We laughed with delight and not a little derision whenever he brought the old thing to Redhill, but Dickie was one of the old school and laughed with us.

BISH LEAVES
I never quite knew how it happened, but suddenly Bish was to leave us to help with the formation of the Seaplane Club, an appointment he was to take up on the 1st May. The impression amongst the regulars was that

some unnecessary politics had been going on, for Bish was very popular and very active. His going was not only regretted but resented.

He was then 62 and continuing to do a wonderful job for the Club he literally lived for. Poor "GB" as his successor took some of the stick for Bish's going but, like the good man he was, bore it all with a cheerful fortitude, but I suspect he was deeply hurt. There was no trace of any resentment though in the official announcement in May.

As you may have heard, Bish has been persuaded to give his experience and help to the newly formed Seaplane Club – so closely allied to the Tiger Club. The seaplane being ready, it is certain that his duties at Lee-on-Solent will shortly mean his absence from Redhill more often than we shall like, and although he is not in any way fading out of the Tiger Club and its affairs, he has felt it reasonable to delegate some of his duties and responsibilities, and thus leave time to enjoy the best of both clubs.

Norman, and indeed all of us, feel that no one can ever quite fill the bill of C.F.I. (Chief Flying Instructor) as Bish has done, and consequently it has been decided to abolish the title which was particularly his.

The Club is now so large, the difficulty of remembering the particular skills and abilities of individuals makes essential a more careful system of type checking. Norman has decided that there shall be what he terms a Senior Check Pilot, who will be answerable to him for all checks by the team of check pilots. Provisionally, "GB" has accepted this, and in his words: ". . . on the condition that he be considered 'senior' on age rather than ability, and that the nomenclature be understood as 'administrator' of the team."

In the same issue of the *Tiger Rag* Bish wrote:

"Dear Members,
As many of you will know already, I have from the first of May been seconded to the newly-formed Seaplane Club at Lee-on-Solent, my job being to help Air Commodore Paul launch this venture, and to help him put it on a sound footing.

This of course means that, for the time being at least, I shall not be seen at Redhill as frequently as in the past, and this I shall very much regret. I have been with the Tiger Club since its very beginnings as a flying organisation, a time when we had but 25 members and four aeroplanes – G-ANSH, G-AOAA, G-ANZZ and G-AODR – and I have seen it grow into its present strength of over 20 aeroplanes and 400 odd members, and to gaining its present reputation as the foremost organisation in light aeroplane flying in England – and probably anywhere else as well. This has been a happy period and I am proud to have been able to help the Chairman, Norman Jones, in the fulfilment of his ideals, and to have had his confidence – and, I hope, yours – as Chief Flying Instructor of the Club. There have, of course, been times when I have had to make myself thoroughly unpleasant to all and sundry; this is very regrettable, but on reflection I am sure that those who have 'suffered' will realise that my words were for the good of the Club and very often themselves as well.

Now the old order changeth. "GB," well known to you all, will be in charge of all check flying. I ask you all to back him up as you have in the past backed me; and for the time being I leave the welfare of the Tiger Club in your hands.

Yours sincerely,

C.Nepean Bishop,

Chief Flying Instructor"

"Who (wrote Barry Griffiths) breathes an atmosphere of flying wires, open cockpits, leather helmets and watch-your-airspeed? Marvellously calm in the right-hand seat when you are panicking in the other trying to remember that you are the captain – God help you – of this damn thing.

The doyen of instructors. Still human after all these years of teaching idiots not to kill themselves and him with them. Still full of youthful zest – whatever he may say – to fly a demanding little aeroplane; none of the comfort of the old man's armchair for him. Still willing – and eager – to pass on to you the fruits of his priceless experience, merely for the asking, and to let you ham-fist him around the sky and to bring you down a better pilot than when you took off.

If he says you're OK, then, by golly, you are. How long is it since you had a check and the satisfaction of hearing him say so?"

Although no one believed it, it was goodbye. Bish served on the Committee for another year but he was seldom seen again at Redhill.

RECORDS, GILBERT AND PANSHANGER AGAIN

The Stampe was unserviceable – wrote James Gilbert in April. Neil had "collared" the Tigers for a formation practice, James B. was entirely involved in practising his gallantry in picking up ladies' kerchiefs, so I couldn't follow him around. All the other aeroplanes were in the hangar, with everybody gone to lunch. So I pushed out the Cub and took off.

At five thousand feet I emerged from the haze. At ten thousand feet it was still climbing well. By twenty thousand feet the performance had fallen off somewhat; engine revs were down by 200 and max. IAS was 65 mph. I continued making tiny upward zooms, gaining 150 feet at a time. I was flying in thin cirrus, but bright sunshine. It was a glorious cold-front-type day, with cu nims around me, I was very nearly level with the anvil tops – I think they were not more than 5,000 ft higher.

I could see the south coast in places, and its line by the pattern of cumulus in others, from the Isle of Wight to Dover. A line of cumulus also showed the coast of France. The view was exquisite, the clouds and haze below the sun being quite golden. Redhill, Gatwick, Kenley and Biggin seemed so close as to be in adjacent fields. Aircraft outside the hangars at Redhill were too small to be distinguishable. I saw a Swissair Caravelle pass 10,000 feet below me.

Assuming normal adiabatic lapse rate the outside air temperature must have been 63°F colder, or about 45 degrees of frost. The heater kept me quite warm, but some metal parts of the cabin were painfully cold to touch.

In spite of sitting absolutely still, and breathing deeply and evenly, my hands and feet were tingling with anoxia by about 21,000 feet and I was becoming dizzy and slow-witted, so I spiralled down to lower heights. The aircraft had been still climbing, albeit slowly, and had ¾-full tanks. I weigh 10½ stone, so a lighter pilot with nearly empty tanks, and perhaps one of the gliding fraternity's lightweight oxygen sets . . .

LETTERS
"Honourable companion and self is reading with astounding interest in Tiger Rag, *Bombay edition, of Tiger Club's member who is being flying to 21,000 feets above Redhill Flying Field.*

It is with horrific surprise we learn that Commonwealth Airspace is being violented we are understanding with sureness that the London Terminus Controlling Area is commencing at lowly flying level of 1,500 feets and at said time was Indian Mike Charlie. Are not also many beautiful colouring airways mixing togetherness over Redhill?

We are noting also with revered interest of esteemed aviator's account flying 10,000 foots above Swissair Caravelle. Much braveness is honoured but more wiseness foreseen flying 10,000 foots below honourable airliner.

Your devoting servants (five illegible signatures),
(Royal Bombay Tiger Shoot)
P.S. We are delighting to exterminate any remaining Tigers on Flyingfield."

James Gilbert was, I like to imagine, a typical angry young man of the sixties. Tall and slim, he was always to be seen with beautiful women with whom he seemed most successfully offhand. His dedication to flying though was anything but offhand for he was a first class aerobatic pilot. His flying was never dull, but never. He drove an old VW, was a brilliant photographer, and was destined to go far. (He did too. He later went to the States, became an editor of *Flying*, wrote successful books, and on his return to the UK put the magazine *Pilot* on the map and rules it today, where he is a reformed character – I think.)

He set up something of a record too in 1963 by flying 143 hours with the Club, much to Michael Jones' delight and resultant poverty to a happy James.

James Gilbert, on going into Lympne: "This is Foxtrot Tango, how do you read?"

Came the reply: "Foxtrot Tango, strength 5 – shall we dance?"

PANSHANGER, FULL DISPLAY, APRIL 1963

It had to happen one day; an organiser's nightmare – half our aircraft missing. To see the patient lines of cars streaming into the airfield conveying a huge teeming gate to line the E-W runway expectantly, and yet to know that half the team couldn't get through . . . This happened. The first to take off from Redhill got through, then the weather clamped for the remainder – but really clamped. Out at Panshanger and north of the Downs the weather stayed clear with visibility of six miles plus. Overhead the cloud layer settled for 3,000 ft and more and the wind blew steadily at 15 knots. Yet the clag had settled over the hills to stay. Panshanger even had some sunshine!

Briefing time came and went, by 2.30 we had to count out the rest of the team; we had eight of our own aircraft (we were later to co-opt a further five), willing pilots and the biggest crowd we are likely to see this season. The decision was: "all systems 'go.'" A quick revision of the programme was initiated. Just how 50/50 was the score could nicely be assessed when the subject of food was brought up. Only soup had arrived, but no utensils, so soup was brewed up in the kettle. For every act we had either the aircraft or the accessories – never both together.

At three precisely we waded in with the flypast, for which a couple of interested visitors were invited to join, one a wondrous Cirrus Moth, which had gleaming brass tumbler ignition switches (and flown we learnt later by DH test pilot Desmond Penrose) and the other a Sywell Tiger – just ten of us. Just as many minutes later John Carter, who had set off 40 minutes earlier, returned triumphant after a round tour of the locality with flour bags and balloons.

The programme timing was carefully adhered to, although the items presented little resembled the written programme word. Item by item went down well, the team work was terrific, with pilots and helpers hopping about like scalded cats. Of Charles Boddington's aerobatics it is difficult to do justice with the mere written word. His display was surely the finest he'd ever done. It isn't often that the crowd, who for the most part are not too knowledgeable on the subject of aerobatics, get quite as excited as they did this day. No one could fail to appreciate the finesse and delicacy with which he led Tiger 'MZ through every point of the compass. Right on time, James Baring let his Turb foursome over the field – with orange smoke streaming from his three followers. Alongside him and closely tucked in were Ian Trethewey and Bill Innes, and in the box Don Lovell.

Thanks to John, the flour bombing was 'on' . . . the Sywell Tiger had a spectacular time, as was expected from Charles and with Barry Tempest as bombardier, but the surprise was Titch Holmes in our Piper with Sam Bee lobbing; they really did score hits! We sorely missed Dennis Hartas, so I was left to stand in for the crazy flying, and then to continue in the dogfight. Since we had no spare Tiger to shoot down, we dived straight into one another and played it 'off the cuff.' Neil Williams in the Active was armed with the latest model – the Mk.II in Spandaus – of Dev's creation firing blanks, but I don't think Neil had a chance to fire. It was probably a hairy draw. Anyway 'MZ was unarmed! This led nicely into a demonstration of the Active which did everything but bring the sun out – how Neil enjoys flying that aircraft, and how well.

Dave Allan and James Baring "hankie snatched" vigorously, but the hastily prepared hankies (the tied together flags) clung desperately to their sticks in a most frustrating way. James Gilbert, who until this time had been valiantly commentating, decided it was half-time and handed the mike over to me for my turn: we had agreed to share this chore.

We'd made the interval . . . A hope that the *Ballerina* might appear at 4 came and went, about 4.20 and with the second half of the display well under way, a lone Tiger slid in. The relief of Mafeking was nothing like this. It was good old 'PRA with Peter Phillips and John Blake: John to the commentary, 'PRA for the 'SOW' rig and Peter to organise the final race.

The day was over; we'd done our best, and we felt the crowd had enjoyed itself. The sun was now weakly shining through and it was noticeably warmer as one by one the planes flew off into the murk over Surrey, leaving the joyriders in their bright Proctor to fly on into the evening . . .

The sight of that beautiful DH.60 Gipsy Moth at Panshanger aroused a lot of interest, but Norman was never tempted to add to the collection by buying one. They were already getting rare, and he reckoned, I suspect correctly, that they'd not stand up to Club wear and tear like the Tiger.

The Club has always been very de Havilland conscious. I suppose it could be explained away as one of original availability, but in fact the Chairman, encouraged by Bish, a staunch DH man if ever there was one, always had an eye open for DH types.

Incidentally another light-hearted view was that Norman, like Geoffrey de Havilland, was a keen entomologist, and approved of Geoffrey's choice of aircraft names. I remember one Christmas receiving an unfortunate Tiger Moth that Norman had neatly mounted under glass. It hung dispondently on a wall for years until one of my sons wanted to see it fly and released it. So now, to add to the Tigers, the Jackaroo and the Hornet, we'd been given the delightful Puss Moth.

Unfortunately it was soon to get bent. A few months after she joined us, she force-landed in France and ran into a cow. 'HLO's remains were brought back by lorry for a lengthy rebuild by Rollason's Chief Engineer at Redhill. It was generally believed that Dev dragged out the rebuild in the hope that it wouldn't leave the hangar in a hurry and get bent again. A fervent DH enthusiast was Dev Deverell, he viewed all his wards like his own children. He still does.

A few years later, and in spite of an anguished Dev, Father MacGillivray, who was over here on one of his RCAF tours, snapped her up and took her back to Canada and there she remains to this day.

The Panshanger Show was a turning point for me. With none of the top brass there I had been unceremonously promoted by Charles Boddington to take over its direction. It wasn't that much of a long shot, for I'd been display-flying for four years. If I hadn't picked up some know-how by then I was never going to. The Show had worked, and I was promptly earmarked to take over from Frank Bigger, who was dying to return to Dublin to open his cake shop. At least that was what he kept telling us, but it was hard to know if he was joking or not, such was his wild Irish scnsc of fun.

He owned a Tiger he'd bought for £100 a year earlier – a rock-bottom price by then – and he then proceeded to fly it in a way that never failed to put the wind up me. To my knowledge though he never pranged it, perhaps it was his undoubted skill as a driver – he'd won the Monte Carlo in '52. I often wonder if he ever turned out the mouth-watering confections he was ever dreaming about.

THE CAITHNESS BUSINESS

The Caithness Saga, as I write, occured some twenty-five years ago. It has, over the ensuing years, become something of a legend. As if the occasion hadn't been memorable enough in itself, it was also recorded for posterity by members with a gift of literacy and who, in the best tradition of the Japanese theatre, were able to see the same events but through different eyes. I won't say such an adventure couldn't happen again, but with bureaucracy working the way it does these days with its stranglehold on anything that flies, the odds are against it.

The *Tiger Rag* of July '63 merely provided a resumé that was to prove to be the tip of an iceberg of later reminiscences. I had written:

CAITHNESS

Redhill to Marseille is a long trip to give an air display, but it's no further than the north of Scotland, yet that's just where we went recently. Caithness, as this jaunt will long be known, was quite an adventure. It all started when some farmers from up there saw one of our displays, met Bill Chesson, and firmly requested us to visit them, all expenses paid.

We left, all eight aircraft, immediately after the display at Sywell on Whit Monday, to fly to Yeadon, refuel, and on to Middleton St. George, our overnight stop. A man-made mist by courtesy of ICI was sweeping across Middleton as we arrived in two formations, first the Turbs and then the biplanes, Tigers 'NMZ and 'RAZ in company with 'ROZ, the Stampe. Beneath us the runway lights of this RAF master diversion station led us in a steady stream landing that left the runway controller nervously playing with his Aldis lamp, obviously unaccustomed to such rapid circuits after the resident Lightnings.

Wing Commander Flying was John Severne, and the following morning we asked permission to snatch a quick practice and at the same time entertain our hosts for their hospitality. I think the sight of Lolita on the wing of 'RAZ waving to the station personnel as she flew over the married quarters and station HQ won't be forgotten for many a long day.

Like the ten green bottles, we were already down one, James Baring had gone into Tollerton with a burst oil lead, down but not out. Newcastle and halfway, and the seven were suddenly reduced to four. James Gilbert couldn't start his Turb, Arthur Humphreys, also Turb-mounted, stayed with him, as did Don and Tessa Lovell in the Ambassadeur. Perth and four of us. The three biplanes led by Neil Williams flew across the Highlands in the beautiful evening sunshine, alternately slope-soaring, then hugging the base of the cu nim that lay across the tops of the peaks, in an endeavour to conserve fuel on this, the longest hop direct to Castletown. Above us, like a mother hen, was Bill in the Mousquetaire.

Inverness had closed, and our diversion, if necessary, was on one of the two disused airfields that lay on the long plain beyond. The promising wind proved fickle, became a steady headwind, a nor'easterly that was to stay with us and to bring some trying weather. We chose Fern and went down. No sooner were we down than a friendly farmer arrived, offered us transport and fuel; they even found a funnel and a chamois! Refuelling over, the three of us (Nick Pocock in the Stampe), flew off into the evening to leave behind some fifty fascinated and friendly people, all of whom had come out to welcome us.

Castletown proved to be a fine surfaced, disused airfield right on the coast, in clear view of the Orkneys and edged by the bluest sea outside of the Med. The local hospitality was red carpet. Not since Cobham's day had a bevy of light aircraft visited this corner of the country; everyone knew about us, everyone bothered and lent a hand to entertain and befriend us.

Two displays had been planned, both in the evening, on the Wednesday and Thursday. Since it didn't get dark till midnight (how much further north can you get?) the seven o'clock start was in plenty of time. On the Wednesday afternoon, to everyone's delight, the three Turbs in close formation flew in low over the airfield, followed by the Ambassadeur. Full strength. The day was fine, brilliant sunshine boosted the air of excitement. A food marquee complete with two field kitchens and Calor gas provided hot food from two until nine each day and the kindly folk who looked after it were forever forcing hot soup and coffee on the crews and helpers.

A pilot's briefing tent was already established. Hugh Neil, from Stirling, had driven up through the night just to be on hand to help, and help he did by taking over all refuelling and maintainance and as happy to be of assistance as we were to see him. Hugh, a good friend of Bish's, had been a chief engineer during the war – I think at Perth – so Tigers were right up his street. (What most didn't know was that Hugh was on duty the whole time, camping out by his aircraft. He was later made an Honorary Member for that remarkable service to us all.)

From fine weather to total clamp – just like that. Twenty minutes before seven a vast fog bank swept swiftly in from the sea. The airfield lay under a pale of damp cloud, the base of which hung around the 100 foot mark. The locals shook their heads sadly as we postponed the start for an hour. To no avail. The show was cancelled until the following night. The same thing happened the next night too, only this time it waited until seven to visit us. We had co-opted a Cessna 210 for the flypast and no sooner was he off than he was in it, up through and was gone, back to Perth and clear air.

It was a tremendous disappointment. 600 miles to show our paces and then this. A "one aircraft up at a time" display was improvised, and for an hour and a half we cavorted beneath the fluctuating base with occasional loss of shape as someone skirted too near the cloud.

The strangest sight, I was told, was when Lolita stood on the wing and occasionally disappeared into the cloud as I strove to stay in touch with the ground, and Nick's slow rolls just above the deck delighted his audience, but it was all below a hundred feet and very spectacular.

Although only scheduled for the two evening performances, considerable pressure was brought to bear for us to remain until Saturday and put on a show in the afternoon. The overwhelming hospitality clinched this, and all but one, 'RAZ, elected to stay on. Business commitments on the following Monday necessitated my return. As I write this some days later there are still two aircraft somewhere up there! The return from Caithness was as full of adventure as the journey up – more so. The trouble was twofold, mainly weather and some mechanical. Perhaps one day someone will write more fully on this trip, of the characters we met, of the characters that went. *(This has now been done – see Tail Ends of the Fifties, published by Cirrus Books in 1999, which contains an additional contribution specially written by Nick Pocock.)* For instance, James B. made a sudden forced landing beside an outback loch. Neil reported that he seemed to be on fire – the smoke being in fact oil streaming out behind him. Neil somehow got down beside him in the special Tiger and then mounted James aboard, the fuselage cover acting like a sort of windscreen, and careered off.

Thus was James transported to Inverness. He later borrowed Horace Henderson's car (Horace was the prime mover in getting us up to Caithness) and drove 700 miles non-stop to London to appear in court, probably to appear on another of his parking charges, won his case, and then immediately returned, complete with spare part for his Turb.

Must ask James to write up the account of his twenty-five mile early morning tramp to Horace's for breakfast, and his attempted conversion by two earnest evangelists (wickedly sent up to his bedroom by Neil) whilst James was trying to sleep off the effects of his walk and the drink of the previous night. One of the shaken women was later to have stammered, after being turned out in no uncertain manner: "He is never likely to see the Light."

It was a great adventure, regretted by none and enjoyed by all. James Gilbert later wrote a long and absolutely delightful account which because of its length I was only able to publish but a section at a time: Here is, without question, the choicest snippet.

THE CAITHNESS SAGA – JAMES GILBERT'S STORY

I borrow a diesel-engined Land Rover and drive through the high-hedged, dewy country lanes to the airfield. No one else is about, and except for the skylarks and curlews the landscape is altogether deserted. I untie my Turbulent, start, it up, and take off towards John O'Groats, almost the northernmost point of the mainland of Britain. Then I turn out to sea, towards the misty shapes of the Orkney Islands. Orkney itself, bigger than the others, is wreathed in harr, a thick, curving mist generated as that moist sea air flows slowly over its shores.

It was my ambition to land there; no one from the Tiger Club ever has before, so remote and strange are these islands. I turn back to Stroma. A little island clear of fog, shining in the sunshine. At one end is a lighthouse, huge and white; I circle it at a low altitude, than drop down over the sea for a low run alongside its beacon tower. Beside it is a monstrous foghorn like a giant's saxophone, and I aim my tiny Turbulent right at it, as if I intended flying down that vast black throat. Just as I pull up over the top, some wit who has been watching me sounds it off, in a monstrous cowlike moo, deafening even above the noise of my engine, a roar that almost frightens me out of my seat and into the sea.

If I cannot land on Orkney, perhaps I can on Stroma. True, it has no aerodrome, or indeed anything else much and, true, it would be an illegal and foolhardy thing to do, but there is one field of short, sheep cropped island turf that looks smooth and level and just about long enough. I have always made it a rule never to land in any strange field I have not walked over first to inspect, but is not today a good day for breaking rules? I drag the field twice from a low altitude, then set up my approach.

Low and fairly slow; it looks plenty long, so no need to slow right up as for a really short landing. Touch down in a perfect three-pointer, and run on, slightly uphill, towards the end of the field. Run on and on, unaccountably she will not slow down, uphill though it is. Brakes on a Turbulent are differential only, for steering while taxying, but you can obtain some braking action with them by pumping the rudder pedals from side to side. I pump, with increasing terror, as the end of the field looms up ahead. With fifty yards to go it is bitter, certain knowledge that I am not going to stop before reaching that solid stake and wire sheep fence. At the last minute I turn the careening beast sharp right towards rough ground and a ditch; she leaps and bounds, the tail coming up, and the whole airplane dives with a deafening crash nose-first into the ditch. There is a rending, splintering sound as the propeller disintegrates, then absolute, stark silence, I am hanging face down in my straps in the wreck of my aeroplane as it sits, tail in the air, nose in the ground. I undo my straps and clamber down over the wing. I sit, near to tears, on the edge of the ditch.

I am an idiot. A 300-hour idiot. I will be drummed out of the Tiger Club. My friends will never speak to me again. It will take a month to get the wreck off this lonely island and back to the shop to rebuild. I will be prosecuted for every flying offence in the book. I will be penniless for years trying to pay for fines and repairs. I have done something so stupid I can hardly believe it. There cannot be more than one boat a week to this forsaken islet; I will not even be able to leave the scene of my crime for days.

The curlews call, and the waves lap against the nearby rocks. Somewhere a sheep is baaing; "baa," it says, "idiot, baa." Mechanically, I take hold of the tail of my Turbulent and pull her out of the shallow ditch. Strange, there doesn't seem to be much wrong with the airframe. On closer inspection, miraculously, there doesn't seem to be *anything* wrong with the airframe. But the propeller must be smashed into a million pieces. But there's only four inches snapped cleanly off the end of the tiny blade. Still, what use is any prop with four inches missing off one blade, Unless, of course . . . and a mad idea begins to form in my mind. Today I must have really gone crazy. Suppose you sawed four inches off the other blade, and could get it to balance?

Normally, these VW engines turn at about 3,000 rpm in this installation. But I own a VW car, and I know the engine in that turns at 4,000 rpm for long periods, cruising flat out, with no damage. At 4,000 rpm I would be getting more horses out of the engine, perhaps enough to offset the inefficiency of the cut-down propeller. Enough to take off from here? For the first time since my recent abrupt arrival I take a good look at where I am. For a start, I was trying to land with a 5 kt tailwind. And this field has a deceptive double curvature, so that the lip over which I touched down was not the lip at the end of the field, but a false one halfway down! I was trying to land downwind, and using only half the available run!

Over the dewy turf, on a tractor, comes one of the island's inhabitants, and addresses me in a Pictish, Gaelic, Orkney accent that is next to impossible to comprehend. Could he, I ask him, find me a hacksaw anywhere on the island? He thinks the lighthouse people have one and drives off to ask. There is a little village of crofts in the centre of the island. It is a medieval village; there are no roads or gardens, each croft being surrounded by a rolling sea of green turf, criss-crossed by tracks where the inhabitants of Stroma have been in the habit of walking to work, or to each others' houses.

Till he returns I burn with impatience. The hacksaw comes, and with it I bite off the other tip. What's left is a sad runt of a propeller, but when I start up the engine it runs smoothly and sweetly. I swear there is less vibration than ever before. Full power revs are not excessive, and taxying up and down the field seems to reveal no lack of acceleration, so far as you ever experience acceleration in a Turbulent. So I strap up, and back up to the topmost corner of the field, and taxy at full throttle down the field. Yes, I think she would have flown there. Once more, and then the real attempt. At first it seems doomed to failure, not to say disaster, then the tail lifts, and we slowly, slowly gather speed; at the far end of the field, yellow with fright, half stalled, we get airborne. Soon we are properly flying, at a decent speed and altitude, very chastened, back towards the mainland . . .

James Gilbert's journey back to base at Redhill – he flew the entire way with the sawn-off propeller – was a long, tedious and occasionally hairy trip. And he wasn't the only one who couldn't hurry. I couldn't, yet I needed to. I had recently opened my Colindale shop, and since it was a one-man business, there was no one else to open it on the Monday; Lolita and I set off in Tiger 'RAZ on the same journey and at an indicated 65 kt. We had to transport the 'SOW' rig in position on top of the aircraft, and such was the extra drag, coupled with the fine pitch prop fitted, it was the only speed available to us. Five more legs and a further eight hours flying were to follow before we got back to Redhill.

The following portion of the Saga was actually published some three years later in the *Rag* under the heading: "Let me off this time and I'll never do it again." It was the first of a series of "I was there" events presented in the belief that it's good for the soul to confess and that others may learn from the lesson. To be honest I don't think it works, for Michael Jones in the same issue had written a stern warning about careless swinging of propellers *sans* chocks etc. He'd also like a pound for every incident since.

THE CAITHNESS SAGA – BENJY'S STORY

We couldn't stay on. After the two abortive attempts on the Thursday and Friday to put on a show, we had to resist the entreaties of our friends and hosts to join them for a third try. It wasn't easy, but we had to be back in London on the Monday.

Farewells, and we turned Tiger 'RAZ into wind at Castletown and hurried back to Thurso and the little harbour to dip our wings in salute and then to head towards Inverness. Above us around 1,500 feet a solid layer of cloud hung darkly. After a while we left the comfort of the solitary Thurso road and climbed steadily to the plateau between the twin peaks of the Caithness range. We slipped through skirting the cloud and sank thankfully down to the coast. Across Dornoch Firth bucking the wind at a cheerful 200 feet to speed across the lowlands towards the airport at Inverness. Cloud base 1,000 feet.

Tea, refuel and a word with the Controller. He phoned Aberdeen. To make Perth direct was out. The rest of Scotland lay beneath a mantle of fog. Only the east coast was clear. Aberdeen weather was down to two miles and a cloud base of 800 feet. We consulted the map and reckoned that, provided we followed the Moray coast and only moved inland beyond Elgin, we'd miss the high ground. It was worth a try anyway. We could always return. it was dank and chilly, Aberdeen was on our way, and anyway it might not be as bad as forecast.

Up past Lossiemouth with the vis dropping as we left the coast to edge inland. No longer the clean definition of cloud and land. Instinctively I wiped my hand across the lenses of my goggles and followed the lonely Aberdeen road. A lorry driver waved. His wipers were busy, the road glistened. I hadn't realised I was so low. The misty drizzle had suddenly reduced our little world to that road and the hills which rose steeply either side of us. The map clearly showed the valley and the big plain beyond it. Too late to turn back and with it the stark knowledge that we either scraped through or we were going to have to climb up through, with the certainty of 8/8th cover beneath us. Vis had nearly gone. The rain beat on my face. I glued my attention to that road and then, suddenly, we were through. Now the road led us to the railway – the very railway which actually crossed the edge of the runway. All I had to do now was to stay with it. Every sense said: "you were lucky, don't push it, get down, make a precautionary, the weather is worsening." But the roar of the engine, the sureness of our position, and with it the knowledge that the airport wasn't nine minutes away weakened my senses.

Just a little further – decide then. And then it was too late. Imperceptibly the rain, the cloud and the fog become one. Impossible now to lob in anywhere. All that was visible was a hazy railway track 80 feet below. Nothing else showed, not even the fields either side, just the wet blinding fog. The marshalling yards – and no more than a mile to go – HT cables, a heave back into the mire and push down the other side. Blindly searching for the runway. A chimney passed. Too late to worry. A huge white numeral; that's all we saw, not even the edges of the runway – just one figure and in a flash we were down on the runway.

They were a nice crowd at Aberdeen. No fuss. "Didn't see you," they said. "Let's get your Tiger in a hangar." I wish now, and I wished it then, that I had stayed in Inverness.

THE CAITHNESS SAGA – NEIL'S STORY

The display had been a good one and the natives more than friendly. Aeroplanes and pilots had been refuelled, and with some reluctance we prepared to leave for our long flight south. We needed two days for this, as we were at Castletown Aerodrome in Caithness – almost as far north as you can go on the mainland of Britain. Benjy had already left on the previous day, as he was only able to achieve 65 kts in 'RAZ with the rig in position. James Gilbert was wondering whether to saw off any more propeller or add wood screws to the other blade in an attempt to stop the engine from shaking itself out of the airframe, while Nick Pocock's Stampe refused point blank to start at all, so James Baring and I decided to leave in formation. We took off, gave the locals a farewell beat-up, and set course across some of the most barren country in Scotland.

Peat bogs, marsh and heather were the order of the day; for mile after mile nothing moved on the ground, no vehicle (no roads), no trains (no railway) – not even a sheep. The sheer desolation was indescribable, and instinctively James and I closed up into a tight formation. I was flying *The Canon*, and it was going beautifully; I felt that James was a braver man than I in flying a Turbulent over such country (incidentally, Norman's own machine loaned to James for the trip).

These thoughts were interrupted by the realisation that James had dropped back a few yards, but was still flying steadily on course. As I watched, he slowed even more, until eventually he was several hundred yards behind. Feeling slightly irritated that he should break formation over such poor terrain, I rolled into a 360° turn to let him catch up. He flew straight past without even a glance at me as I levelled out alongside. "Miserable blighter," I thought, when suddenly I realised he was in trouble. The next second, my heart nearly stopped altogether, as a great trail of white smoke erupted from his engine. "You're on fire!" I shouted, realising in the same instant that he could not hear me.

The ground was completely unsuitable for any sort of landing, but the map showed that the coast was only a few miles ahead. James was obviously trying to reach this area but surely he would never make it? The smoke became thicker and trailed forty feet behind the aeroplane, when we suddenly crossed a low hill and there below us was a clear, calm loch. But more important, alongside the loch was a beautiful field, big enough to land a Turbulent. James shut the throttle and spiralled left, while I followed him down, carefully keeping out of his way. The picture is still imprinted on my mind: the loch, the hills covered with heather, a tiny dark blue aeroplane with a white smoke trail and a beautiful green field. James straightened low over the water, his reflection almost touching him, the smoke still persistent. As I got lower, I saw that the field was very rough – apart from a narrow strip in the centre.

Suddenly I realised that what I thought was smoke was in fact oil. The Turbulent's windscreen was black with oil and I feared that the landing was rapidly becoming impossible. But with falling oil pressure there is no choice, and with relief and admiration I saw the skid bite into the turf just inside the field. What a sight I saw as I overshot: cowlings, wings and windscreen were glistening black with oil, but James sat there unconcerned and waved.

Now it was my turn! I brought the Tiger in as slowly as I dared, low over the water, and as the grass appeared behind my wing cut the throttle. *The Canon* bounced, touched down again and lurched to a halt. The silence could almost be felt when I switched off, for there was no sign of life apart from a few sheep who stared at us dully.

We took off the Turb's cowlings, cleaned off the oil and started up. Immediately a jet of black oil squirted into the air, and we quickly switched off. We found that we needed a new oil pipe; it was fractured and impossible to repair. Darkness was a couple of hours away, but I didn't want to leave James alone in that wilderness. Looking at the map, we found that we were exactly on track; the other pilots *en route* to Inverness should have spotted us, but we had to console ourselves with pointed remarks about their navigation. We saw nothing and needed a two-seater aeroplane to get James back to civilization.

As I cursed the fact that I was flying a single-seat Tiger, a crazy thought struck me. This was a special Tiger, stripped, light and with a powerful engine – powerful enough to lift both of us (one in the slipstream) over the hills which surrounded the loch? It was worth a try. We picketed and covered the Turb and removed the luggage which occupied the space normally taken by a standard Tiger's front cockpit. James found that, by standing on the pickets and holding on to the centre section struts, his head was level with the top wing. He was game to try it. We paced the field and found that the level strip was fifty yards with a good overrun. We started the engine and James climbed in. He packed himself in with all the baggage and, last of all, took on board the wooden cockpit cover which he wedged in over his knees as a sort of windscreen. James pronounced all systems "go," and I prepared to take off. Even the sheep were taking an interest by this time.

We taxied downwind towards the loch and turned into wind. The idiot sheep stared blankly as James pulled down his goggles and nodded. The wind was about 15 knots as I opened the throttle. The tail rose slowly and the flock of sheep got nearer. At 25 knots I started pulling, and with a final bounce we were airborne! The sheep did a very creditable bomb burst beneath us as we slowly gathered climbing speed. James hung on grimly, with beard and moustaches fluttering, and his flying jacket billowing out behind him. Surely his ancestors must have sailed in long ships – he looked the picture of a Viking, thirsting for the spoils of war!

Meanwhile the Tiger circles, climbing slowly. What an aeroplane! But now I was becoming concerned, because I was using full throttle and the slipstream and cold would be weakening James. But at last we cleared the hills and could throttle back slightly. Every now and then James half turned and nodded, signifying that he was OK, and soon Inverness appeared before us. The Tiger handled almost normally, in spite of its unusual burden, and as we taxied clear of the runway, James was grinning; he seemed to have quite enjoyed the experience! Not so Don Lovell, who had almost given us up. The expression on this face when we arrived made it all very worthwhile!

THE LEGAL FUND AND SHAUN

The Legal Fund, now so well established and so much an integral part of the Club, came into its own during July '63 in unfortunate circumstances. During the previous summer the Tiger Club had been over to Eire and whilst there were invited by the Shannon Aero Club to fly their six Turbulents in a formation over Limerick. In spite of a careful pre-briefing to keep clear, an Auster had joined the formation and collided with Shaun de Salis's mount, resulting in an accident from which Shaun did not survive. Shaun would not even have seen the Auster.

In the subsequent inquest the Irish Inspector of Accidents stated that the accident was caused by the Auster pilot permitting his aircraft to collide. A contributory cause was the negligence and incompetence of the Auster pilot who did not appear to have any formation experience. In spite of this conclusive evidence of outrageous bad airmanship by the Auster pilot all the Turbulent pilots were prosecuted over here on the dubious grounds of flying below the regulation height.

Jack Piercy, a most respected member, took it upon himself to write the membership personally.

"Dear Member,

Please read the enclosed notes. They concern the recent prosecution in England of five of our member, for an alleged flying offence in the Republic of Eire. If these notes had come from a casual observer they would have been moving enough. They were, in fact, written by Mrs Fane de Salis, mother of Shaun, who so tragically lost his life during the flight in question.

Of course, Mrs de Salis' excellent observations cannot be regarded as a record of the trial, which lasted five long days; further, they apply to a particular case and a particular jury. Another jury might have returned a very different verdict. The notes do, however, serve to bring home to us, very forcibly, the anomaly in the treatment of those who sail and those who fly. Unlike mariners, who are tried by specialists in Admiralty courts, flying people have to face an ordinary court whose members almost inevitably display the laymen's prejudice and ignorance of flying matters. It is small wonder the average flyer of modest means, when faced with the truly formidable cost of fighting, is often obliged to accept a magistrate's conviction, although he knows himself to be innocent.

But not everyone is prepared to take this treatment lying down. Our five members, convinced of their innocence and determined to make a stand for a principle, elected to go for trial, although warned beforehand the minimum costs would be £200 each, win or lose. In order to give evidence for the defence, another member took two weeks off from his employment and paid his own fare to and from the Lebanon. The case was lost and their public-spirited action has resulted in costs and fines totalling about £2,000.

The Tiger Club Committee has decided to form a Legal Defence Fund with the object of making a contribution towards the costs of the case already fought, and to provide a continuous reserve to be used (at the Committee's discretion) in helping members who may find themselves involved in air rule proceedings.

I don't think you will want me to employ the usual appeal language in asking you for your contribution. You are almost certain to want to join in fighting for the just treatment of the pilots. The Legal Defence Fund gives you the opportunity of doing this. In addition, I believe we are all selfish enough to consider such a fund as a form of insurance. You or I may be the next!

The Fund has already opened spontaneously. Without being asked, six members have each sent me cheques for £10, and the Meath Flying Group has most generously volunteered 50 guineas. Our Chairman has handed over a magnificent cheque for £100. What should you give? Only you know what you can afford, but I suggest nothing less than the equivalent of a couple of hours in your favourite aeroplane. It hurts a lot more to stand in the dock alone and unsupported. Mrs de Salis had, more in sorrow than in anger, revealed the shortcomings of the so-called witnesses' evidence. The case had left us badly shaken and very wary of the law. A fear of its ignorance has stayed with many of us ever since."

Norman Jones our Chairman wrote:

"There are sad hearts and aching pockets to be found in the Tiger Club. We are licking our wounds after our first battle with the law. The sad hearts we do not expect to last long, but the aching pockets may take longer. The law looms very large in the life of the private flyer – and a law which is made and administered by those who have no practical knowledge or experience of our difficulties and temptations is certainly more than likely to be the proverbial ass. But it is a poor faith which fails at discouragement. People may measure themselves not by what is done to them but by what they do to others. That we should use this case to try and get a square deal for private flyers in the future is right and wise. But to allow it to discourage us, or still worse, for it to give us a 'chip on the shoulder' would not be in the Tiger Club spirit!"

In going through my papers for the period I came across a lone 1963 raffle ticket in aid of the Legal Fund. It revealed I was the organiser – I'd forgotten – and that the first prize for the 5/- (25p) ticket was a "fine teenage Sunbeam Talbot 10." Heaven knows what that lovely old car would be worth today. Bill Chesson had presented it. Norman Jones had presented the second prize, a magnificent open 1934 MG Midget. I do remember though that Mike Jolley won it; I remember that ruefully, because I had fancied it. The total money raised in this raffle either indicates that I was a disaster as an organiser, or no one else tried very hard, because we only raised £23. The event was considered a bit of a flop. If only we were gifted with hindsight.

THE SEA TIGER AND THE BRITISH SEAPLANE CLUB

Early in '63 I had written:

Recently saw the Tiger floatplane at Croydon. First impressions (surely wrong): it'll never leave the water, and that if it does it'll only live to get down again. She's an impressive size, and looks very nearly ready to fly. There's a great number of VIP-ish folk in line to fly her, my sympathy goes out to the luckless pilot who must one day dent her – there's only one set of floats. One doesn't hold spares at £2,000 a time.

Can't help feeling the Tiger Club needs a weekday London base. Redhill is a great spot for the weekend, but it's a dickens of a way to go just for a gossip, and that's all lots of us make the journey for with so many weekends at this time of year. What we need is some sort of liaison with an established London Club (with like ideals) so that we can be armchair pilots of an evening as well as the weekend!

We can't all be prophets, for the floatplane went on to be a great success, but I scored on the later idea. We were much later to get our London HQ, the Kronfeld Club.

The Tiger Club seaplane was to begin an important part of the Club story. To start with, the Tiger seaplane was, and was to remain throughout its near twenty years of its life, the only floatplane in Britain. Norman, whose brainchild she was, presented her to the Seaplane Club.

The first meeting of the British Seaplane Club was at Croydon on the 20th April '63. The Chairman, J. Lankaster Parker, paid tribute to the Club's Patron, aviation pioneer Oswald Short, and no doubt to his useful contribution of £500. G-AIVW in its land form was already a famous Tiger, for one of the Club's founders, Jimmy Denyer, had won the King's Cup in her back in '58. By the way the only Tiger to win this famous race. He did so at a speed of 118.5 mph and for a Tiger that was moving.

Air Commodore Chris Paul, a noted test pilot in his day, and staunch supporter of the light aircraft movement, became the new Club's first secretary. To be precise, he was probably the second, for Ann Carter had efficiently dug the Club's foundations in that position, but she handed over the reins when the Club became operational. It was Chris who first flew 'VW off at Lee on Solent on the 20th July in a most successful and much publicised flight. 'VW was later to be ceremoniously named *Oswald Short*, but somehow the name never caught on and she remained known to one and all as the Sea Tiger. Some years later the Seaplane Club quietly folded and the Tiger Club welcomed the Sea Tiger back, where she remained with us under the auspices of the Seaplane Section until her final demise in the 80s.

AN ACCIDENT, AN EMBARASSMENT AND SUE AGAIN

The Sywell display in July wasn't one of my favourites. I had taken on the extra job of the crazy-flying slot and my regular display spots by then were the Tied together, Balloon bursting, the Dogfight and the Standing on the Wing. I was never happier than when I was flying, and that day I was as happy as a sandboy climbing in and out of aircraft, shouting for a prop swing one moment, and lending a hand to swing someone else's the next. I was hyperactive, all keyed up and heading for a fall. I got me a beauty.

I was flying one of the single-seat Tigers of which only four were ever built. They were a delight to fly. There was power enough for a top speed of 120 mph, yet the wing loading of this lightweight was so low that the stall nearly didn't happen.

The Sywell Display was a popular venue with us. There was always a good crowd from nearby Northampton and we had become regulars there, but this year, for some reason or other, the 13,000 spectators were lined either side of the grass runway. It was in the momentary lapse of concentration in the crazy-flying slot, as I pondered my positioning, that I lost control.

Crazy-flying takes considerable skill to keep the right side of an accident. Without doubt the slow flat turn downwind was on the wrong side, and a deliberate spectacular manoeuvre swiftly developed into a 200 foot one-way dive into the ground. It was accompanied by a concerted "Oh!" from the crowd. I sometimes think spectators secretly love a good old-fashioned accident to go home and talk about over tea. I didn't fail them. My last thoughts as I plunged downwards were spared me. I woke up in an ambulance.

The photograph of Tiger 'NMZ going in vertically, feet from the ground, didn't say it all. Some of the later comedy behind the scenes was priceless. It's true, I did come to in the ambulance and with the traditional words "Where am I?" addressed the tearful blurred face of my young bride who was leaning over me.

My next words however caused absolute panic. "My balls, my balls," I moaned. Immediately I had their attention, everyone became very interested and came over to have a look. With that I passed out again. Fortunately the general consensus gave my wife hope. But what no one realised, and I was past telling them, was that the tender skin was being burnt by the high octane fuel into which I'd been plunged when I was catapulted into the fuel tank.

When we got to the Northampton General I was still unconscious so can only relate what happened next second-hand. As I was being wheeled into reception, our *cortège*, now several strong, were met by the emergency team hurrying out to help. They were headed by a coloured doctor who swept everyone to one side and began an immediate examination.

This was too much for Sue Phillips, who had up to now accompanied my wife and maintained the three Cs. She stepped forward and in a loud ringing voice cried: "Take this black man away and fetch a proper doctor."

Variations of this opening gambit have delighted members for ages.

There was a shocked silence. Still according to legend, the good doctor smiled and replied in the purest of Oxford accents: "Please acccept that I am well qualified to attend your friend."

For a moment Sue considered this statement, and then with a toss of her lovely head, as if to say: "You may carry on," stood back and graced them all with an angelic smile, and everyone breathed again. And attend me he did with remarkable skill. I've always been grateful to that unknown doctor and to the good Lord for the blessed state of unconsciousness. Conscious, I'd probably have had a relapse.

I read of my passing in bed the next day. A Sunday newspaper prematurely recorded my death and the subsequent letters of sympathy came as a bit of a shock to my parents. Some days later I discharged myself to escape from a sadistic Sister. I was aided and abetted by Charles and Diane Boddington, who sensed I'd be happier in my wife's and their care, so they all spirited me away to convalesce with them nearby.

Fifteen days after the prang I staggered down to Redhill and was promptly helped into the Jodel Ambassadeur – I say that literally – by Pee Wee Judge and made to fly. He was acting on the assumption that, in common with horse riders, the sooner back in the saddle the better. What really hurt me though was when, in the September, Bish wrote up the next year's pilots' availability list. He'd deleted me for flying and was canvassing Dave Morgan to replace me. Dave wisely didn't follow up Bish's offer.

Of the only two other pilots marked for the act at that time, only Dennis Hartas was to remain unscathed. All he ever did was to tip a Tiger onto its nose, and he blamed a hole in the ground for that and Bish believed him. The other, poor Neville Browning, also made a most spectacular ending to his spell for crazy flying and he wasn't asked to do it again either. The act continued to break planes, we never did seem to learn.

Some years ago during the winter of 1977 I was staying with John Gurney in California sampling Cliff Robertson's fleet of Tiger and Stampes, when over dinner John mentioned that he had always wanted to meet the pilot who had reputed to have survived a nose dive in a Tiger. Before I could stop him, he shot off to find Bunny Bramson's book *The Tiger Moth Story* which featured that awful photograph of the Tiger and I poised vertically three feet from the ground. It made his day and dampened mine.

OF CHARACTERS AND COMMITTEES

One of the most remarkable facets of the Club has always been the diverse nature of its members. It collects quite effortlessly "individuals" in the truest sense of the word. If at times I appear to harp on this aspect of our Club, please bear with me, because I have never ceased to marvel. Without going into deep definitions, I'd consider an "individual" to be someone with a mind of his own, while a "character" is someone who also has a mind of his own but is an unwitting extrovert into the bargain.

So at a guess I'd say the Tiger Club had, and probably still has, a collection of 90% individuals and 10% characters which, when you consider it, could be something of a social problem. For instance, who was going to lead, when and where. If it was ever a problem no one was ever aware of it. To start with, the Club ran as an autocracy. The fact was accepted intelligently, and the undemocratic environment even seemed to promote – for the sake of a better word – a togetherness. There were no opposing camps, no ambitious cliques, and above all there was always an air of camaraderie unique in my experience. Much of this delightful state of affairs was the direct result of Norman's belief that everyone could do as they liked, providing they did what they were told.

On the third Tuesday of every month the Tiger Club Committee would get together. Much has been written on this institution, some of it wry, and not without good reason, but all without malice. Norman, our Chairman, had retained quite a bit of his abrupt Naval demeanour and it was never better expressed than at one of his meetings.

He generally regarded Committee meetings as a necessary evil and his time was to be used sparingly. It wasn't that at times we weren't allowed to express our views – at times we weren't – but his military manner commanded us to mentally stand to attention, and woe betide anyone who rambled. His Committee meeting minutes were always brief and written within the compass of one side of paper. He would quote Churchill on this.

Then again the meetings have always been at 6.30 pm. Norman once observed that hunger concentrated the mind, and even today it's a 6.30 start and dinner comes later. 1½ hours is still par for the course. Some of the members came from quite far away to be present, but no one would ever willingly forego the occasion, for that short period was nothing if not invigorating. When one considers that the average attendance was some fifteen or more, the meetings must on any count, be considered extraordinary to cover so much ground in such a short time. Autocracy does help.

Some of the best remembered meetings have not been without humour. There was one occasion when for some reason or other Norman was being a bit short with us and a sort of nervous energy was building up. It was as if we were back at school and we feared that some little thing or other would act as an unwanted catalyst which would invoke laughter and bring the Master's wrath down upon us.

And so it was that night. And the catalyst was being passed from hand to surreptitious hand around the table. I could see laughter well up and be subdued on face after face as the slip of paper came nearer to me. Norman, who couldn't have been unaware of the ripple of movement and stifled laughter, pressed on firmly. The newspaper cutting, for that was what it was, was slipped into my hand under the table. Norman, who now knew full well how far the thing had travelled, gave me a baleful look. Look or not, I edged it onto the table in front of me, and behind the cover of a raised copy of the minutes, read it.

It was a cutting from the *Telegraph* about a German couple whose kitchen sink had become blocked. It was late in the evening and the husband promised to have a look at it in the morning. However, later on, after the wife had retired, he realised he had to get away early the next day and phoned instead for a plumber.

The next morning the wife went into the kitchen, and seeing her husband on his knees under the sink, playfully grabbed a handful of trouser. Taken by surprise, the plumber shot upright and knocked himself out. The distraught wife phoned for an ambulance. Since the plumber was still a bit groggy when the two ambulance men arrived they insisted on carrying him downstairs on a stretcher.

On the way down, they asked him what had happened, and when he told them they laughed so much they dropped him. He arrived at the hospital with concussion and a broken arm.

This was too much for me, and I burst out laughing, immediately joined by the others, all except, of course, those who hadn't seen it; and Norman.

"Let me see it, Benjamin," he ordered.

Like a naughty boy I handed it over. He read it.

"Very funny," he said and went on with the meeting.

"Pass it on," hissed the member the other side of me. I was glad to.

Until 1984 the Tiger Club had never a General Meeting or an election for any office. The Chairman's practice was to co-opt any promising members to the Committee when a specific job presented itself. It was usually a spontaneous act. Nor did Norman waste volunteers. To make a suggestion at a Committee Meeting was to get the job, and newcomers quickly learnt the rules unless they wanted a further workload. If all this sounds undemocratic, it was, but then it also worked. At no time was there any power lobbying within the Club for station, and there were no side-taking factions. Everyone supported one objective: the Club. Self did not come into it. This remarkable state of affairs was accepted without question, and if the degree of Club pride was anything to go by, it was by no means a bad system.

SHEILA, *MYTH* AND DREAMS

The *Tiger Rag*, by now a regular monthly, ran a Mutual Aid Column, a feature which has appeared every now and then ever since. But in '63 it was going strong and clearly showed, not only the individualism, but a strong camaraderie as well.

The April issue saw:

"Dreamers' corner. Are there two people in the Club willing to seriously contemplate a two year cruise in new yacht. You'll need at least £2,000. Not cheap but what an experience! Box 24C."

I had seen the most fantastic new 40 ft catamaran which cost, believe it or not, under £10,000. I'd always loved sailing and immediately saw myself sailing into the blue. Richard Ball instantly agreed to join me, even though he didn't have a penny either. My brother, who I appreached, said something like: "you must be joking," and the idea fell through. Years later fate took a hand, and Richard and I did set off into the Atlantic in a catamaran, but that's another tale.

Another read:

"For Sale: Happy and well cared for Jackaroo seeks kindly home where she'll be given the sort of treatment to which she's supposed to be accustomed. Box 44."

This of course was Sheila Scott's *Myth*, and she was willing to haggle at £800 for that strange half-breed.

"Wanted. Lonely field wishes to share 450 yards of lovely strip with 2-4 seater with view to Guildford. Box T42."

This was Wright Field, which was near Cranleigh in the depths of Surrey. There was never 350 yards, much less 450, as the many visitors who came to grief there will feelingly confirm. John moved away to squire it somewhere down in Devon in the early 80s.

Sheila Scott, who was one day to enter the record book as one of the most courageous airwomen of our time, was a dear friend of mine. I'd first met her in 1959 when we shared our first air races. She had entered her biplane *Myth*. Her mentor and flying instructor, John Heaton, sat in with her, for in those days Sheila lacked confidence. However, John wasn't the most patient of men and, knowing him, I just don't think he would have sat there and let others overtake. He didn't. To see *Myth* hurtling around the course meant only one thing: John had taken over, although Sheila laughingly denied it.

The Thruxton Jackaroo was an ungainly contraption and not the equal of the Rollason-modified version, but for a tight cabin four-seater it took some beating for value, for they used many parts that were interchangeable with the Tiger, which it closely resembled. Strangely enough the performance was in no way inferior either.

I'd flown over to Thruxton, near Andover, where Sheila had learnt to fly, to say hullo and try out her aircraft. I wasn't a potential buyer, but Sheila had asked me over because I might know someone who was. Sheila flew it first.

For someone so versed in Tiger Club ways I wasn't prepared for what was to happen. Sheila hadn't a lot of hours to her credit so she quite properly pre-flighted with great care, and taxied out with even more. The going was very slow. I began to get impatient and fidgeted in my seat and earned a black look from the pilot.

We lined up eventually on the duty runway, and Sheila began chatting to the tower. I didn't even know they had a radio there, for it wasn't usually manned. I suspected John had turned it on to reassure her. He reported "all clear," and she could take off. But she didn't. Nervously she waited on the deserted airfield until I could contain myself no longer, and burst out with: "For Christ's sake, Sheila – go!"

"I can't," she wailed; "it isn't clear."

She pointed. High up and far away and at a good 3,000 feet up were some jets, probably destined for Farnborough which was on at that time.

John's patient voice came back. "It's OK, Sheila, you can go."

She looked at me and smiled nervously. "You are sure?"

I gave the empty circuit another once over. "Yes Sheila," I said: "go."

Yet within a year Sheila was to be a world figure. She never completely conquered her nervousness, yet flew alone over the longest and toughest routes on earth. That in my book is the mark of a brave lady.

The finances of the Club we flew with were seldom discussed. If once in a while we reflected on our good fortune, it was usually over a hot curry at one of the many South Kensington Indian restaurants we frequented, where we made as little as we decently could of those questions that niggled our consciences. One popular explanation was that the Tiger Club was Norman's hobby and that with the conceit of youth considered us his favoured children on whom he lavished the profits of a big commercial enterprise. Another was that we were benefiting from some tax loss; any excuse to shrug away the simple economic facts that we, in our perpetual impecunious state should have been all too well aware of, that the Club didn't ever pay for itself and we were getting our flying on the cheap. But to be fair to us there did seem to be a big untapped reservoir of money and the Boss never disillusioned us. Come to think of it he never did and never has. Norman simply didn't and doesn't talk about money. I take my hat off to him for he's the only person I know who doesn't. Like it or not, the blasted subject is never far from my lips. Shame on me, and the rest of us.

It was many years before we learnt that money didn't grow on trees, even for the Tiger Club, and it was events like the air racing at Coventry in '63 that commanded our attention instead.

RACING AND CHEAP TIGERS

The long summer weekend once a year at Coventry was always great fun; it was the one chance in the year to meet everyone. Food, gossip, the Shell tent, where food and drink was all on the house, and the parties in the evening never failed to draw the *aficionados*.

Visibility that year was poor all the Saturday with intermittent rain. After weeks of fine weather it waited until the competitors had booked in on the Friday, and then clamped. Coventry can be a fiesta of colour and animation, but not in the rain. Dreary low cloud, umbrellas, with everybody scurrying around from shelter to shelter waving red airfield passes at damp policemen. Sunday was much the same. No racing. The poor Royal Aero Club officials with infinite patience pacified, helped, arranged, and tried the impossible to get all the racing in on the one day left – the Bank Holiday Monday.

The first race, the Air League Challenge Cup, brought cheers from every turning point for Dave Morgan in a Turbulent; he was the first off – and led all the way. It being a handicap race, the slowest got away first and if the handicappers got their sums aright everyone should cross the finishing line together. Pure fiction of course, but until the advent of Formula Racing all racing was handicapped thus and many the strokes we pulled to kid the handicappers – who in turn kidded themselves they knew it all. The Tiger flying of Dennis Hartas was positively exciting and did nothing except arouse misery in the hearts of at least two grounded competitors condemned to the turning point pylons . . . either of whom would have given anything to have been up there. John Donald got lost, he was an early member of the Club and getting on a bit, and had a reputation for getting lost, not that the reputation ever bothered him one little bit. So did Neil Williams, and we sorely missed the Arrow Active to liven things up. Dennis came in second, closely followed by Bill Innes, also Tiger-borne. The Condor piloted by Norman averaged 110 mph and the winning Turb 103 mph.

That year saw all the entries "mixed up" into just two races, so in the second race, the John Morgan Trophy, we again saw Tigers and Turbs, Airedale and Cessnas, only this time the Hon. James Baring was flying the Cosmic Wind. First away was, as in the first race, the ultimate winner. Did feel sorry for poor Beryl Saunders second away behind the Tipsy Nipper, for she was obviously flying a cooking Turb. There was no mistaking the verve of David Phillips in the Tiger and Bev Snook in the Jodel 117. Incidentally eleven out of the fifteen entrants in this race were Club members . . . including the pilots of the three new Airedales.

If ever there was a thoroughbred on the course it was the *Ballerina*; James took her around the course in immaculate style, and put up precisely the same time as Pee Wee Judge the year before. Sheila Scott flying the Ambassadeur came in second and Ranald Porteous was third in the Airedale.

At 7.30 that evening they flew off the final race – The King's Cup. There were thirteen Club members out of a total entry of twenty two. First home was Peter Bannister in his Tipsy, Ranald in the Airedale second and A.J. Spiller third in his Cessna 180 – a considerable improvement in speed on his old Proctor. All honours to Dave Morgan in taking home the Air League Challenge Cup and Dennis Hartas in collecting the de Havilland Tiger Moth Challenge Trophy yet again . . .

Those events recorded at the time of the '63 National Air Races genuinely conveyed the atmosphere and were typical of the period. Within a few years public interest as opposed to regional had gone. No more the TV cameras, they went away in '61. The Press coverage in the "populars" the year after and, saddest of all, the sponsored support of the great prewar houses of Shell, Esso and Dunlop was soon to fade. Handicap racing was no longer news, and stayed that way until the revived Schneider Race struggled back in the '80s to capture a fleeting interest.

Useless to reflect on the immense public awareness of the prewar King's Cup when the pilots were national heroes, who flew before hundreds of thousands every year in a blaze of publicity. That was yesterday. Times change, and although today's pilots continue to have a wonderful weekend at their own expense, no one else seems interested.

"We're out, snooker's in," said one pilot sadly.

Tigers were once very cheap and they certainly weren't overpriced in '63. Frank Bigger had bought a rough one for £100 and I bought a really good one for Cliff Robertson for £280. Cliff, a well-known American actor, was over here making the film *633 Squadron*. I collected him at Denham airfield after filming one day and we flew down to Stapleford Tawney to see a Tiger that was up for sale for £350. I reckoned that it might go for less if they didn't recognise Cliff either as an actor or as an American, so with some urging he put on a pair of dark glasses and promised to keep quiet.

As it happened I had heard of a new buying ploy and decided to try it out. Someone had claimed it was Chinese and it always worked like a charm. I later learnt it wasn't, it didn't, but fortune smiled this time.

To the nervous owners I smiled winningly and, having assured them that I could fly, took off for a test trip. Everything seemed OK and nothing fell off so I landed and got out smiling. To the visibly relieved owners I reported it was perfect and worth every penny they had asked. Out of the corner of my eye I could see Cliff hopping from one foot to the other, but he gamely kept to his side of the agreement and kept out of things. The only trouble, I explained, was that I hadn't expected it to be so good, and had only come along with £280 which was all I could raise at the time. Quite obviously, I continued, they could never accept that, but if they did consider it I at least had the cash ready in my pocket. Delighted at meeting such an appreciative punter they put their heads together, conceded the difference, and the deal was struck. Cliff, Lollie and I ate and drank away the difference that night celebrating at the Dorchester.

It was around this time I asked Michael Jones, who was Norman's son and now running the firm of Rollasons as well as managing the Tiger Club, how much he'd charge for a reconditioned single-seat Tiger with the 1C engine and metal prop. The word "reconditioned" was very nearly a misnomer for the airframes, instruments and engines were all likely to be nil-hour, and in fact the Tiger was virtually new. A Rollason Tiger was considered by the professionals as the Rolls Royce of rebuilds. They were, and still are, reconstructed to a high standard. The resultant Tiger was a work of art, and the Rollason boys were justifiably proud of their work.

Michael looked at me uneasily, no doubt sizing up my pocket in the near certain knowledge it was empty, but answering just in case I'd had a windfall he hadn't heard of: "£1,000."

And, seeing the look on my face he added: "of course, it'll come with a years C. of A." (Certificate of Airworthiness.)

"Cor," I said unfeelingly: "you must be joking."

Michael looked hurt. "It's cheap," he added sadly. Within a couple of years the price was £3,000 and has been going up a thousand a year ever since.

The Rollason team at Redhill of Dev Deverell, Jim Ellis, John Sarrett and Ted Carman, coupled with the Rollason Engine Division men down at Shoreham of Frank Hounslow and John (brother of Jim) have all been together without a break for over 30 years.

This collective expertise on DH, Stampe and the Jodel range, both engine and airframe – must be unequalled. Even the administrative teams of Mavis Harriott and Tessa Lovell, her part-time helper, at Redhill, and Frank's wife Lottie down at Shoreham have all been together just as long.

It speaks volumes for the loyalty and service they have all given to both Rollasons and the Club. Whilst it is the glamour boys who fly that comes to mind when the Tiger Club is spoken of, believe me it's that sort of backup with its remarkable continuity of management and engineering that is the very backbone of whatever success the Tiger Club has ever had.

A CHANNEL FRIGHT

Twenty-five years later I look back through my log books with some incredulity at my seeming indifference to a succession of flights all clearly marked with a touch of bad airmanship, yet at the time I thought I was the cat's whiskers. In 1963 alone there had been that trip home from Caithness, the crazy-flying prang at Sywell, and in the October an unequalled act of lunacy over the English Channel. My flying log books record none of the real facts, I barely used the 'remarks column' provided. By that time I had a thousand hours on single-engined aircraft, and still wasn't paying attention to that notice writ large on the instrument panel of all Club aircraft: "All Aircraft Bite Fools" – notices are always for the other chap. If there is to be an exception to prove the rule, that there are old pilots and bold pilots but no old bold pilots, then that exception could be me. Air BP – a wonderful aviation magazine that for quality and style was years ahead of its time – had published an article which was to cause something of a stir. I'd written:

We were going to Belgium. Just the two of us. Gatwick control were as friendly as ever and accepted our tiny Jodel two-seater without question. But the forecast they gave us was drab, belying the late October sunshine. Low wet stratus stretched over the Channel, with visibility down to a mile in places; above the 8/8th layer it was clear. Lympne was still open – just – and the whole lot was moving our way. Weather the other side was clearing.

I muttered 'normal weather' and mentally plotted the pros and cons. The Channel crossing was no stranger to me, nor was bad weather. As a matter of fact I could recall only one occasion when the visibility had ever been good over the stretch of water, and I had felt so uncomfortable at being able to see so well that I spent the entire time expecting the engine to stop. I decided to go.

Getting to the coast was easy – simply follow the railway line, so that if things got too bad and Lympne was closed I could easily backtrack. As for the stratus, I expected a clear layer beneath – at least it was worth a look. Anticipated better weather the other side, and the lure of a week-end in Brussels, enticed me on.

As we neared Lympne at 1,000 ft it looked awful. The hangars on the hill were just visible from a mile away, and visibility seaward was much the same – dull grey and very familiar-looking. I called up Lympne and promised to report over the Varne lightship. That was a laugh in these conditions; never mind, I'd call up after a bit of DR.

Beside me, my wife sat relaxed and trusting – she'd been out with me in worse than this. My thoughts were more direct. It was quite on the cards that the weather would worsen, and I had to have a plan ready for every contingency. I was fairly sure that a couple of thousand feet above us the weather remained clear, and even at the worst – if the weather on the other side did not break up as forecast – I could about turn and get a let-down into Gatwick. They couldn't have helped us at Grimbergen, our destination, and I hesitated to inflict my rusty RT procedure on any other international airport – Brussels for instance. But breaking up through the cloud was to be only the final move. I prefered to fly by the seat of my pants, nice and low; upstairs I'd have to mix it with the cross-Channel airways and more unaccustomed RT.

I was still pondering this when I realised that we were gradually getting lower. The visibility was still two to three miles, but the cloud base was coming down – 800 ft . . . 600 . . . For a while it steadied at 500, and since we were two-thirds of the way across I thought we'd got it made. Then it went down again, to 400. I tensed a little; decision time was coming up. Then, quite suddenly, the visibility dropped too.

Secretly, with stealth, the cloud had fooled me, and I was in it and on instruments. This worried me not one jot because, mentally, I was ready for it. A couple of thousand feet, even on limited panel, was no skin off my nose. I no longer considered dropping below and climbed for the sunshine above. Needle, ball, airspeed. I went through the same routine that, 20 years ago, the RAF had so carefully taught me.

Outside the little canopy, the wind shrieked like a wild beast. The noise and shaking imposed itself on our small world and beat a tattoo about our ears, shouting "beware." My mind didn't comprehend; something was wrong, I knew – but what? I clung desperately to routine and repeated: "needle, ball, airspeed" and conscientiously cut out the alarm within me. We'd made no more than 800 ft and the ASI was touching 125 knots. Reason said we were diving, but no matter what I did I could not get the airspeed back.

Noise was all about us, like devils trying to get in, and the little compass spun wildly. I understood that. The needle is sensitive on south and my over-correcting wasn't helping. Forget the compass, just concentrate on the first essential – climbing. The turn needle was giving me hell, indicating a constant turn to port which I couldn't get off.

"Get it straight, you fool," I shouted to myself, and stood a bit more on the rudder. As I did it, I knew I was losing – nothing I did was going to make this work out. There were no dramatics. I was spiralling down fast. At the best I had 400 ft left.

My wife screamed briefly, the 'g' forces were alarming her.

"She's not the only one," I thought bitterly. I realised clearly what a fool I'd been. Here we were about to die; all because I had been over-confident. The fear of death didn't worry me, just that my incompetence was going to kill an unsuspecting dear one. I remember glancing at her. Survival was unlikely. It was extraordinary how clear my thoughts came to me, but all the while I retained my grip on reality.

What to do? If ever I needed to remember my "recovery from unusual positions" procedures, this was it. There was one recovery I had never forgotten and could do with my eyes shut – I was going to have to. I pulled up hard into a deliberate stall.

In the sudden hush my wife turned to me and said: "Darling, I wish you wouldn't do loops in cloud."

It was ludicrous – the classic line-shoot to out-do all other lines. The ultimate in sick farce. I can't remember my retort – if I made one. Since I've told this to no one, I haven't heard the laughter it warrants. For myself, a long time later, I can see the funny side of it – but I've never been able to laugh.

Up . . . up . . . until the ASI needle fell off the clock. Now at the top, with a clean stall, I could wipe the slate clean and start again. Wings level, some reassuring silence to think in, and the plunge downward the last gambit before oblivion. It worked. It worked first time. I can still remember the relief as the cloud broke and there was a glimpse of the sea, nature's built-in artificial horizon – even though it was under my propeller and only about 200 ft down. I pulled back as hard as I dared – no prayers – just using all the skill I could muster – no high-speed stall now, and a rapid orientation. The 'g' pressed us in our seats, the water passed under us and before I could embrace the visibility we were climbing into cloud again.

If to have been granted one's life was ecstasy, to have it snatched away was damnation. Men have gone grey over less. If it worked once *it must work again. Deliberately I climbed the speed off and stalled again, knowing full well that there couldn't be 300 ft beneath us. With a growing rush of air we again broke out of cloud and skimmed the grey water of the Channel. This time I held it there.*

"I think it's time to go back," I said. The wife didn't answer. It was unanswerable – the understatement of the year.

The compass steadied on north and at 100 ft we sped back. I kept asking myself what had happened. All instruments read correctly, innocent little faces openly reproachful that I could suspect them of lying. Mentally I went back through that initial climb into the cloud. I had opened the throttle fully and eased back. Trim. I hadn't trimmed it out. No wonder the stick pressures had fooled me; and I recalled more. The Jodel on full throttle needed a lot of right rudder.

The unforgivable thought still haunts me – it had never entered my head that I couldn't cope, that I hadn't questioned my competence. Perhaps I thought that IF (Instrument Flying) once learned is never forgotten, like riding a cycle.

Back at a drizzly Lympne, the controller said: "Not nice, is it?"

"No," I replied, "so I thought we'd come back." I'd have given everything to have said that with conviction 20 minutes earlier.

To say the least I wanted a low profile, so I asked John Taylor, the Editor that, if he published it, would he please not reveal my name. Unfortunately he forgot, and in no time at all pundits of every type were rushing into print. When the dust had settled an uneasy truce remained. I'd pointed out a bit defiantly that although my recovery was a bit unorthodox it had worked, a point of view to which there seemed no answer.

"It was luck," someone finally said. "It wouldn't have worked the second time."

I argued weakly that it had; but I've avoided clouds like the plague ever since. I still have the original artwork John sent me as consolation, and it still dumbly accuses me.

TOP: HRH Prince Philip flies 'PNZ at White Waltham in the autumn of 1960.
BOTTOM: Norman Jones looks on as HRH receives last-minute briefing from John Severne.

TOP: Jack Piercy checks over Jodel 140 G-ARDZ outside the hangar at Redhill. Probably in the summer of '61.
BOTTOM: Turbulent line-up of nine. Pilots visible are Barry Griffiths, Ian Trethewey and – just behind him – James Baring. Circa 1962.

TOP: A spectacular air-to-air by Vic Blackman of Lollie greeting her fans at Fairoaks in September of '62.
BOTTOM: Some of the display team at Leavesden in September '64. L. to R.: in the cockpit Peter Phillips, Gavin Dix, Lollie and author, Bruce Cousins, attractive companion and Bill Goldstraw.

TOP: A tied-together *post mortem*. Author back to camera, Dennis Hartas, Clive Elton and Pee Wee Judge during the summer of '62.
BOTTOM: The much-loved Jodel 117 G-APOZ outside the hangar at Redhill in the spring of 1960.

TOP: The first Condor, G-ARHZ (still in primer) reached Redhill during May 1961. Viewers (L. to R.): a small Paul Conyers, Arthur Humphries, Frank Hounslow on wingtip, Bish, 'GB' and the back of James Baring.
BOTTOM: DH Hornet Moth G-ADNB at Redhill in the autumn of 1960.

TOP: DH Puss Moth G-AHLO takes off from Redhill in February 1963. It's also a good view of the old pumphouse, and the narrow peri-track off which we often flew in soggy conditions.
BOTTOM: Redhill in the early sixties. 'CDC overflies the E-W runway.

TOP: Sywell, July 13th 1963. Author no doubt thinking of John Blake's memorable 'think cloud': "If this doesn't kill me, Norman will."
BOTTOM: Another Blake 'think cloud' adorned this delightful shot of 'GB' and Bob Winter when it adorned the notice board at Redhill around 1964.

TOP: Stampe aerobatics at Little Snoring in May '65. L. to R.: David Timmis, Robin d'Erlanger, Martin Barraclough and Neil Williams, probably on the occasion of the McAully Aerobatic Competition.
BOTTOM: Super Cub 'RAM on skis in January '63 at Redhill. Note the Dexion mountings – crude but effective.

1964

ON COST, SAFETY AND A WILLING WILLIAMS

Flying cost a bit more in 1964.

SUBSCRIPTIONS AND FLYING RATES – 1964
(Subscriptions to take effect on 1st January, 1964)

Associate Member	£5.5.0
Full Member	£4.4.0
Passenger Member	£2.2.0
Overseas Member	£1.1.0
Temporary Member	5.0

Flying Rates to take effect from 1st February, 1964

Tiger Moth	£3.10.0
Turbulent	£2.0.0
Condor	£3.10.0
Jodel D.117	£4.0.0
Jodel DR.1050	£5.0.0
Jodel D.140	£7.0.0
Super Cub	£5.10.0
Stampe	£3.15.0
Jackaroo	£3.15.0
Arrow Active	£3.15.0
Cosmic Wind	£9.0.0
Night Flying	5/- extra

Foreign Touring. An extra charge of 7/6d. will be made on each individual trip to cover administrative expenses.

After 50 hours flying in one year with effect from 1st January, 1964 a member will be allowed 10/- per hour reduction on all flying rates (excluding glider towing etc.).

The membership had risen too. A total of 450, comprising 312 flying, 107 passenger and 31 honorary. The increase in flying membership included a guinea towards the block subscription to the Royal Air Force Reserves Club in London's Park Lane we had taken out the previous year. From now on we, as affiliated members, were free to use the Club's facilities, but it was never a popular venue and the arrangement didn't last long.

Down at Redhill, where the dreary weather hampered flying, some of us with typical impatience formed a new section – we called it the Tiger Shooting Club. It all started when I impulsively bought a powerful air rifle, and then talked three others into sharing the cost, and we started lighthearted target practice. The idea caught on, and in no time at all there were two more air rifles and an air pistol. Gerald d'Arcy, a brother of one of our members, who farmed land adjoining the airfield, all too aware of the increasing noise of the bigger guns and thinking of his livestock, wisely offered us facilities for clay-pigeon shooting and twelve bores became the order of the day using a trap lent us by the late Donald Campbell. Everyone had a lot of fun and made a lot of noise. Then as suddenly as it began it finished. The weather cleared and guns were forgotten. We were busy practising for the forthcoming display season.

The new season was important for us. To start with, it was to be my first as Display Director, and after some of the fiascos of the previous year we were determined to make it as safe as we could. Letters flew about, all full of good intent, and perhaps the most important was the suggestion that we form a Display Committee to accept responsibility for flight safety. Dennis Hartas agreed to become Safety Officer to follow things up, and he would submit a list of safety points for display briefings. To all these suggestions Norman agreed with his normal brevity; however, he assured us, he would also be a Safety Officer AND with overriding veto. He wasn't going to let go of the reins.

It is probable that the current CAA guidelines to displays had their foundings in Dennis's first proposals, the earlier guides used quite a lot of it near word for word. From the word go we had kept the Ministry in the picture, it was politic to do so. The Ministry of Aviation of course hadn't been unaware of our mishaps, and had had a quiet word with John Blake, who was then with the Royal Aero Club. He had wasted no time in passing the word on. By March we had established the procedures that were to become the routine in the years to come. In a letter to N.H. Thompson during that March I outlined our plans:

"May I outline our approach to flight safety. It is of course, far more than that, for we have a definite plan which has been in operation since January. It must first be stated that responsible members within the Club were appalled at the incident rate last year, and immediately resolved to put matters right. The proof of the pudding is of course in the eating, but we are confident that the measures we have taken are the right ones, and will again produce the incident-free displays we have been accustomed to over the previous five years.
The plan is as follows:
***Pre-season:** Early in January we formed an experienced Display Committee (five out of the six members are professional pilots) and elected a Safety Officer. All practice flying is carried out under the personal supervision of Team Captains (Committee members). Although unconnected with the actual display flying, but definitely with safety in mind, was the appointment of a Chief Check Pilot and the now*

established practice of regular six-monthly checks on type. We have laid down three basic conditions for pilots in all future display flying:

1) The best available (this final selection of pilots is the responsibility of Team Captain and Display Director).

2) Considerable practice.

3) a regular routine.

Pre-display: *The Safety Officer will visit every venue, decide course of race, assess hazards, local conditions, and report back. A full rehearsal to establish that each act is not only attractive show-wise, but carried out in a safe manner (by safe we mean to pilot, aircraft and public).*

Display: *A full briefing is always held at which the display director runs through the entire programme emphasising the following points:*

1) The met. condition.

2) Adherence to timing.

3) No unauthorised manoeuvre.

4) At no time to fly towards or over the crowd.

5) Maintain the agreed safe distance from public – as with item 6 this distance varies with every act, a distance that has been previously discussed and agreed in committee.

6) Maintain agreed minimum height and emergency procedures. The Safety Officer always speaks on these occasions.

Post-display: *A debriefing is carried out at the home airfield and any lapse of flying discipline will certainly be acted upon. Incidently we have already clamped rather hard on two occasions with long suspensions and restricted type of flying to others. We only mention this in order to emphasise our determination to be better safe than sorry.*

In case we have made display flying sound rather a forbidding affair, we hasten to add we all do it because we enjoy it (we are amateurs and NOT paid) because we all believe in the future of light flying, and anything that jeopardises this future deserves to be taken seriously."

His reply was typical of the close support we always got from the so-called powers that be in those days. Even then it was stylish to knock Civil Servants, yet in my experience these quiet men not only had the knowledge, but the common sense to go with it. If they regulated they did it for the common good and they did so selflessly. The empire builders came later. He replied:

"Thank you so much for your letter about the Tiger Club's approach to flight safety. It was very kind of you to give me such a full account of the measures you and your Club are taking to produce incident-free displays, and all concerned with flight safety will be interested in them. I am glad that the enjoyment you and your colleagues get, and give,

with the flying displays will not be effaced; otherwise this too would be fatal!"

Do our Civil Servants write in such friendly vein today, or with such sincerity? I hope so.

We were undoubtedly on our best behaviour at Panshanger in Hertfordshire for our first display of the season on the 30th March. To pass it over as just another display would be to ignore that it marked a turning point in display safety procedures that would be the pattern for the future. The acts had been well rehearsed and it showed. For the highly critical observer, and we were never short of those, there were few moments that dropped below a very high standard of airmanship, and it was to be the memory of this day that was to spur the pilots to do even better.

Panshanger firmly established a display criteria that was never to be surpassed. Future historians will probably consider the decade that followed to be a classic period of flying excellence, for it was obvious that a few regular display pilots were in a class of their own, and the Tiger Club provided both the stage and the opportunity to develop their talents before an eager public. That there was an availability of exceptional pilots at the time has never been in doubt. Even without the Club such men would have eventually received the recognition they were due, but the Club with its policy of active encouragement in the sport of flying provided the springboard such men needed.

PANSHANGER 1964

It proves little by way of consolation to learn that Easter this year was the coldest and wettest since 1886. To put on a show was an effort, but to good cause – especially since there was a goodly crowd. With tongue in cheek, I'd reckon on 6,000. It will long remain a mystery why so many came at all; it rained on and off the whole day.

But the show was a good one and the crowds must have gone away feeling that it had been worth while, for they had seen some superb flying. Whilst rummaging for a scrap of paper on which to record this event, I came across an old programme – just two pages of it – for the Easter display of '61 held at the improbable Snoad Street Farm. I couldn't believe we had progressed so far in 3 years. There were 14 events (three of them races, and those were rigged), two aerobatic, one by Sue Burges and the other by Peter Phillips (Tigers), Balloon Bursting and Flour Bombing, and a Pupil and Instructor act, Tied-together and a long forgotten item, "McKenzie's Secret Weapon." Does anyone recall what that was?

153

Three years later the crowds were to see five aerobatic performances on three different types, a Race, Standing on Wing, Parachuting, Formation aeros, Crazy flying and Sailplane, radio controlled model aircraft plus all the old favourites. 1964 began with two converging formations of Biplanes and Turbs through which a Cosmic streak of lightning fairly sizzled. For six minutes Peter Phillips gave the crowds something to gasp over as he flew that fine aircraft all over the sky. A smooth 16-point roll and he'd gone, and along came James Baring with his three fellow Turbulators to dive and punish the streamed rolls of paper, to formate and delight, chugging low and sedately before us. George Bottomer led a tight three in echelon through broken cloud at 1,500 to drop the parachutists. Stampe aeros by Peter followed by Pee Wee Judge's Tied-Together and this time with two new wing men, Bill Innes and Sam Key. Unfortunately their tapes broke, and through no fault of their own; the tapes, weakened by a long damp winter, just gave up the ghost; we MUST use nylon next time. Balloon Bursting was hectic, and most spectacular, perhaps as much as the spirited crazy flying by Neil Williams. He mentioned afterwards that he was just warming up when his time was up – it would be hard to imagine anything more hair-raising.

In the interval Robin d'Erlanger and Martin Barraclough completed a Voltige Competition, one which was judged by the Chairman and John Blake – never did find out who won. Talking about John reminds me to mention his consistently fine commentary and his running buffet in the Pilots' tent. This was an innovation, and one that seemed popular. The constant supply of hot tea and food throughout the afternoon was most welcome and did much to cheer wet pilots and crewmen during the rainy spells. Our thanks to Mrs Jackson, France Seignol and Ninnie Fisher.

A cold wind blew steadily, occasionally bringing with it rain squalls that swept across the field, making life difficult for pilots and spectators alike, but the ranks held – a tribute to the flying, which every now and then was rewarded by encouraging applause. Neil Williams in the Active; a stirring sight as he looped and rolled, seemingly off the ground. Of all the Club's aircraft this must surely be the most exciting; and not a little frightening. A double formation of four Turbs weaved and crossed, a mass of colour bucking the wind, their engines rising and falling with throttle to stay in position. Neil in the Cosmic Wind with his startling new introduction of an upwards 'S' for which he needs 240 mph, hard won from a cloud base of 1,500 feet. No sooner had he gone – whirling like a dervish (whatever that is) – than a sailplane, noisy in the silence, gently looped and turned in a graceful display. Our thanks to "Lefty" who was towed through some wet stuff by Mike Jolley all the way from Bicester. James Gilbert in a Stampe and a well-balanced and positioned aero display which marked his entry as a first class performer. 'SOW,' or Standing on Wing, encountered a bit of a setback when trouble was had affixing the rig to 'CDC in time, and what was to have been a double act resolved itself into the familiar husband and wife act; Lollie reports it was COLD, and as I write this she is comfortably curled up in bed with the flu and I'm doing all the cooking and housework!

The newest act we'd left till nearly last – it was Neil's brainchild on its first public airing. In his formation aerobatics – all five of them – Peter Phillips immaculately led his wing men, James Baring and Neil Williams in loops and wingovers, whilst Bill Innes and James Gilbert co-ordinated aerobatic runs from either side of the field in support of the formation. Their mirror act went down well, an act that has already gained considerable publicity both in the National Press and on TV. The flour bombing by Dennis Hartas and Pee Wee Judge kept the fun going until the Race brought the show to a noisy end . . .

In passing it is worth recording that the 'mirror' act, an aircraft in tight formation beneath one inverted that is now so familiar in Europe, was first ever seen at Panshanger. What isn't so well known is that the two originators were Bill and James. An excellent quote came up some time later. Two pilots were discussing their mirror act.

Said Neil Williams, who was the pilot underneath on this occasion: "James, you weren't straight, you were slipping."

"I wasn't," replied James Gilbert. "You were – I could see your ball wasn't central."

My debut as Display Director was successfully behind me. The only trouble was that I had to stay on the ground, only getting airborne for the Standing-on-the-Wing act. However, in my enthusiasm that day to put on the best possible show I made what in retrospect was to prove a dangerous mistake.

Everyone had practised hard and long before the big day, no one more so than Neil Williams. Neil was one of those extraordinary mortals who never seemed to get tired. He would without question tackle any task given – as long as it was flying. A strong, very strong man, with super-sharp reflexes, Neil was every inch the dedicated pilot, and since he never refused any assignment he was a tower of strength to the new Display Director. My mistake was to fail to see that I was over-using him, an oversight I repeated at the Sywell Northampton Display two months later during which Neil nearly lost his life.

On the face of it, six slot times of around five minutes each flight didn't seem much. Norman however warned me in a letter after the show in which he wrote: *"I think it important that no one pilot takes too big a part in the show."* Peter Phillips, who was equally worried, wrote in similar vein and named Neil. Yet Neil's apparent calm and downright professionalism – he was currently an RAF test pilot at Farnborough – allayed any qualms that would have arisen with a lesser pilot. At Panshanger he flew six five-minute slots throughout a show that had lasted three hours. On paper that didn't seem excessive, but it was. I overlooked the many changes of aircraft, the time preparing, positioning, and the essential five minutes peace sitting in the cockpit before take-off, the absolute minimum to familiarise to craft, act and surroundings. The outcome was two dangerous moments at Sywell where the previous year I had made such a fool of myself. If poor Mike Newton, the airfield owner, took heart when he learnt I wasn't doing the crazy flying that year, he must have lost it completely when he watched unbelievingly as Neil Williams took my place. My report in the May *Tiger Rag* makes no mention of the dangers; there was never any sense in washing our problems in public, but in private the debriefing was down to earth, a lesson had been learnt. Never again was any one pilot given more than four display slots and only then if they were well spread.

The Sywell Display was a winner but the day was very windy – gusts of 30 kt prevented parachutists and put an extra notch in the display pilots' awareness. There was a new act. It was one Barry Griffiths had been planning for a long time. It was introduced by Professor Griffinsky. Barry had invented an extraordinary contraption – a mysterious black box, and in flamboyant dress he entertained the crowd preparing the device for a radio transmission to the tolerant veteran Tiger 'CDC that stood by with its safety pilot – a fellow foreigner named Williamsky. To everyone's huge amusement the box exploded in a cloud of red smoke and 'CDC got cheerfully out of control and proceeded to attack its controller! In the second half of the programme, during a sizzling session of aerobatics in the Cosmic Wind by Neil, he made our hair stand on end with a dead stick landing that wasn't on the menu. He pulled it off superbly . . . so I wrote at the time.

That mysterious black box was only seen once. It cost £40 to concoct – a fortune in those days – and the idea was to produce something between a mad scientist's brainstorm and a clown's show stopper. For some reason Barry Griffiths dressed up as an old granny complete with bonnet and voluminous skirts. In spite of its smoke and bangs the box didn't live up to its inventor's promise, and for years afterwards Norman would periodically ask what happened to it. A not unreasonable request since he'd had to pay the bill. Barry's alarm at being the target for Neil's crazy flying was real enough, for a determined Neil Williams always flew to the limits in display, and his crazy flying was sufficiently hairy for fellow pilots to look away. It was immediately after this frightening series of near misses on Barry that Neil hurriedly clambered into the tiny and very fast Cosmic Wind *Ballerina* and, with no time to gather his wits, flew off for his aerobatic slot that wound up with a manoeuvre at too low an airspeed which in turn induced an already overworked engine of only 100 hp to throw in the sponge. Neil's subsequent forced landing from only a few hundred feet was nothing short of brilliant in the circumstances. A downwind turn is a no-no in normal conditions in that taut racer, but a death wish in the winds that prevailed. I got another letter from Peter Phillips. It was brief: "I told you so."

QUOTES FROM SYWELL

"This bossing business makes me savage" – attributed to Bruce Cousins i/c crewman.

Margo McKellar on her new Turbulent: "She goes so fast I daren't race her."

Neil Williams had the power of descriptive writing and his memorable contribution after the Panshanger show will forever stand as a most remarkable and evocative declaration of a top display pilot's thoughts as he goes through his act. His opening paragraphs should have rung alarm bells . . .

". . . What a hell of a way to spend Easter Monday! So run my thoughts as I strip off my heavier flying kit and, considerably lightened, sprint across to the *Ballerina*. Tony has the canopy open and the straps all laid out ready. Thoroughly out of breath, I scramble aboard, cursing all displays, directors, and close time schedules. A glance at my watch – eight minutes past four; my display starts in nine minutes time. What if the engine won't start?

I force myself to concentrate on strapping in; if Tony can't start it I'll eat my helmet! Lap straps first – tight! Can't afford any loose movement here; shoulder harness tight; that b***** parachute box is crippling me; I'll have to move it – ten past four – no, dammit, I haven't got time. Switches off, throttle closed, cold air, cylinder head temperature selected to No. 2 – set, contact. My legs are trembling as I hold the toe brakes on – 'still on' from Tony – my God, it isn't going to start. No sooner the thought than she fires and I just grab the canopy in time as the slipstream tries to slam it down. I close it and slide the bolts home, oil pressure O.K., oil temperature 250°C, eleven minutes past four, I check the stopwatch on the panel, and set the altimeter to zero. Mags dead and alive and I wave the boys away, 1,600 rpm and she rolls forward waggling her wings and giving me a resounding clout on the ear as she bumps over the grass. Checks as I taxi, make a rude sign at John Blake. He says something into the mike equally rude no doubt, but I can't hear anything inside this flying echo chamber.

Twelve minutes past four – five minutes to go, never thought I'd make it, must complain to Benjy, extra heave on the harness adjusting straps and we're ready to go. The two Turbulent formations are running in, I'll have to wait, God, this cloud looks low. I tie the loose strap ends together, mustn't have those in my face during the display. The Turbs cross and I open up to 2,000 rpm, check mags, full power and off we gallop. Airborne, just behind the Turbs, turn away, keep it low, clear of the field, phew! Airspeed 130 into the climb, and run through the pre-aerobatic checks – hullo, cloudbase 1,500 – not so good. Still there are breaks, and I climb in a gentle spiral, 3,000 feet in the clear, but it's a pretty small hole I came up through. A couple of rolls to make sure the harness is really tight and to check for loose articles – two minutes to go, I'd better get into position, throttle back, the slipstream whines mournfully around the canopy as I break out beneath the – where in hell's the airfield?!! It can't be far away – 90 seconds to go – how am I going to explain this away? Turn into the wind, fingers crossed, a wave of relief, there it is, what a devil of a place to try and find, even then I could only see the crowd – 60 seconds and I'm right out of position, full throttle, come on airspeed, 150, 160, 170, the staccato engine note changes into a blare of sound – the noise is terrific, 30 seconds to run and I pull up into cloud – let's hope I've judged this right, on instruments, give it ten seconds, ease forward, needle in the centre and down we go. 1,800 feet, 1,600 – 1,500 and the airfield is dead ahead – airspeed 190 increasing. A wave of fright – the sky is full of Turbulents! What the hell are they playing at?

I must have got the time wrong. Shall I keep going, shall I break off – airspeed 210 – height 1,000 feet – too late, I'm committed, check my watch, five seconds to go, the noise is devastating, airspeed 230, the crowd changes from a coloured rectangle to a sea of upturned faces, she's snaking now, very sensitive on the rudder, clamp those pedals hard, throttle back a bit, the revs are nearly off the clock, bang the stopwatch – start pulling, airspeed 240, brace hard against the lap belt, she's really moving, the nose is up, my breath comes in gasps as the 'g' builds up, vertical, full power, the 'g' is very high now, as the horizon comes in – push!

From plus 9 to minus 4 as we go up into the second half of the 'S,' the engine cuts, bang the throttle shut, keep pushing and she comes over the top at 50 indicated. There's fuel everywhere, it's streaming out of the filler cap. I can't see ahead, the windscreen is running with it, the cockpit is thick with petrol fumes, I hope none gets onto the exhaust pipes – the prop is slowing, it's going to stop, ease back on the stick, gently, gently. She judders on the stall but I get in a quick pump on the throttle which helps me over the top with a sudden burst of power. The engine cuts again but now the nose is down, 70 knots (the straight and level stalling speed) 80, 90 – vertical. God, that ground looks close but whatever you do don't push or she'll stall inverted. 120. 130 and push gently, she's coming round, that ground looks desperately close, gently does it, the negative 'g' is up to 4 and the nose is on the horizon. I roll as smoothly as I can to straight and level flight – 400 feet, plenty of room actually. So the show goes on for another terrifying four and a half minutes, flying the aeroplane to its limits, knowing that every mistake is recognised by fellow pilots – this to me is the biggest ordeal. Nearly over – a wingover into ten successive aileron rolls – if this one doesn't topple your gyros nothing will! I level out for a fraction and then go into a tight turn – this is because I'm so dizzy that I couldn't fly straight and level if I wanted to!

Relax boy, this is the final manoeuvre, right on the deck, full power, airspeed 170, that's plenty. Keep it going and as the centre of the crowd comes up a quick check on the stopwatch again, it shows fifteen seconds to go – that's about right, pull up at about 7 'g' and check vertical (and if James Gilbert thinks I'm gong to tell him how I do a Lomcevak he's had it!). As the rotation stops I pull out of the dive and bang the throttle shut. With the engine popping and banging I pull up and round into the downwind leg as the sailplane releases high above me. All attention is on the quiet grace of the glider as I cross the threshold and ease down onto the grass.

I switch off and open the canopy, sweating, deafened and completely exhausted.

"Quick," says someone, "you've just got time to get into 'OAA, we've kept the engine running!"

As I said before – what a hell of a way to spend an Easter Monday.

DAWN-TO-DUSK, TIGER TAG AND ROCHESTER

"Just because I come down to Redhill every week it doesn't mean I'm keen, it's just that I've nothing else to do!" – Tom.

The origins of the Dawn-to-Dusk contest were probably based on the usual seasonal wish by pilots to fly into the still of the night and beyond. In July I'd noted:

June turned out to be a bit of a corker, warm days but not always, it seems, in the early mornings. It happened last year, the usual routine, it goes like this. It's late evening – all is still and the heat of the day is still softly caressing. The lights of the village twinkle and beckon; a night for a walk and quiet-spoken friends. Someone always says: "Let's get up at the crack of dawn and fly to meet the sun." Someone says it every year. June had its quota. They'd had a wonderful party up at Kidlington, full evening dress, dancing in the moonlight until the early morn and a dawn flight back to Redhill. To Tom Storey, Ninnie Fisher, James Baring and Martin Barraclough our condolences – they took hours to defrost. It was no far step therefore to the announcement that Norman Jones had issued a challenge. He offered the free use of four Turbulents in a Dawn-to-Dusk Endurance Competition.

I'm not so sure about the free bit but it could have been. I wasn't alone in suspecting it was a ploy to better aircraft utilization, but it was an inspired idea.

The Dawn-to-Dusk must now be the best known national competition outside of the King's Cup. Little did those early contenders know what they were starting. It was originally an endurance contest for Turbulents, with hours flown as the primary aim, distance covered was secondary. With the longest days being around the middle of June most of the competitors flew that month. The winner of the first contest was Don Lovell who flew 1,003 miles in just under 13 hours. Only four started, Beryl Sanders came second and Bill Goldstraw third. John Mimpriss retired. His subsequent report: "I was forced to retire with engine failure'" – it was a bit more than that – was a classic of understatement. He'd made a start from Redhill before light, and whilst still in near darkness lost power over a remote part of Kent. His blind forced landing wound up with him trapped upside down in the plane and sinking into mud. John, who was then a serving helicopter pilot in the Royal Navy, just managed to cut his way out of the wreckage with a survival knife strapped to his naval overalls. It was a close call.

The Club News each month always provided a touch of gossip – nothing malicious of course – but like the tip of the proverbial iceberg there was often much left unsaid, leaving the knowing to fill in the blanks. There was for instance a fisherman's tale that was perfectly true, even if the pilots concerned denied it all, but most of us knew better.

The incident occured during the *Daily Express* Air Race with its spectacular dash around the south coast at the height of the holiday season. Two Tigers were having a neck and neck private race on the side and they flew so low across Brighton Pier that one of them took a fishing rod along with them. Later the irate fisherman claimed that the line ran out so fast the reel began to smoke, and when the rod and line tore from his hands it wound up in the water and sank with a big sizzle. It cost one of the pilots a new rod and several drinks to hush the matter up, and much diplomacy.

No names, no pack drill, but diplomacy must have stood them both in good stead in later years. One of the duo finished up as the Chairman of the Royal Aero Club and the other became the Lord Mayor of London.

Peter Harrison, the CFI at Rochester, was recently elected to the Executive Committee of the Medway Chamber of Commerce. His first public appearance was at Chatham Dockyard – the occasion, the launching of a submarine. As the sub slipped down the slipway the CFI was heard to mutter: "God bless this ship and all those who fly over her."

QUOTE: Michael Headfort: "I tried to tune into Rochester NDB but nothing happened, not even a smell of burning."

Tiger G-ASES never did join us, but G-ASKP did. This welcome relief for hard worker 'CDC wasn't particularly attractive with its odd paintwork of dark red and yellow. Quite early on in its career – in fact *en route* for its first display at Rochester carrying Neil Williams and Roy Davis, it no sooner got airborne than the engine began to misbehave– so audibly that everyone gathered on the tarmac to watch the fun. While Neil was coaxing revs from the engine, which was shaking fit to leave the airframe, he spotted a hand in front waving a piece of paper. With commendable patience he took time off to read the message: "ENGINE MISSING?"

It was after the Shoreham display in the August that Neil Williams put pen to paper to record his impressions of the Formation Aerobatic slot. If there was ever a man who could talk you through an experience it was Neil, it was the next best thing to flying with him.

TIGER TAG (Formation Aerobatics) as seen on the day from the No. 3 Position

So far, so good; just another formation take-off. Looking to my right, I can see Peter Phillips' head moving from side to side as he positions us for the start of the display. Beyond him a black and silver Tiger sits glued to his wingtips; from here James Baring looks like a bearded Viking – pity he hasn't got horns on his helmet! The waiting is the worst, as we gain height. And it's so easy to hold position too, when Peter turns with only 20° of bank! Oh, well, if he kept it down to 20° it wouldn't be an aerobatic formation! Hullo, this is it, here we go; Peter looks at each of us in turn and we nod confidently (liar, in my case; I never felt less confident about anything!) Again Peter signals, making a circular motion with his hand (we know he's going to start with a loop, but with no RT we've decided to retain all hand signals).

I ease the trimmer fully forward – I find it helps to hold a steady pull force, and as Peter nods his head we ease forward into the dive. I have full power and I'm only just holding him – and he's supposed to be flying the slowest aircraft! Surely we might be approaching 120 knots now if the roar of the slipstream is anything to go by. There is an almost overwhelming temptation to glance at my A.S.I., but sure as fate if I do that I'll be on my own! My aircraft has eased up a couple of feet and I can see James on the other side of Peter's fin and rudder. He appears to be completely at ease and is as steady as a rock. Very gently I press forward on the stick and start easing down into position, and of course this is the moment when Peter nods again and two aircraft leap upwards away from me! I pull hard and I can just see Peter's undercarriage below my top wing as we enter the loop. James and I are now gaining hand over fist as we approach the top of the loop, (our spacing in time is always the same but as our speed changes our actual distance apart varies). I start throttling back, but too late – Peter's aircraft appears to rush towards me and in sudden fright I bang the throttle shut. Peter's tailplane hovers between my wingtips and I am aware of a baleful eye glaring at me – I can just imagine the language in his cockpit! This is one time I'm glad we have no radios! My ailerons still roll the aircraft, but as the 'g' drops towards zero and the lift falls off, there is no lift component available to enable me to turn away. At the same time, I know that unless I open the throttle, I'm going to get left behind. James is still sitting there making it look easy, blast him! Well, it's now or never; full throttle and – I knew I'd left it too late – Peter starts to move ahead. A touch of rudder does the trick – I ease out a foot or so and find I've been holding my breath! I crouch in the cockpit, trying to coax an extra knot or so out of my aircraft; I glance across at James and am relieved to see he has the same problem. Peter meanwhile is throttling back as he knows that we could never catch him on the way down otherwise. This is no time for finesse; again I throttle right back and at the same time I can see James's prop slow down.

As we approach level flight, I know that Peter is going to increase power, and in anticipation I start opening the throttle. We're still pulling about 4 'g,' and I for one have had enough for one afternoon!

Thank God for that, straight and level and we're still in formation! Well, I might have known it was too good to last; Peter's signalling a wingover right. This is a manoeuvre I detest, being on the outside, as I don't have any power to spare. As he signals I open throttle wide – this make no appreciable difference as our drag is so high at this speed (120 kt). Sure enough I start to fall behind. Cheating furiously, I edge in closer and drop down, hoping that Peter will notice my problem and throttle back a bit. James, on the inside of the wingover, just gains – he's got plenty to spare! As I finally get into position, Peter signals "straight ahead" and indicates a second loop. We roll out and this time it's James' turn to sweat as he swings up from the inside with his throttle wide open. That'll teach him to grin, I think, gaining in turn. The loop goes OK until we reach the top and both James and I virtually fall across the top, both banked away from Peter and unable to increase our separation. We have a choice here: either we pull back hard, at which point the wings will start doing a job of work again, or sit here with our eyes closed and our fingers in our ears and hope for the best. James appears to be sticking it out and so I decide to do likewise. Later I find out that he's been waiting for me to break away. Peter twigs the problem and pulls tighter, and we heave a sigh of relief as control returns. This time we already have full power on, and we cut the corner slightly to catch Peter on the way down. Another wingover, this time to the left and I'm looking straight up at two Tigers apparently hanging in space. This is impossible, I think, they're bound to fall on top of me. I have to concentrate hard to try to fly steadily, and not to cross my controls. It occurs to me that James doesn't appear to be having any trouble on the outside!

I still haven't seen the crowd yet. I suppose we're still over the airfield! Well, that's Peter's problem, I've got enough trouble! Yet a third loop, wonder of wonders, no complications. Why can't we do them like that all the time?

A steep turn to the right and – there's the crowd, we are in the right place! Not that there was any chance that we wouldn't be, but it's nice to see them anyway! I wake up with a start as I realise that Peter is signalling to me. He points at me and waves his arms across to the right – echelon starboard – go! I throttle back a touch, drop down and put on about 30° of bank – this change is going to be snappy. As I slide across behind James, my port wing tips encounter his slipstream and I find myself straight and level much too soon, well stepped down and too far in. I slink furtively into position, hoping nobody will notice. My neck is stiff from looking constantly to the right, it's a pleasant change to turn my head the other way. I am startled at the sudden appearance of a Tiger Moth in plan view, which disappears instantly as Peter breaks hard. I start counting – one – two – three, and James goes after him – four – five – six and open the throttle wide and apply full aileron.

Below and ahead I can see James diving while ahead of him Peter is curving around the field, his yellow and black machine contrasting sharply with the green countryside. I suddenly feel very small as I look around, as after five minutes' formation one tends to forget the exsistence of the ground, the airfield and the hangars, and the only real objects are the aircraft in the formation. It's akin to walking along a cliff and coming suddenly to the edge. I can't recommend that for a pastime, either!

But to work! Peter appears to be trying to get on my tail while I am desperately trying not to lose James. At the back of this mad follow-my-leader, I have two slipstreams to contend with, and I spend most of my time trying to prevent my aircraft from indulging in a series of flick rolls. Finally we run out of altitude and Peter rocks his wing.

At full throttle we join up and sure enough we tend to overcook it. Peter, however, is watching and opens his throttle to prevent us shooting past. Into a steep turn to the left – oh, when is this going to stop? I am soaked with perspiration – yes, even in a Tiger, and my arms and legs are aching. I force myself to relax my vice-like grip on the control column and to uncurl my toes from the rudder bar. Peter signals a "Prince of Wales" as we enter a dive and we nod our understanding. This is one of the most exciting parts of the whole display as we sweep across the field only a few feet up. Peter starts to pull up and, as James breaks, I go with him. As I near the completion of my *chandelle* to the left, I look across at James and attempt to maintain the same height. I am aware of Peter completing a roll off the top between us. As he finishes he dives to his right beneath me and I see James start to follow him down. At the same time I go into a 270° turn to the left, relaxed for the first time, since now the actual formation is complete. James is dead ahead as I roll out, and we turn round the field and finish with a good low beat up in line astern. I make sure that I stay well away from slipstreams at this height! We pull up individually into stall turns, and then it's every man for himself as we slip in for the landing.

Peter walks across as James and I climb out of our Tigers discussing the finer points of the loops. "That change into echelon was a bit ragged," he says! . . .

There were six Full Displays in 1964 which for my money was two too many. I protested to Norman. The difficulty was getting the best teams together so frequently during the holiday months, and he finally conceded the point. In later years the number went down to four, but in the meantime it was hard work and I for one spent more time burning the midnight oil than my shaky business could afford. Pointless to do more after all these years than to highlight the occasion or incident, for so much of what we did were repeat performances, yet moments survive in one's memory . . . and the high plateau which was Rochester was ever a favourite with the pilots.

ROCHESTER '64

Our third Full Display of the '64 season was at Rochester, that plateau skirted by the new M2 and topped by Elliott's white buildings – a reliable homer installed long before the NDB. Writing this report some weeks later isn't so easy if I'm to detail each item – although I could. I watched it all, but now only a few items remain outstanding – it was, for instance, a display that throughout its length of two hours was never more than 60 secs late. And that for a non-radio set-up is darn good teamwork.

Then I recall the tail end of Neil's crazy flying act. The end of it, because it's an act I prefer not to watch, but whatever it was that made me take a peep I don't know, all I do know is that when I did I wish I hadn't. Neil was diving over the side of the airfield. My heart stopped beating, the dread mantle of utter helplessness was heightened by the instinctive reaction of some of the spectators who began to run across the field, led by the two lone Club members who had helped in the illusion of the learner out on his own. It was an act. I knew it was an act, I arranged it as an act yet I fell for it

– I have always done so. Neil had dived into the valley as he, and the rest of us before him, have always done. It's good sound flying, it's just that I'm developing into a terrible back-seat driver. And of Peter, whose supreme aerobatics in the Cosmic Wind never fails to leave me excited anew: "I doubt if there is anywhere else in the world one could see such an exhibition"; not my words but those of another fine aerobatic pilot.

I'm conscious, as I write these words, of the effect they must have on others who have never seen performances such as these, and who perhaps might accuse me of blowing our trumpet a bit too loud, yet to blow too softly is not to be heard(?). I am bold and express my opinion, after all the *Rag* is but a sounding board.

We all cheered when the diminutive Flying Flea appeared bubbling down the slope onto the field before us, and, as Ralph gingerly opened the throttle it hesitantly hopped and bounced so happily that its magneto nearly fell off! As a postscript, it is good to learn that some weeks or so later the tiny noise had been so cleaned up and encouraged by all this attention it proudly hopped about 15 feet and then, well satisfied with itself, allowed Ralph and his boys to put her away. She hasn't flown since. Rochester was fun from beginning to end . . .

There is no question that the displays we witnessed that year were pure vintage, perhaps unique, and the pilots exceptional. Two pilots stood out. They always did, in spite of the fact that all the Tiger Club pilots that season were outstanding men. In any other company Dennis Hartas, Martin Barraclough or James Baring would have been head-and-shoulders above others, but even they were overshadowed by Peter Phillips and Neil Williams.

To one who not only flew with them but had been friend and witness over the years to their display flying, their styles were absolutely different, and each flew with a signature that was unmistakable. There is no doubt in my mind that until around 1974 Peter was the better pilot – his 16-point rolls in the Cosmic have never been equalled – and even until Neil's death in early 1978 when his skills were at their zenith, there was nothing to choose between them, but such was their ability that each shone in a different manner. Anyway, it would be churlish to differentiate, such was the unmitigating pleasure they gave us all whenever they flew.

There was a great and politely unspoken rivalry between them. Peter was aloof, even languid, the epitome of the public school image of the elite fighter pilot, an image he never quite shrugged off in civvy street. Neil, on the other hand, seemed almost eager to demonstrate his humble beginnings. A Welshman to his finger tips, he was proud of the valleys and his unquestioned skills. Whilst Peter gave the impression that flying wasn't everything, Neil bluntly dedicated his every waking moment to the one and only subject that mattered: his flying. The question will always be asked, was he a natural pilot (for such men do exist), and for me the answer is probably "no." He made his mark by a single-minded determination to be, and to be seen to be, the best. Within him dwelt a competitiveness that was unquestionable. His progress through the RAF was meteoric, but it was sheer hard work that did it. Had he been a leader too, the RAF would never have let him go for he would have shot to the top. But Neil was ever a rugged individual who flew best on his own. A sort of latter-day Mick Mannock. Sadly his obsession excluded his home life and his lovely first wife Jean must have suffered deeply. The freedom that he experienced with the Tiger Club after the restraint of service flying was instrumental in giving Neil the direction he was unwittingly seeking. It was the golden opportunity to exploit his great skills, and he exploited every minute of it.

He'd stay on at Redhill till the very last light, willing to fly at the drop of a hat. And if encouraged, would talk on right into the night with only one thought and only one subject, I never heard Neil expound on any other. But back in the year under review he was still a dozen years from his unforgettable best. Both Neil and Peter feature strongly in the tale of the Club in the years to come.

BEAUVAIS

Certainly by 1964 there were already clearly defined sections of the Club with established form and ways. The touring pilots of the Club may not have had the glamour of the display and aerobatic boys, but they certainly knew how to enjoy themselves. Throughout the summer there were many long and cheerful journeys. The new Jodel Mascaret had already several non-stop flights of over five hours to its credit.

Michael Jones and Bill Chesson did the 600-mile trip from Wick back to Redhill in her in four hours flat – tailwind and all. But the big event of each year was the annual tour and occasionally a special weekend away. We were not unaware what they got up to, so every once in a while pilots from the other disciplines would join Don Lovell, the touring boss, and relax a bit too.

In the September I was talked into a cross-channel break from display work. All the touring aircraft had been booked so I organised a Stampe, my wife the passenger in the front seat. She had a bit of a thing about appearing feminine and always made a point of dressing up rather than down for Redhill. I did apologise for the open cockpit but she only grinned a knowing grin. Our arrival at Beauvais caused a mild sensation. Lollie asked if I could park a little away from the others, and when the prop had stopped she nipped out on the blind side and began a quick change. Overalls, slacks, pullovers and helmet sailed over and disappeared into the front cockpit at an alarming rate. In no time at all she stood awaiting me. She was like a plate out of Tatler (she had graced the cover the previous year). Her slim legs were enhanced by high heels and the eyes, when they got around to it, took in the tailored skirt and silky white blouse as well. She was stunning to behold. "That'll show 'em," she muttered triumphantly.

The dinner in honour of the Tiger Club was a gourmet's dream. A long leisurely parade of good food . . . the six glasses before each place silently expressed the French view as how to help it down. For five hours we had battled manfully with our imperfect French and the magnificent food until in the fulness of time came the speeches. Unexpectedly member John May rose to reply to the President. In glowing words he toasted them all: "The Concorde, the Queen, the Beauvais Club, De Gaulle." He was more French than our hosts. I didn't understand a word but he was obviously doing jolly well. When he sat down someone whose French was in my class but hadn't met John murmured approvingly to her husband: "Darling, shouldn't a member of the Club reply now?"

The Beauvais weekend was a classic. For all of us it was the most memorable ever. That so much was done for us left us feeling positively guilty at our "tea and sandwiches in the hangar" hospitality. At Beauvais we were welcomed with champagne and there were all of two dozen of us. Cars were allocated and the drivers were to become our personal guides, friends and constant companions.

That evening we drove at a furious rate into the countryside to a tiny village where we dined. The evening was warm and clear after the haze of the day. Somewhere around a hundred visitors and guests sat down to dine and drink the evening away – and a good bit of the morning.

Then the equally furious drive back to Beauvais. I needn't have feared for our skins; the French seem able to drive well, even after drinking well, but those tall, dark avenues of trees between which we tore at 140 km/hr seemed to one speechless passenger, stiff and sober, an endless series of beckoning ghostly fingers. A fertile imagination and a touch of indigestion makes a coward out of anyone. The party atmosphere stayed on at the two hotels where we had been deposited. Who wanted to sleep? It was only three in the morning! Back home, like a well-regulated pub, my eyes close at 10.30, but in France . . . The tumult and the laughing died; it simply had to. We were to attend the Mayor's reception at 10 am.

Beauvais is proud of its famous tapestries and at the Exhibition in the Town Hall we spent a sleepy morning downing champagne and viewing the fine collection of tapestries. One awed young lady was heard to mutter: "I once did a tapestry but it was nothing like this." Twelve o'clock Sunday, the weekend was nearly behind us. Rumour had had it that there was to be a bit of a barbecue just before we left. But after the previous night's adventure we were no longer thinking in terms of food. At the airfield the day was perfect. The large rambling expanse that is Beauvais, is, depending on how you look at it, a fine airfield equipped with vast terminal buildings and runway, or a meandering pasture with sheep and shepherd – the one intermingling with the other. How is it that the French can mix the old with the new without trace of incongruity?

We stepped out of the car. The aircraft, those that had been hangared, were now being pushed into line. The indefatigable George Crucifix was everywhere – like an affable rubber ball bouncing in every direction.

Someone said: "How's your stomach?", and pointed weakly to a group of Algerian soldiers slowly turning the carcases of three sheep over smouldering ashes. Unwillingly, for the sheep were being roasted whole, and our tummies weren't that stable, we closed in with all the others, hypnotised by the process. For eight hours the soldiers had been roasting the sheep, for eight hours the carcases had been basted with a potent-looking red concoction (no one asked what it was), brushed on with the sheep's own tail. Over the loudspeakers came the sound of urgent Algerian music and in this off-beat spot the only thing missing was the dancing girls (next year they'll probably have them). You haven't lived until you've heard the discordant North African "Top of the Pops" version of *Smoke Gets in your Eyes*. It was hot and the sun blazed onto the oasis. Shades of Lawrence; everything was becoming more and more unreal. Over at a long trestle table two huge Algerian sergeants were ladling our drinks. I earned a shrug which eloquently wrote off all English soda-water drinkers. What else?

There were nine opened bottles of Scotch; and more. Black olives, peanuts, shishkebabs. They were the genuine thing. No need to ask where the delightful bits of offal came from. The morsels that were skewered between the bits of fat that everyone was surreptitiously dropping all over the place. Our host and friends of the previous evening were there in force urging us to eat this and that, and with the occasional assurance that the fun had yet to begin. The sheep were delicious. The few who had penknives used them, the rest picked off the hot flesh with their fingers under the guidance of friendly Algerians. The move to the long hut behind us came as no surprise, we were getting beyond surprises. There, in a gaily decorated room, there were young trees all over the place, were at least one hundred places set at tables – two very long ones indeed – tables all of nine inches from the floor. Long lines of palliasses invited us to sit down cross-legged. This was a feat I no longer thought I was capable of, and what's more, we all made it – but not without a few grunts.

The extraordinary nosh outside was, it seemed, merely an *hors d'oeuvre*, although the meat we'd put away would have made portions at

Simpson's seem mingy. The same genial soldiers now served us huge helpings of what appeared to be a finely-grained sweet rice. Our friends assured us gleefully it was cous-cous. Whilst we were waiting for the boiled fowl to go with it, the President, a big jovial man who sat opposite James Baring, exhibited his juggling skill with a plate of cous-cous. Not to let the side down, James managed a quick loop with his and as an encore attempted a slow roll. He fell out of it and covered himself. An Algerian laughed so much that he dropped his urn of the potent-smelling stew at poor Harold Hargreaves' feet, and we were so helpless with laughter we could do nothing but watch the steaming rivers of red, complete with cauliflower, creep over the floor; it was still there when we left . . . although, needless to say, no one wanted to go.

The weather was perfect as we all set course – different directions – for a more subdued clime. No anti-climax this, the English coast could be seen from the deck at Cape Gris Nez. Beauvais was surely Don Lovell's *pièce de résistance* – the visit supreme, but oh, will we have our work cut out devising the hospitality that these generous folk deserve, when they next visit us. To the Beauvais Aero Club the only word I know in French – *formidable*, very *formidable*! And my undying thanks.

ARTISTS, "GB" AND A LOOK-BACK

The *Tiger Rag*, which for many years was duplicated, was never a suitable medium for illustrations. The best we could do was the heading and the occasional line drawings. They were first introduced in the sixties, a series of humorous cartoons of a little bloke called "Ace High" – and he loved Tigers. Ace's creator was Maurice Page, who was cast in artistic mould and only worked to eat, which he didn't seem to do very often. He was always uncomplainingly broke. His technical aviational knowledge was of a high order and through the cartoons' fun his little details were worth studying. He led a shadowy life and lived no one knew quite where, but it couldn't have been far from Rochester airfield where he could usually be found. Temperamental and hard to tie down, his offerings became scarce and he faded from the scene a year later pursued by wild rumours. I liked him and his work, but probably due to a complete indifference to other opinion he never gained the acclaim he undoubtedly deserved. His bold new heading for the *Rag* was first seen in February '65 and replaced the machine worn-out one by Chris Wren.

Apart from Chris Wren, the Club had the services of another remarkable artist. John Blake was the Royal Aero Club's PR, general factorum and librarian. Not only was he a walking encyclopaedia of flying information, he was also a prolific photographer of considerable ability. The results of his work – and I do mean work, for he processed and printed all his own film on full plate – he then handed out every weekend with a generous abandon. "When do you find time to do all this?" we'd ask. Then when he won an award at an exhibition of aviation art at the Kronfeld Club we were introduced to the artist John. His works, mostly in water colour, have become collectors' items. If there was a man of many parts John was to fulfill yet another role.

In the summer of '64 he managed and led the British Aerobatic Team into the World Contests in Bilbao, and his reports to us back home were a joy to read. What mattered was not that we did terribly well – we didn't – but that what we did was done with style and great heart. They took to Spain the new Cosmic Wind in which both Peter Phillips and Neil Williams enchanted their international friends from eleven nations with magnificent flying in an uncompetitive but graceful mount. That the Cosmic was never designed for aerobatics in no way held our pilots back, but as an indication of its unsuitability consider the fact that in one sequence, Neil had to turn the inverted system on and off sixteen times. Sandwich that into the complex Aresti diagram that each flew, and appreciation of their efforts becomes apparent. Third pilot in the team was Bob Winter, who wisely stayed with the Stampe which he shared with member Nick Turvey the Lone South African entrant.

Before the end of the year Barry Griffiths had written about "GB" (Golding Barrett). Sadly "GB" is no longer with us but his contribution to the Club was considerable and in '64 he was in full flow, and Barry captured the essence of "GB" with an unerring touch.

CHARACTER REFLECTIONS by Arthur Non.

He has been mistaken variously for the British Ambassador to Nicaragua and a tramp about to doss down in the back of the hangar; which only goes to prove that it is all in the eye of the beholder.

The two highlights of his life of which we know – although there must be many more in such a rich and varied past – are when he (as a Pilot Officer) told an erring Air Vice Marshal to get out of his aerodrome, his circuit and his life, and when he (as a civilian) was allotted the Admiral's sea-cabin on one of Her Majesty's aircraft carriers on an exercise at sea.

His aeronautical experience remains comfortably anchored at about 300 hours solo – he having conveniently "lost" his log books for the past thirty years – so that he is nicely in touch with both ends of aviation. The discrepancy between his admitted total flying time and his easy familiarity with the semi-mythological creatures of the dawn of aviation is one of the many contradictions which he assiduously cultivates and which are an essential element in his character. Show him some misty old photograph of a thing of vaguely aeronautical shape and his reaction will be immediate. "Avro Hawk-Moth," he will say promptly; "Pobjoy Niagara" (or some such unlikely-sounding power plant). "Splendid little machine. Saw old Puffy Prendergast write one off at Heston in twenty-eight. Smashed it to bits; wasn't hurt, of course, couldn't hurt yourself in a Hawk-Moth, no matter what you did – gentle as a lamb." One is left wondering at the miraculous escape of Mr Prendergast and the somehow quite different characteristics of aircraft built today.

Known cryptically by the only two initials appropriate to the type, he likes the company of aeronautical infants, from whom he loudly and constantly demands instant respect but receives only ribaldry, a state of affairs with which he is greatly content.

He is the man who – the legends are legion: for example, he is the man who flew a Tiger Moth, waving a genuine Charles II candlestick, over the heads of the astonished onlookers; combining, he explains, his interests in the best of the old and the best of the new.

He drives his own car with care and restraint and yours with the verve of a racing driver, demonstrating (for the loss of a couple of teeth – your car's, not his – how unnecessary to the use of the gears is the assistance of the clutch.

He is vintage Englishman. A rich, ripe, mellow, dyed-in-the-wool eighteen carat Englishman, with a built-in distrust of the "Abroad," its citizens and all its works. His tweeds, like his hats, are superb and, typically, he disappears at intervals, this kindly gentleman, to go off and murder things in remote parts of the country. Those who have entered his garage after his return from one of these forays, and been confronted with the corpses hanging by their necks from the rafters, will not quickly forget the experience.

There are no half-measures about this man. When he laughs, he does it properly. He is not merely amused, he is ravished by mirth. Weeping copiously, he is overtaken by apoplexy and asthma together, his urbane countenance distorted into the face of some laughter-tortured gargoyle. When telling him some particularly hilarious story, one wonders whether one is doing him a favour or an injury. He acts as a buffer state between warring tribal chieftains and, as one-man U.N.O., rushes between them and persuades them to put their *assegais* away.

He is believed to have invented radar, air traffic control and daylight. So we owe him a lot, really.

Tom's grandmother's char recognising a photo of "GB":

"That's "GB"! she exclaimed; "my husband makes antiques for him!"

"GB" phoned a would-be new member to question the absence of flying times on his application form.

He asked: "What are your hours?"

"9.30 to 5.00," was the response.

1964 was a year to look back on with a lot of satisfaction. It was a period of much recognition and great endeavour by our members. Early on Charles Masefield and Lord Trefgarne had flown their prewar twin-engined biplane, the classic DH Dragonfly, back to England from Australia – they were to later take it on to America in what was nothing less than an epic adventure. Then C.A. Nepean Bishop, or "Bish," was recognised by the Guild of Air Pilots and Air Navigators with an Award of Merit and a Silver Medal. Nick Pocock, that shyest of members, went to go cropdusting in the States and promptly came back with a beautiful bride, and having said hullo went back as promptly. James Gilbert flew 167 hours in Club aircraft in '64, and "was that a record?" he enquired? It was, and still stands in 1988.

Richard Cox reporting the troubles in Zanzibar for the *Sunday Times* scooped the headlines and flew himself out just in time. From what I was never quite sure, but he gave up frightening himself and became instead a writer of best-selling thrillers. Nick Carter designed the Tiger Aerobatic Plotter, and the Annual Dance at the Albert Club in the Embankment had Dick Emery in the home-made cabaret – he was also popular for letting us fly his Miles Magister, aptly registered 'ITN. "Jacko" Jackson, who was in charge of the glider towing section, beat the 1,000 tows-in-a-year by a handsome margin. And Bunny Bramson saw his now famous book *The Tiger Moth Story* published. It's been in print ever since.

Over in the States Texas member Frank Price was seen towing a banner with *Vote Goldwater* on it. Poor Frank; wrong side again. And Sheila Scott, whilst there, received the Amelia Earhart Medal for her extraordinary achievements during her stay. She obtained, within the period of three weeks, her Commercial seaplane and helicopter ratings plus her multi-engine instrument rating. Sheila also found time to take a High Altitude Course in a pressure chamber and also qualified for jet flying. In three weeks? If you believe that you'd believe anything, we said, but Sheila was on the way to proving us wrong. Robin d'Erlanger began looking for a flying boat. He'd nearly got his feet wet earlier in the year when his Turbulent came down in mid-Channel and he hadn't forgotten.

Ted Baillie-Reynolds flew a tiny Danish KZ.III solo to Redhill from Malaysia breaking every record in the book for an aicraft between 500-1,000 kg all-up-weight. All that on a Cirrus IIA of 90 hp. It was a wonderful achievement to round off a fine year and it prompted Norman our Chairman to suggest to some of us that we do something similar in a Turbulent. I for one pretended I didn't hear.

Overheard in the local pub. Time 13:00 Sunday:
Sam Clutton: "I think we'd better get back, I'm supposed to be relieving the Duty Pilot."
Michael Jones: "That's alright – you're taking over from me."

We admired Sue's off white budgie. "Actually," said Sue, "the bird is white – it's just that I don't dust the flat enough."

TOP: *Tiger Rag* headings in the '60s. The top one is by the late Chris Wren and was used by the *Tiger Rag* from March '63 till Janaury '65. The lower was by Maurice Page and was first seen in February '65.

BOTTOM: A youthful Brian Smith clears the chocks from Stampe 'SHS. Redhill '65.

TOP: Roy Davis, our ever-happy ground chief, outside the Redhill hangar prior to a display practice. Circa 1965.
BOTTOM: Barry Griffiths attacking balloons at the Shoreham display. Note the hook attached to the wing with remnants of balloon still on it. Suspect it was August 1965.

TOP: Redhill Airfield around 1963 and quite unspoilt. Landings were often made across the short neck of the north end of the field.
BOTTOM: A low-level turn upwind. The Tower is well shown, as is Brian and Pat Iles' M.18 and the Jodel 140 G-ARDZ.

TOP: The dogfight duo. The author, wearing the Tiger Tim helmet, is in *The Canon*, and the Arrow Active with Neil Williams rears up behind. Just discernible is the black cross on the rudder.Redhill summer 1963.
BOTTOM: Getting ready for an aerobatic sortie. Robin d'Erlanger about to get in, and Dave Allan with seat pack cushion. Just visible in the cockpit is the Aresti sequence.

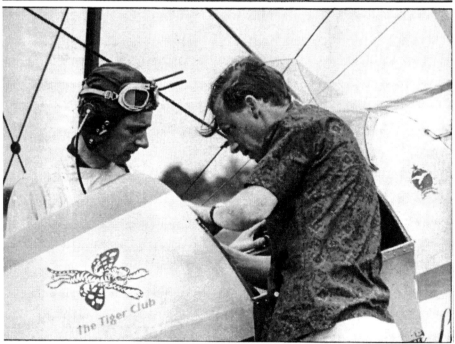

TOP: May 1963 at Fairoaks. Lollie on top of Tiger 'RAZ gets ready for her TV debut on *Tonight*. The *Ballerina* and the Active lend colour.
BOTTOM: Bob Winter and Peter Phillips. The Stampe 'ROZ was for a while named *The Leon Biancotto* in honour of that great pilot; the lettering can just be seen. The year was probably 1966.

TOP: The first of Maurice Page's cartoons of Ace, from a short series during 1964, and Chris Wren's Tiger Club Xmas card for, I believe, the same year. Norman, 'GB' and John Blake are recogniseable, as indeed are some of the pilots.
BOTTOM: The Arrow Active in her new livery. Neil Williams is leading a formation take-off.

TOP: Some tight formation by Neil Williams in ski-Turbulent 'RRZ over a snowy Surrey during 1963.

BOTTOM: Tony Haigh-Thomas's bent Tiger G-ASKP in the vast Hatfield hangar. Tony can just be seen contemplating the wingtip. 21st July 1965.

TOP: Confrontation. Norman Jones and Tiger, Redhill. The Tiger's head, which usually lived in the Clubroom, had been donated by Major Bill Foster who had shot it way back in 1924. At that time it was a record size.

BOTTOM: Hartas, author and balloon, Redhill. Presumably we had to do something; it was too misty to fly.

1965
MEMBERSHIP PARTICIPATION AND
FOREIGN TOURING

1965 saw the membership pass the 500 mark. I recorded at the time:
Membership now totals 500 plus. The present breakdown is as follows:

Founder	5	Hon Members	16
Associate O/seas	48	Hon. Members O/seas	6
Associate	144	Passenger Members	115
Members	136	Passenger Members O/seas	9
Members O/seas	12	Hon. Passenger Members	2
Hon. Passenger Members O/seas	2	TOTAL:	503

There was a scale of membership that, for the flying types, began with "Associate." An Associate, once he'd passed his initial flying check, was fully accepted. If after a year the Associate Member hadn't put up a black, flew reasonably often, and was a nice fellow, he was upgraded by the Committee to Full Member. The only obvious benefit was that his annual subscription now cost 4 guineas instead of 5. Even so Associate Members would breathe a sigh of relief when they were upgraded. Somehow they then felt they really belonged.

The term "'Passenger" was a misnomer and was patronising even if it was unintentional. Yet the anomaly stuck with us for many years. Originally it meant exactly what it said. The term used to apply to those who wanted to join in the Club fun, but were carried from A to B. For this privilege we charged them 2 guineas. But the term was later applied to anyone who hadn't passed the flying test. And since the minimum hours we required for Associates was 100 in charge, which in light aircraft usually meant solo, quite a number of so called "Passengers" considered themselves anything but, with, as so often happened, a current pilot's licence an aircraft of their own and over 80 hours solo.

Maybe Norman knew what he was about when the title was introduced, because it certainly acted as a spur to get the hours in. Not that we benefited for the hours could only be obtained outside of the Club. We had no facilities then for amassing hours, for unlike conventional Clubs we didn't do *ab initio* training, and anyway only experienced pilots could join. However to be an Associate Member of the Tiger Club was proof of one's flying status. You'd arrived.

January and February were the months we really got stuck into practising for our forthcoming display season.

Apart from a brief cold spell the weather in January continued mild, and with a spring-like burst of enthusiasm display practice set everyone scrambling for aircraft. Tigers and Stampes with Neil Williams at their head joined forces with Clive Francis and his Turbs to present some great formation flying . . .

The Club's second Stampe 'SHS was just about to be upgraded to what we called Super Stampe, to be armed with a Gipsy Major engine instead of the original Renault, the front cockpit faired over, and a similar sunburst colour-scheme to her older sister 'ROZ. The Active was near the end of its refit: the fin had been extended in the belief it would help directional stability (it didn't) and it was resplendent with its checkerboard tips to the wings and fin and rudder, all reminiscent of prewar RAF markings. And to the aerobatic chaps: the Cosmic was due back with a new engine with fuel injection.

There was of course more to be considered in the display scene than the Full Shows which were exclusively Tiger Club affairs. If everyone was practising it was often as much for the smaller, and unsung events that weren't always reviewed in the *Tiger Rag*.

During the season small teams of pilots and aircraft would fly off from Redhill to appear just about anywhere within a 200-mile radius. Usually to participate at someone else's show, where a spot of expertise in formation or aerobatics, or to show the Cosmic, would brighten the more mundane. Then too, there was no shortage of requests to appear at non-flying events. The Round Table, the Young Conservatives, Farmers' Union and Village Fêtes would happily pay up to have as a highlight a 'SOW' or Turbulent Formation.

There was by now a routine of booking these 'participations' as we called them. Organisers would write months earlier to the Club and Michael Jones would channel the requests to the various team leaders for action. At this stage they were noted as Provisional, but once the Committee had okayed them, they were entered in the Book as confirmed. From then on the arrangements were left to the individual teams to make final arrangements, and in time get paid for their efforts.

The payment side was always considered a bit of a delicate subject. Since we were all amateur display pilots as opposed to professional (virtually an unknown breed then) we asked little, content to reclaim our flying and out-of-pocket expenses. Certainly the Club didn't want to know. Michael quite rightly considered we should get on with it ourselves, he expected us to uphold the Club's good name, pay attention to good and safe airmanship, and pay for our flying. It was always costed at the standard rate, regardless of what we got up to; even air racing, when the engines at full throttle gulped twice the normal amount of fuel. Remarkable, but true.

These 'participations' were an excellent example of Norman's belief that since we were responsible pilots – he assumed our competence – we were well able to make our own decisions. We were never asked when or where we landed, nor was any prior permission sought to take aircraft once the act had been confirmed by the Committee and booked to that pilot or pilots. It was as if we personally owned the aircraft ourselves. A delightful state of affairs.

But not everyone viewed us through rose-coloured spectacles. There was always an element of jealousy among some of the pilots of Flying Clubs where, unlike the Tiger Club, tuition was the everyday bread-and-butter. To have a Tiger Club member nip in and execute a neat tight circuit with a short three-point landing off a slideslip was not, some instructors thought, a good example to their students who were drilled in leisurely circuits we called cross-countries, and the temptation to slip in ahead of one of those tedious long finals was ever strong and inevitably practised.

It wasn't for many years either, that there was any Club use of radio at Redhill. Apart from the Jodels, which had indifferent 6-channel units, the Club aircraft didn't carry them. Even the variable circuit at Redhill didn't come into being until a year or so later. A big 'T' in the landing square was all we glanced at as we flew our left-handed circuit around the airfield. It was a blissful state of affairs for with flying the Tiger at £3.17.6 (£3.85 as near as damn it) an hour and the little Turbulent costing but £2 we had it made.

Our composure was shaken somewhat when in February the petrol rebate was suddenly cut off with only four weeks' notice. The rebate, a small concession to encourage the rebirth of private flying, varied from 12/- (60p) an hour on a Stampe to 2/6 (25p) on the Turb. The new flying rates were eventually introduced in May. The Club and its members were never noted for anything political unless it affected our flying. We got a bit upset back in '59 when Croydon closed, and now I wrote:

"The unwelcome news that the Ministry has removed the petrol rebate for Clubs has come as a severe blow. Hard on the heels of the annual increase in rates, it must surely push the flying rates up yet again. This column has never before mentioned politics during its five years but it ventures now to break this rule to say that Wilson's 100 days will be recorded as the most humiliating and disastrous period for both light and commercial aviation this country has ever known."

Had I extended the period another 60 days I'd have hit the jackpot as a prophet. In the April the Labour Government of the day cancelled the TSR.2 programme.

To give an idea of Don Lovell's Foreign Touring programme he offered us some tempting titbits each year to join their merry throng. It was irresistible except to the financial strugglers, but even there we pooled our resources and joined in whenever we could. 1965 was a typical year.

FOREIGN TOURING 1965 by Don Lovell

4th April: Lunch at Berck. An early start to the season with this popular annual event.

1st-3rd May: An Invitation Weekend at Kells. Our host will be the Marquis of Headfort. Display pilots seeking an early holiday will be particularly welcome to help with the air show on Sunday. I look forward to this, my third visit, and an opportunity to fly the Lake LA-4 Amphibian.

26th-27th June: A Weekend at Beauvais.

3rd-11th July: The Annual Tour.

4th-5th September: The Tiger Club "At Home" to Overseas Visitors.

11th-12th September: A Weekend Abroad. The new foreign touring list of approved names began with the new year. All members wishing to be placed on this list should apply to Michael Jones or myself when a charge of 10/- will be made for the "hospitality fund." This fund, you may remember, is to assist with the costs involved during our annual "At Home."

WINTER WEEKEND, WINTER AEROS, JACKOS TOWING

Socially the Club was very close. We did a lot together, which was surprising when you realised that the membership was far from local. Many travelled considerable distances to make weekends. For instance a couple of months earlier Jack Piercy and Pee Wee Judge had organised a winter weekend in Brighton. It was a complete shambles but what mattered is that we had a go.

SHOREHAM WEEKEND

Given brilliant weekends for some 30 consecutive weeks and yet bank on *just one* being anything like reasonable – just when you need it to be . . . The weather was so bad on Saturday, 5th December, that even Neil couldn't have got through. Not that he was trying for Shoreham at the time but it just goes to show. The Tiger Club representatives drove down by car, even James. By the time the writer joined the party they were going strong, making amends for the weather by overeating at Wheeler's. At 30/- (less wine) a head they couldn't have done badly.

Out at Shoreham the Southern Aero Club had their monthly Party to which all were invited. We had hardly got there when the band went home. With much noise and the inevitable shouts of "Where are we going?" everyone got back into their cars and the party divided neatly into two – suddenly we were all together and then we weren't. Nothing planned, just the usual chaos. Some of us found our way to Jack Piercy's place – a drink and Jack's tale of his business trip, BUA and Capt. David Phillips a combination that proved good for a bit of VIP treatment.

The following morning was simply windy and overcast. Vis was good and it didn't rain. When I arrived everyone was busy with maps and bits of paper. Pee Wee Judge thrust a piece into my hand and said: "Get a half million map and go!" He had organised a navigational exercise, and then threw the contest open to everyone at Shoreham. I teamed up with Jack Hamblett in his Jodel 117. We clocked the fastest time of 45 mins, but missed a clue.

Not so Jack Piercy, who navigated for Jimmy Edwards in Jimmy's new Cessna 180; they came home in 45½ mins with all questions right. However, the moral victory must surely go to Tom Storey who used his head and flew the course the reverse way in the Tiger and clocked a time of 47½ mins! It didn't dawn on anyone else that the strong wind could be taken advantage of. Unfortunately Tom, who flew solo, missed a couple of clues, the paper with the questions on flew out of the cockpit . . . at least that was his excuse!

Robin d'Erlanger did well in a Turbulent; he took the hour and came home second. Back home to Redhill to round off with a showing of *Way to the Stars*, a coordinated programme by Ken Smith and yours truly. How well that film wears. Our thanks to all who helped beat the weather to make the weekend the cheerful success it was. Now who is organising the next?

In no time at all Charles Boddington answered the call on behalf of the Tiger Moth Club up at Poddington for a get-together in the March but in the meantime there was the ever-popular Annual Ball. There was always an effort to hold the event on St. Valentine's Day, or at least as near as possible, and indeed 23 years later we still do. It came about this way. When, asked Norman, should we hold our Dinner? The Committee considered. Before Christmas was socially too busy, immediately afterwards we'd all be flying. Said Bev, all romantic-like: "Let's make it a St. Valentine's Night Ball." At least that's how I remembered it happened.

For the last time we held the Ball at the Albert on the Embankment. But it was far to small for our growing Club. The Awards were handed over by Norman with, as ever, just one brief speech by the Boss, another tradition that's hung on to the present day.

Bob Winter, a keen aerobatic man, became the first Aerobatic Secretary to join the Committee, the latest to join the Secretaries of the other departments which by now had grown to a long list. To the Chairman, the Hon Sec, CFI and Treasurer we now added Chief Check Pilot, Membership Secretary, Display Director and his Assistant, Display Promoter, and no less than six extra secretaries (Overseas Touring, Parachuting, Aerotowing, Aerobatics, PR and Legal Fund). Throw in an

Hon. Physician, a Legal Adviser, and five extra Committee men without portfolio, the three on the House Committee and the *Tiger Rag* Editor and you had enough for a cricket match, an umpire and a teamaker. Norman never wanted for an audience.

The Hon. Physician was Peter Chapman, who used to give free licence medicals in the Clubroom at weekends. No one today, versed in the expensive performance of getting a flying medical, would credit the effective simplicity. Afterwards it was the done thing to make a £1 contribution to the Legal Fund. Another one-off was our Display Promoter, Bill Chesson. He would fix up the venues, and for a modest fee, would lead his determined gang of followers to rope off enclosures, erect some of the shabbiest tents you ever did see, provide refreshments for the crews, take the money at the gate, direct the car parking, install a PA system, and –when we'd all flown home – wearily clear up after us. Bill also flew with us, was no mean rally driver and skier and he used to claim he'd fought pirates in the South Seas. Good value, was Bill.

But back to Bob Winter. It was he who so keenly got us all involved with the smaller aerobatic contests that sprang up, and so helped to provide the basic and intermediate training facilities necessary for the up-and-coming contestants.

TIGER CLUB AEROBATIC COMPETITIONS, 1965
by Bob Winter

Our good friends the McAully Flying Group have again invited us to hold the McAully Aerobatic Competition in May, at Little Snoring Airfield in Norfolk. We can be sure of their usual excellent hospitality. This competition is specially designed for beginners.

The East Anglian Flying Club will be our hosts for the de Havilland Trophy in June at Ipswich Airport – I really must remember to tell them how many to expect for lunch this year! The competition is flown to the same rules as the Lockheed International Trophy and so gives good practice to Lockheed entrants; other pilots are most welcome to take part.

The final Tiger Club Aerobatic Competition is the Esso Trophy to be held at Rochester Airport in September with the help of Rochester Flying Club. Esso provide most generous cash prizes for this event as well as the Trophy; it is hoped to award a special prize to the highest placed newcomer. The competition takes the form of set sequence followed by a precision landing . . .

The McAully was so named after poor Mac killed himself in the first special Tiger, the *Bishop*, a few years earlier. Mac it was who had flown her inverted across the Channel – never did discover if he was the first to do so or the last.

The Esso Trophy was then in the form of a *voltige*, a word I thought I'd look up. It wasn't to be found in the Concise Oxford, so I turned to a French dictionary and found that it meant "a tumbling or vaulting," and a voltiger was someone who fluttered or flew about.

Which I guess was near enough. My memory can no longer recall the exact sequence, which in any case was very simple. It began at 1,500 feet with a waggle of wings then into a loop, followed by another with a half roll on the way down, and then a slow roll, a stall turn and a spot landing from whatever height you had left. It could be done in three minutes and that's from take-off to landing; with five minutes in hand it was positively leisurely. The single-seat Tiger climbed initially at 1,500 feet a minute, so rapid *voltiges* were certainly on the cards and were always great fun.

The late A.J. Jackson, "Jacko" to all of us, ran the Glider Towing contingent of the Club for several years. He was a teacher by profession, but an aviation fanatic at heart. He was happiest flying the Club's vintage machines, and his knowledge of them and their history was remarkable. His wonderful series of books published by Putnam, of which his British Civil Aircraft A-Z in three volumes was his greatest triumph, established him as a leading historian. He was a cheery friend to everyone and is much missed.

GLIDER TOURING – A.J. Jackson (Glider Towing Sec.)

Although a quick look through the current Tiger Club booklet shows that 75 members are qualified to tow gliders, there are many whose homes are remote from the Redhill/Fair Oaks area and many whose prowess lies in other fields. In fact, very few are left to carry out the Tiger Club's not inconsiderable annual glider towing commitments.

More are needed urgently and anyone with the urge to qualify and have that coveted little "g" against his name in the next booklet can now do so through the good offices of Roy Proctor and his colleagues at the R.A.E. Gliding Club, Farnborough. Roy has kindly agreed to provide a glider towing check-out for Tiger Club members and has arranged a course consisting of at least 12 tows (the first three under the supervision of himself or P.P.L. examiner Dick Thomas), and comprehensive briefing to cover handling, emergencies, and the airmanship of towing. The u/t tug pilot will also be given at least one tow in a two-seat glider so that he knows the other chap's point of view.

Candidates will be accepted one at a time so that each can receive individual attention and be checked out in a reasonable time. This also has the advantage that Farnborough's security system will not become confused! Although security problems can be overcome without difficulty, it must be emphasized that this is only possible without embarrassment to our good friends at the R.A.E. Gliding Club if members will **refrain entirely** from contacting Farnborough direct. Application for the course should therefore be made direct to me, and all will be well.

Qualified tug pilots wishing to offer their services for flying Tiger Club aircraft at the National Gliding Competitions at Lasham 16-24 May, or for any of the other Tiger Club towing sessions, are requested to put their names on the sheet at Redhill, or drop me a line . . .

During November of the previous year the Crabb brothers, well known for their gliding interest, got "Jacko" to tow one of them off in their new Slingsby Dart at Redhill using the 1,500 cc version of the Turb. They made three tows altogether. It was purely an experimental trial, and the Turbulent was probably the lowest powered aircraft ever to tow a glider.

A LIKELY STORY

I make no apologies for including "A Likely Story." When it was published in the March *Tiger Rag* its humour was so infectious I was besieged for extra copies and further instalments. Only wish I could say it was written by a member, but it wasn't.

A LIKELY STORY

We are indebted to Malcolm Fisher for introducing us to this magnificent letter which appeared in *Amber 2* and obviously originated in Elstree. It is with considerable regret that we cannot reproduce the item in full, space doesn't allow, but the following extract more than justifies a belief that it will one day rank with the all-time-best in flying stories.

"I do hope that I am not being oversensitive but I think I detect an atmosphere of resentful criticism on the part of the Club and School towards me since that eventful day last week. In order that I may do justice to myself and preserve the good relationship that we have always enjoyed, it is right that I should acquaint you with the facts in the order in which they occurred.

At 0900 hrs I arrived at the airfield to find Chipmunk Tango Golf authorised to me for a cross-country to Southend and a pre-flight check suggested moderate serviceability. To dispose at once of the incident concerning starting, it is conceded that the young man who swung the prop DID lose the index finger and thumb of his right hand but all his other fingers are intact and completely serviceable. He is very young and will soon accommodate himself to his new condition. I strongly resent any implication of negligence on my part, since the magneto switches proved to be upside down, having obviously been miswired to be "on" in the up position. The responsibility for this laying squarely upon the shoulders of the engineers; it is simple, though regrettable, justice that one of their number should be sharply reminded of his deficiencies.

I am surprised that so much should be made of the take-off affair, My instructions, although conveyed in Liverpudlian tone were, nevertheless, explicit, viz: Taxy 17 left; QNH 1012; now, on taxying to the left from our solitary northbound taxyway, one must arrive at the west end of our 27 runway which is perfectly logical, so that I had no doubt that I was to use 27 starting from the west end. It is a demonstration of my advanced airmanship that despite the difficulty of a downwind take-off (a surface force of some 15 knots), and although I unstuck only where the runway declines into the frying pan and ditch, I succeeded in clearing the public highway in a magnificent climb. The resulting stall from 300 ft was easily overcome since the farmer's barn was open at both ends and more than adequate in width. I then ascended into the circuit.

Despite his adroit airmanship, the pilot of the two-tone blue Cessna 310 twin who took off in the opposite direction as I was endeavouring to achieve an airborne condition should be severely censured – possibly expelled from the Club.

As to that circuit trouble, I can prove that, on my previous flights on the preceding day, Elstree circuits had been right-hand. No one mentioned any change and I had no reason to expect one, therefore I flew right-hand. I cannot help it if others mistakenly flying left-hand do not know their rights from their lefts.

Referring to the complaint from London Control, they make altogether too much fuss about V.F.R. and controlled airspace. How can I tell what height the cloud is unless I climb up and find out? Of course I saw an aircraft on my starboard side, but am I to be intimidated by size? The Vanguard was an awe-inspiring sight at close quarters, albeit the pilot flew very dangerously, crossing my path so that I encountered severe turbulence from his slipstream.

When I had recovered from a number of unusual attitudes, I found myself temporarily confused. However, upon consulting the compass I noticed that the little line with a twig on the end was pointing to 090 degrees. Since this was roughly the direction in which I wished to fly, I set the D.I. and opened full throttle. I always do this on cross-country flights in order to make a fast journey before fuel gets low.

I was soon passing over a very large town which I thought was Harlow, but my suspicions were aroused by the presence of red buses. Throttling back a bit, I banged down half flap and made cautious inspection. There was a bus going to Camden Town. Restoring flap I returned to full throttle and circled to ponder the situation. It was then that I discovered a fault in Tango Golf's compass. The little scale on the top can be moved around so that the little twig can be made to point anywhere. It was clearly not to be relied upon. I considered following the bus to Camden Town whence I knew the road to Southend quite well, having driven the route many times, but after a short trial, I rejected the plan as impracticable due to constant circling while the bus discharged and acquired passengers.

About then, the 707 passed directly above my canopy. It took considerable experience to recover from the ensuing disorder and I thought it prudent to return to Elstree to set a fresh course. Fortunately I saw at that moment some eight or so miles away a small cloud which I was sure I recognised as having been overhead the field of my departure. Full throttle I pointed the Chipmunk at the cloud and relaxed. It was very pleasant.

I do wish someone had mentioned the Purple Airway. I did not intentionally fly close to the helicopter and I must remark that your hysterical outburst when you waved that crested notepaper at me was entirely unwarranted. I did not, repeat NOT, make the gesture of which I am accused – quite the contrary. When I recognised the passenger, I at once attempted a regulation military salute. However, the Chipmunk cockpit being a trifle restricted, on performing that motion which requires 'longest way up – shortest way down,' I slammed my hand painfully against the panel and when HE glanced my way, I was holding up my fingers in agony.

Soon after I entered the cloud. This in no way foxed me. I have always considered IF training to be quite unnecessary provided one has studied the panel closely. This I have done in extreme detail and I looked onto instruments at once. Considering my aptitude for instruments, you may imagine my astonishment upon emerging at 1,000 ft to see the earth above my head advancing towards me. My reactions are very quick and swift, intelligence told me I was descending in an inverted attitude. Appreciating the necessity to climb, I slammed in 'Carb. air cold' and hauled back on the stick. To my amazement, Tango Golf pointed herself directly at the Earth, revs needle spinning while the altimeter cringed. As I deliberated the next move, the sky suddenly assumed its normal location and I found myself passing at some speed and at zero feet between some masts festooned with wires. It flashed through my mind, 'Rugby or Daventry' just like that, and although I realised I had slightly overflown Elstree, I felt encouraged that from here I might find the M1. I am sorry the BBC was unable to transmit the Morning Story; personally I always enjoy it."

I no longer have the extract that fitted between this section and the next. It's hard to recall what happened after so many years, but I seem to remember our hero ran out of fuel and landed on a stretch of unfinished motorway, where some of his new-found friends, the construction workers, managed to find some fuel for him . . . now read on.

"I returned to find Tango Golf's tanks moderately charged with what I was assured to be high-octane fuel direct from the tank of a crested Aston Martin parked near to the administrative buildings.

It should be stressed that I could not possibly have known that the Purple Airway had any connection with a series of V.I.P. public works inspections to be concluded at this site later in the day, although I regret the visitor concerned was obliged to cycle from the site to a local railway station. With the assistance of my good friends, Tango Golf was pushed onto the southbound shoulder of the M1 where, after production of more paper money, a jeep loaded with exclamation marks and yellow panels proceeded to shut off the slow and centre lanes for some half mile, leaving the fast lane open. Meanwhile, having failed to find a volunteer prop-swinger, I set fuel, switches and throttle, walked around to the prop and tugged heartily.

I had the presence of mind to throw myself flat. The port wing passed over my head and when I got to my feet Tango Golf was parading in stately fashion at some four knots onto the M1 proper, where commenced a starboard drift towards the central reservation. Girding up my loins and R/T leads, encouraged by cheers from the crowd, I gave immediate chase, overtook the beast, leapt onto the wing root, chopped the throttle and scrambled aboard. Once in command I straightened her out, lined-up and opened the throttle but as the airspeed indicator rose to 25 knots I became aware of a hideous noise behind me. Glancing over my right shoulder, I saw in the fast lane an open Jag going like the clappers, the driver's hand flat on the horn button and a dazed expression on his face. The Jag was followed by a rather smart looking Mercedes 220SE and one of those patrol cars with an attractive little blue light on its roof, flashing away merrily. Horns were blowing and bells were ringing.

Wishing to extend to them the courtesy of the road, I whizzed the canopy right back, changed hands on the stick and made the appropriate Highway Code overtake signal. Meantime, Tango Golf was gathering speed.

You will now understand why the canopy tore off and take a more reasonable view. It was a bit tricky after that. My specs blew away and a right-hand bend approached with a bridge beyond. At 40 knots I.A.S. I nudged the stick over, got Tango Golf neatly balanced on her starboard wheel, applied a bootful of right rudder, skated round the bend and hoiked her off. It was not really difficult! I have done many take-offs like this at Elstree.

As I passed low over the bridge, some fool drove clean through the barricade and plummetted down onto the M1. Airborne once more, I could now follow the road to Elstree whence I might set a new course for Southend. This was necessary as my flight plan only worked from Elstree. At 1400 hrs Watford was in sight and I felt confident that my difficulties were resolved.

I do not know why the aircraft caught fire. Suggestions that tapping cigarette ash and ends over the side should be discounted, for I have done this over many years with my car, and THAT never caught fire. Fortunately, the coincidence of my violent sideslipping and the drying up of my acquired fuel at the same moment resulted in only minor scorching of the aircraft, which I flung straightway into the nearest field, almost within the Elstree circuit.

Having retrieved their horses, the Young Conservatives, who were holding their Gymkhana in the field, were delighted at this unexpected novelty, being most generous in suggestions and assistance, so much so that by 1600 hrs Tango Golf rested once more upon Elstree's welcoming soil.

You may say, indeed you have said, that it can be unbecoming, degrading, disgusting and many other words which I cannot spell to see on Television News an Elstree pilot in a Chipmunk cockpit being drawn slowly along the Watford bypass by two chestnut Geldings flanked by whooping horsemen and grave-faced policemen. You may be right, but I suggest that when the tantivy of the post-horns brought you to your office window to see those fine beasts, ridden by their young postillions, appear through the gates drawing an exhausted, but triumphant Tango Golf, you were very relieved. If you were not, you should have been. No other pilot could have done what I did.

Why control fired the Very I do not know. Perhaps it was misplaced high spirits or even a genuine aid to airmen, but it is reasonable to suppose those geldings had never before seen or heard this signal. As you know, they at once threw their postillions and broke into a gallop towards the airport centre. As that well-known hazard south of 27 approached, they divided in opposite directions, the lines parted, Tango Golf ran onward, crashed the barriers and tipped gently on her nose into the "pit." Peter Laffy's remark that it was the best thing since *Ben Hur* was not in the best of taste and his subsequent observation that he always knew I would finish up right in IT was frankly objectionable.

I remember little more after the sight of senior members of the Staff restraining you from rash and ill-advised courses of action. I trust your well-being is now reasonably restored, although mutual friends tell me the outbursts of violent breast-beating are still much in evidence. No doubt, in the light of this reasoned explanation and full knowledge of the facts the whole affair will present itself in true perspective, you will appreciate the unjust prejudices attaching to me and dismiss the matter from your mind.

My solicitors tell me I will get bail while on remand for the sessions. I have advised them that you would be happy to assist in this direction and am confident you will speak in my defence at my forthcoming trial in the interests of justice.

Cordially yours,

A. Twytte"

EAST ANGLIA AND AN IRISH WEEKEND

The *Tiger Rag* each month endeavoured to keep the membership in touch with each other; engagements, marriages, births and, sadly, sometimes deaths, were all recorded. It was as if we were a big family. Not "if," we were.

In April there was a "News of Members" section. Down at Shoreham George Lowdell had been appointed CFI, and we had a card from Jimmy Hoseason in Suffolk telling us he'd quietly got married to Lesley. Brian Iles had been promoted to Wing Commander and he and Pat had been posted to Bicester. In fact a typical quota of monthly gossip, but these little snippets of news kept us together in a remarkable way.

George was an old hand in the flying world, and he was one of the first I got to sign Bunny Bramson's book *The Tiger Moth Story*. The tale of George's Tiger with its Paraslasher deserved his signature in a book that was destined to be a present to Cliff Robertson. The idea was to get about everybody mentioned in the book to sign it somewhere. For months the book travelled around the country, each signatory in turn passing it on to the next. Cliff, who had just finished filming *633 Squadron,* was delighted with his present when it was eventually given him. It had taken nearly a year to collate. I can't remember now why we bothered, because it was all in vain. He lost it.

Jimmy Hoseason was also an active member of the Waveney Flying Group. When I think back, I can only recall us having close ties with two Clubs, and both were in East Anglia. The Waveney Group was based at Seething, a dozen miles west of Lowestoft. The other was the McAully Flying Group at Little Snoring, some 25 miles NW of Norwich. It was originally known as the Fakenham Group, and when Mac their CFI was killed, they commemorated a good friend by changing the Group's name.

Both were very popular venues, not only for their frequent get-togethers and rallies, but also for the freedom of their skies. So much so that it became the haunt of the aerobatic pilots, secure that over those big flat farmlands and ever-friendly farmers they were beyond the usual restraints and could get down to business in earnest.

It was during a rained-off weekend at Seething during May that Jimmy Hoseason let nine of us loose in one of his boats on the Broads. We meandered at four knots, popping in and out of the cabin with our cups of tea, to gaze around us at the soaked silence of those beautiful waterways. We eventually flew home determined to come back one day and look into this boating business. And many of us did.

Over at Little Snoring were our other friends, among them Barbara McAully, Bridget and Tony Southerland, along with Denis Kirkham, who'd been a Tiger Club man since 1960. After one visit in the same month during which they'd held the McAully Aerobatic Trophy (winner Martin Barraclough) we got a protest from Tony:

" . . . From the terse statement in your last newsletter announcing the hard cold facts of who won the McAully Aerobatic Trophy, how could any of your several hundred readers get any idea of the drama that was unfolded on that weekend?

YOU COULD HAVE TOLD THEM how we were fortunate to have the remaining aerobatic Hurricane doing aerobatics and landing at Little Snoring, and how, as it was taxying out on the runway to take off, one of our budding aerobatic pilots decided to stop his prop and make a dead-stick landing beside it, causing a stampede of scores of people through a farmer's corn, supposedly to pick up the pieces which fortunately did not materialise.

YOU COULD HAVE TOLD THEM of how Michael Jones said the Tiger Club members would be going home after the event and not to arrange accommodation or entertainment for them, and of the ensuing rush to book rooms for them after I casually said to Bob Winter: "I expect you will soon be off now?"; his reply, "Oh! but we're staying," made my next statement unprintable!

YOU COULD HAVE TOLD THEM how Bob Winter was off at the crack of dawn with our most treasured possession, the wonderful picture of Brigitte Bardot, and of how, at considerable expense, four of us drove down to Redhill the following weekend to retrieve her, only to find she was strung ignominiously to the girders in the hangar roof.

YOU COULD HAVE TOLD THEM of the even more incongruous sight of myself perched on two sets of steps on top of a table cutting her down, and of how we nearly pinched a Turbulent to even things up.

But no: just the hard statement of facts. SHAME – SHAME – SHAME!!!"

Glad to say they remain to this day our great friends.

MAY – A lot has happened since the last issue. Where to begin? Chronologically one should begin with Radlett, the display that wasn't. For the first time in the Club's several years of displays has a display been cancelled – as a matter of fact, I can only recall a cancellation happening on two previous occasions and then the aircraft were actually at the display field. We didn't even leave Redhill. The weather conditions were extraordinary. Charles Boddington took a tiny and intrepid band up to the Midlands for a small display on that day. They laid on ten men per Tiger to ground handle. Barry Tempest's tale of coming in with engine in the teeth of the wind and of being pulled out of the sky by these stalwarts makes a great line – we suspect it was true . . .

Bish and his wife had moved down to Bognor where he commuted to the Seaplane Club by a small car which he drove with great caution. He wrote in May:

"As you may be aware, the Seaplane Club of Lee-on-Solent, Hants, is being amalgamated with the Tiger Club of Redhill, and it is planned to commence operations under the new arrangement early in June 1965.

Marine aviation has a fascination that is all its own, as those of the Tiger Club who have already savoured its joys will well know, and in addition to flying, there is the added enjoyment of manning the safety launch whilst flying is taking place."

HOVERCRAFT PILOTS REQUIRED FOR SUMMER IN SOLENT. NO EXPERIENCE NECESSARY. CONTACT CLUB MEMBER MR DON ROBERTSON.

The bit about the hovercraft is now a vague memory. Don I know had constructed an earlier model at Redhill and we all had a go, but I think the one now referred to was an improved version, but if they had the same problems the Sea Tiger had in its operations from Lee, I shouldn't think they stayed there long either. The problem was twofold. The first, the difficulty of launching and retrieving into and out of anything but a calm Solent, and the adverse effect of salt water on engine and airframe. The Sea Tiger was eventually to be restricted to operations from inland fresh waters with the odd excursion into brackish estuaries.

By midsummer poor Don Lovell had nearly given up on overseas touring, plagued as he was by bad weather. However it relented enough to allow a third stab at Berck for lunch in July, and when they got there, they nearly didn't get anything to eat. The restaurants were full! Yet there was one good weekend away that escaped the weather, but to this day I don't know who wrote it up. I wondered at the time if whoever it was even remembered it was his contribution.

AN IRISH WEEKEND.

"Come to Kilkenny," the notice board at Redhill said; "free landings, free Customs, free fuel and a fabulous Whitsun. Proceeds in aid of Cancer Relief," so we went.

"At Holdensruth Field Kilkenny has the finest licensed aerodrome in private Irish hands": so said the programme. It is mostly grass, partly bog and the major excavations lie, like bunkers, just clear of the main fairway. The welcome was terrific, a rainstorm and a car with a bottle on each seat and no Customs officers within 50 miles. We told the Garda we had arrived, but the sergeant had a beer festival in town and didn't need any more troubles.

Holdensruth has two runways, the main one is only slightly curved and quite serviceable. There is, however, a marked taper at the northern end and it is a little too narrow for a Turb. Our Ambassadeur took the surface well, although a 'Schhh 175' gave up after 50 yards or so and knelt in a player to the Great God Coke (or Concrete). That was Heresy as the town's beer festival swam steadily towards Sunday afternoon and the Air Display. The Whiskey was good too.

The Welcome and Hospitality were incredible. If you don't know what we mean, ignore these notes and go to Ireland immediately, or you could wait until the weekend. Oh yes, the airfield; well it is unique in that landing may always be made uphill and take-off downhill. As the aerodrome owner says: "This *does* increase the safety of the manoeuvres, but leads to unusual runway gradient figures." The hospitality really was superb; someone had left a dozen new caravans on the airfield, so we slept well until breakfast, which was followed by beer and lunch and the flying show and beer and dinner and whiskey too. Sunday afternoon saw 30 aircraft sightseeing over Kilkenny Town and Castle, the Irish Parachute and Skydiving clubs exercising, some rain, and an excellent flying display. The aerobatics in a cooking Tiger made one wonder why we need Supers. We returned to London via Dublin on Monday despite advice to return direct and pretend we hadn't come (off Customs man), and were surprised to find little evidence of Customs vigilence and no interest in our story of inbound clearance at Kilkenny.

Returning English travellers have brought back many charming tales of the Irish character and we find no fault in them. There has been no exaggeration. We recommend Ireland as a destination to you all. The Irish sea is wider than the English Channel, but just as busy, so let that not deter you. Even a demand for Customs overtime at 18.05 and landing fee at Bristol didn't seem to matter too much, but complaints that an 18-minute radio warning was not prior permission for landing at RAF South Cerney upset us. After all, they could have said: "No," but perhaps the RAF is Irish too?

THE WILLOW WREN AND THE ODD MINUTE

A look back through the Committee minutes for the year never fails to break out a smile. The very brevity of the items still takes the breath away for understatement. And there were some beauties. One for instance read: *"Aero Club Dinner: Importance of good manners and of avoiding 'cliques' discussed."*

The Dinner in question was as usual a riotous affair. The good manners bit arose over a roll-throwing episode in which Neil Williams got a black eye, and I should imagine the clique referred to our preference of sitting together, as far away as possible from the top table and Norman's eagle eye. That was a long minute, most were no more than 3-4 words. Typical examples "to be accepted" or "very good." The occasion on which we got our first and only glider was recorded in five words: *"Willow Wren Glider: to be accepted if possible."*

John Anning wrote of the glider which we did and didn't get . . . didn't get because it was suddenly withdrawn, and since we weren't over-keen on powerless flight, no one missed it. I think the lack of enthusiasm and the shortage of hangar space put the kybosh on it, that and a general feeling that the thing might not stay glued together. There was no rush to fly it. Sad really.

The Tiger Club has recently taken over the responsibility of a most attractive and beautifully restored old aeroplane, the Willow Wren glider. This actual machine was well known to gliding enthusiasts at Dunstable many years before the war and is thought to be the oldest high-performance sailplane extant in the country capable of flying.

A recent visit by the author to the home of the designer and constructor provided a pleasant evening full of stories from SE.5s to the early days of gliding where much information has been obtained.

The machine was designed and built entirely by Mr W. L. Manuel (then corporal, RAF) while serving at RAF Hawkinge during the early part of 1931. He had been building gliders of some sort or another for ten years but it was not until he had seen Kronfeld demonstrate soaring on the Wren and Professor sailplanes that he decided to have a go himself. He settled for a small single seater and the Crested Wren was the result which was seen on many occasions at Dunstable. The next machine, the Willow Wren, incorporated many improvements and, influenced by German sailplane practice, set the general design trend for future British gliders.

The traditional methods of aircraft construction were used on the Manuel design; spruce, ply and casein cold-water glue which showed no deterioration 34 years later . . . The wing loading is 25 lb/sq ft with a 180 lb pilot and the best speed is about 32 mph. No instruments were fitted except an early variometer, and air speed was assessed simply by listening to the "tune" of the external drag wires! However an ASI has now been added.

In those early days no one had ever heard of tows, so the machine was built and "bungee"-launched over a hill. A simple hook at the front was all that was necessary and perfectly safe. Airfield-type launches, towed from a car, are also practical, but the speed must be carefully watched.

In July 1933, piloted by Flt. Lt. Edward Mole (Tiger Club member and later a Group Captain) the Wren remained airborne for 6 hours 55 minutes, making a new British endurance record. Later he planned to break the world endurance record by flying across the Pennines for at least 30 hours but no suitable weather was now forthcoming. *(Edward records all this in his delightful book* Happy Landings *which was published in 1984 by Airlife – Ed.)*

The machine is now assembled at Rochester and is available for members to use, from a towed launch by car across the airfield. It is thought that soaring may be possible from the ridge to the west of the airfield. Recently Norman Jones did the initial test flight and remained airborne for some 1½ minutes after which he staggered us all by saying it was only his second flight in a non-powered machine!

QUOTE: Lollie: "How do you stop a glider from stalling if you haven't got an engine?"

Every now and then the Committee would face cryptic minutes under the heading BAD AIRMANSHIP. "Ran out of fuel" – fined £25. "Taxying accident" – fined £5. Nothing about the reports that were submitted, or the repairs necessary. Norman never wasted a word or ever laboured a point. It was done; it was discussed briefly, and then there always followed the same question: "Was it bad airmanship?" If we decided it was it warranted a fine. There was a graduated scale, all very modest. £50 was the most, and it was years before that sum was increased. The known form was, of course, to own up and apologise. Norman Jones always liked that, and mentally wrote down the offence, so the fine never got anywhere near the cost of repair.

If we thought the pilot could afford to help out, Michael Jones was directed to suggest that a contribution wouldn't go amiss. Knowing Michael, who on occasion could be every bit as forceful as his father, the suggestion could well have been couched more firmly than intended, for as manager of the Club only he knew how much time and effort was spent on putting things to rights.

We had some regulars as well. Some never learnt. We had one, who will, I know, forgive me quoting him, for I do so as much in fondness as in reproach; he was Arthur Tyrrell. Arthur was older than the rest of us, an inventor, a bit absent-minded, and the owner of a Turbulent. He cherished his little machine, and polished and maintained it whenever he had a moment. But he had one bad habit which he couldn't cure himself of. He'd switch off, and then climb out of the cockpit and go around to the front and thoughtfully pull the propeller through. And as he did so he'd put his ear close to the cowling to listen. I never knew quite what he expected to hear but when asked he would mutter "compression." The danger of turning a hot engine simply didn't register. As a skilled engineer he should have known better, but he couldn't kick himself of the habit. Worse, he would usually do it with the tiny aircraft facing the hangar. To my knowledge the engine fired on at least two occasions, and the aircraft proceeded to taxy into the hangar with Arthur in hot pursuit. His face was always a study of disbelief when a concerted cry of "Arthur!" echoed over the tarmac. It got to the stage that whenever he taxied up and stopped, one of us would gently lead him away from his love and put her away in the hangar for him.

GEOFFREY DE HAVILLAND AND TOLLERTON

June. There are times when to be at Redhill is to turn back the clock. Such a time was early in June on a sunlit morning, for there on the green stood the bright lines of old friends resplendent in their many colours. At a time when more and more airfields take on the 'tin look,' and the radio chatter of the self-important ATCO seems more urgent than flight itself, that picture of fabric and wire was a sight to behold. I heard three people say what all must have thought: "we'll not see a sight like that for much longer . . ." They were soon to fly off to the first full display of the season, after the Radlett non-starter, at Sywell.

June was a month of sunshine, of grass cutting at Redhill and bales of hay stacked perilously near the marked runways, a successful Beauvais tour and the greatest of good news, the announcement of "GB's" forthcoming marriage to Veryan . . .

Fred Marsh phoned early one morning to tell me the latest: He and his sausages made the front page of the *Cambridge News*.

Headline: *PIE IN THE SKY*. Extract: *"Over the Whitsun Bank Holiday the demand for Winton-Smith's sausage rolls and pies at Woburn Abbey was so great that the catering company on the estate asked for a special supply to be rushed to them. To beat the road jam on Whit Monday, as soon as a fresh supply of pies and sausage rolls had been manufactured, Mr F.O. Marsh, MD of Winton-Smith, had them taken to the local airport, loaded into his two-seater aircraft and landed 8 minutes later in the grounds of Woburn Abbey. There he was met by the Duke of Bedford. Said the Duke: 'With the thousands of people we have to cater for over the weekend, this is the sort of service we appreciate!'"*

This was a typical Fred Marsh scoop. There was a delightful story about him going the rounds about then. Our Fred, complete with monocle, had attended a reception given by the Duke and Duchess of Richmond down at Goodwood House. I can't recall now why we were all there, but there we were making small talk in the magnificent reception room when a small lady carrying *canapés* gently offered her plate to our group.

We helped ourselves, then Fred put a fatherly arm around her shoulders and asked: "And what do you do here, my dear?"

"I'm the Duchess," she murmured, gave a beauteous smile and moved on.

"Just testing," said Fred – or that's what it sounded like.

It is planned to put up a nine-Tiger formation as a small gesture of our appreciation to the late Sir Geoffrey de Havilland on the occasion of his Memorial Service on July 21st. James Baring is in charge. The idea seems to have been arrived at simultaneously by John Blake and Martin Barraclough.

The nine-Tiger formation was well received. Charming letters were later sent to us from Joan de Havilland, Rod Banks and George Errington expressing their warm appreciation of the Tiger Club tribute in moving terms. One of the pilots recorded the event from the number 3 position.

Pilot's eye view. The idea met with universal approval. Firstly, Martin was i/c, at least until he had to fly to Japan or somewhere, and James B. took over. Three things were needed, nine pilots, nine Tigers and good weather. James tackled the first two with increasing vigour right up to 30 minutes of our take-off. Even on the eve of the 20th the presence of nine pilots was in question, to say nothing of the Tigers. The final line-up on the night before was: James Baring, Neil Williams, Barry Tempest, Martin Barraclough, Clive Francis, Tony Haigh Thomas, Dennis Hartas, Peter Phillips and me, Benjy. Neither Bev Snook, David Phillips or Pee Wee Judge could make it, as it was it was a squeeze getting nine competent pilots together midweek. The problem was matched by getting nine serviceable Tigers. The Club raised six, including the black Rollason one, Rochester and Fair Oaks one each and Dicky Reid lent us his. Barry Tempest's mount from Norfolk was to have been reserve.

De Havilland's were expecting us at Hatfield by 11 am on the Wednesday, and the photographic ship, the Super Cub, was to be crewed by Ken Smith and John Blake. And that's how things stood 12 hours before the "off." The weather stood fair and James slept soundly that night.

21st July, 1965. 8.30am. Sent Lollie off to work – someone has to do it . . .

9.30 am. Redhill, dank hills lost in mist and five Tigers being refuelled. Gipsy engines can be heard and suddenly two slip out of the mire, it's Martin and Clive from Fair Oaks closely followed by Peter from Rochester.

10 am and no sign of Barry from Norfolk – if anyone can get through, he will, but we watch in vain. The phone, and Barry who got 30 miles in our direction has had to return, weather on the deck. It's only 600 feet at Redhill, but lifting slowly. James begins the briefing one pilot short. John Thomson, who is on leave and who had come to see us off, volunteers. Strong coffee and through the windows we watch the damp clouds. Hatfield is still 400 feet and 800 yard vis. Eight pilots eye Dennis with some sympathetic amusement. Poor Dennis, a difficult decision . . . no one will say a word if he cancels.

"We'll try it," says Dennis. "I'll lead the five vic, James lead the box four – close up into a nine if you're happy."

We take off in two formations. I fly No. 3. I've followed Dennis in that position many, many times. I glance across at Peter, No. 2; he catches my look and grins. I can see Martin at No. 4 and can sense Neil on my left; 900 feet and Dennis is skating through the bottom of the stuff, I instinctively close up . . . and out of the corner of my eye I see James slot in tight. This is going to be a sweat. I talk out loud . . . Half the time we're in the stuff, Dennis is too good a leader to jig about. His head is in and out of the cockpit as he map-reads with a visibility of half a mile and that mostly downwards. The cloud alternately envelops him and then clears. I rub my goggles, it's instinctive, I know they're not misting up. We've crept up to 1,500 feet and I keep thinking of the Crystal Palace masts. I'm actually enjoying myself, that is when I'm not asking myself what the devil I'm doing up here with eight other lunatics in such diabolical weather. All of a sudden there's a wonderful smell of freshly ground coffee. From a warehouse – dockside? We're on course and over the Thames. James is firmly in box, his face grimly set and he is right under Dennis's tail.

My admiration for Dennis is tremendous. He is leading eight aircraft in tight formation and half the time he is on IF. Nearly every time he looks down at his map he pops into cloud. He throttles back! Quickly, I drop back too. If we weren't all working so hard it would be funny. James and his three have all concertinaed up alongside trying desperately hard not to overshoot. They've dropped back and Peter waves – the moment passes.

Beneath us is a familiar line of poplars, a main road and a railway all together. I think: "Well, if he's lost, this should help," and then there's the end of a runway.

"Oi, Dennis!" I shout, "it's on your left." As if he hears me, we wheel, break into the pre-arranged flights of three and thankfully stare down at Hatfield. One by one I see the others stream-land onto a swath of green before the Tower. Turn finals and follow Tony in 'SKP and see him touch down suddenly stop and swing around into a bit of a heap. As I slip past him

I make a rude gesture, he's obviously OK. This is a terrible blow. Tony has flown into an ILS marker.

There, but for the grace of God, go any one of us. "There's a Tiger in your ILS," says John to cheer us up a bit, but no one is feeling cheerful, least of all Tony. Hatfield is wonderful. Another Tiger? One of the controllers has one at Panshanger and there Desmond Penrose gets out his lovely Cirrus Moth to make up the formation in care the replacement doesn't get over in time.

Ken Smith in the Cub ferries the owner over. The first five are waiting to take of when the replacement drops in. I see James clamber into the front cockpit and we are off. Can't see the photographic boys. We are circuiting Hatfield, all nine tighten up for the pass and head for St. Albans Abbey four minutes away. Keep in position – unwind man – relax. On our second pass, the sun weakly breaks through, the first and only time that day. Back at Hatfield and a miserable Ken Smith, and an irate John Blake. Poor Ken had missed his way returning those few miles from Panshanger. It is quite understandable. Then rain. But we'd made our objective. We fly home in loose formation between the rain showers. Collectively pleased to have shown our respect and individually proud to have been part of such a good team . . .

October. It happened last year. Just when we were getting settled in for a long winter the weather relented and we basked bewitched in an Indian Summer with a backdrop of golden leaves, lingering sunsets and the warmth stretching out its fingers into October. No complaints; just an eager move to make the most of things. For instance, James Baring flew his Mascaret home from Majorca to Gatwick non-stop in 6 hours 10 minutes, a distance of 800 miles. If only to encourage a rival challenge, I'll venture to suggest he broke two Club records, non-stop and duration. This year James has flown 300 hours in his Potez-engined Jodel. For an amateur that's some going. He must have just about equalled his endurance record when early on October 21st he set off at 6 am from Redhill to climb above the mists to a vantage point so that his passenger could film the comet. I don't think they saw it. But the fog which was late clearing kept them airborne till midday . . .

And another Condor with some improved features, not the least an easy-to-get-at trim and a rakish two-piece windscreen. Another three DC-4Ms have made the last flight into Redhill; it's all rather sad to see these fine aircraft destroyed.

After Neil's success at Dax, he came fourth and topped the biplane contingent; it's rumoured he and others are angling to get a Zlin . . . Back home the Esso contest at Rochester was won by Bob Winter with Tony

Haigh Thomas second and Charles Boddington third. It was good to see Frances Macrae in the lists. It's been a long time since there has been a woman aerobatist in our midst . . .

Letters from Dave Allan are now arriving with alarming frequency. Several readers have asked the origin of the expression in Dave Allan's letter from Australia: "P. Oing again so soon." It is, of course, an abbreviation of "Peninsular and Oriental Line" and implies a journey.

The year had produced just four full displays: Sywell, Shoreham, Fair Oaks and now Tollerton just south of Nottingham. If we all got together at our full shows – and they had absolute priority on both aircraft and pilots availability – we also met each other at lesser shows nearly every weekend. A glance at my log book showed no less than 12 'SOW' appearances – sometimes for TV – and others such as the two-day event at Farnborough's *Queen's Parade*, a tree lined park within the town which the *Daily Telegraph* had organised.

Tiger Club flying was for real. It was every weekend. I remember a few years earlier taking a weekend off and being reproached by Bish for not being around. I burst out laughing and asked if my attendance of 51 out of 52 wasn't enough. He shook his head seriously. *He* never missed out.

WE ENJOYED TOLLERTON.

September 19th. Tollerton, and a misty warm day, just the sort of weather to lose your way and at the same time be convinced it isn't possible. Tollerton, and a spectator set-up not far short of ideal – grass into wind, sun behind the customers, and excellent PA. Tollerton and no Cosmic, and at least four of the regulars away on holiday, yet one of our best shows. We started early, 2.30 instead of 3.00. We had to. Had the weather been dull, it would have been dark at 7.00 and with a two hour haul for the Turbs we had to be on our way by 5.00. So we started early, scrubbed the interval and startled Bill Chesson with a full-length programme that ended at 8 minutes past 4. It did too. Timing was magnificent and then there was Bill running around looking for something else with which to entertain the crowds, all 6,000 of them. The parachutists obliged with the aid of Chrisair's big biplane and an eager commentator who seemed set for hours. His potted history of parachuting was good fun, whether his tongue was in his cheek or not.

No Cosmic, and no Peter to open proceedings – sad because the combination would have excited the crowds, unaccustomed as they would have been to this whambang intro. The eight-formation served instead as our opening, with as neat a showing as ever. Eight? Robin d'Erlanger and Martin Barraclough were entertaining Spanish girls in Majorca, and we hadn't the heart to recall them 700 miles (I was outvoted). Perhaps the most memorable events were the aerobatics. Against a lovely blue sky Charles Boddington, Barry Tempest, Neil Williams and Bob Winter twirled and danced to everyone's delight. Tony Haigh Thomas, deprived of his Cosmic, sat and watched enviously.

John Blake, our unsung good provider, did as great a job as ever. Taffy Taylor commentated on all things aerobatic, and Mike Jolley, our PRO, talked about most of the rest, a happy arrangement. A lovely summer's evening to fly home in. Maybe the weather gods felt sorry for some earlier misbehaviour; they couldn't have made it up in a nicer way.

OUR "AT HOME," RESUMÉ

The Dawn-to-Dusk competition was being arranged for the coming year so it was appropriate to include Mike Jolley's observation:

Thumbing through Terence Boughton's wonderful book *The Story of the British Light Aeroplane*, I came across a reference to the first ever 'Dawn-to-Dusk' which took place nearly 40 years ago. The pilot or, more appropriately, intrepid aviatrix, was one Sophie Elliot Lynn who was Irish and a qualified parachutist; evidently her first jump was frustrated by engine failure, and she underwent the alarming experience of undergoing a forced landing while standing on the wing and clinging to the side of the machine! Anyway, this splendid woman took off from Woodford Aerodrome, Cheshire, in her Avro Avian at dawn on July 27th 1927, having spent the night on the hangar floor, and proceeded to carry out a complete tour of airfields and private strips in England south of Manchester and then flew up to Newcastle. She covered a total distance of 1,300 miles and made 79 landings! Not a bad effort by anybody's standard. Will this stir us to greater things in '66 . . .?

Tim Lodge wrote up the Club's "At Home" for the *Tiger Rag*. His title *How I flew from Paris to London in 8 hours 22 minutes* is a bit obscure, but he certainly captured one very good day out for all of us.

Anyone who did not know that the Tiger Club was holding an "At Home" for French visitors on the 4th September would surely have guessed it when they arrived at Redhill by the number of aircraft spotters. There seems to be some form of magic intelligence network, which, despite Michael's attempts at security, signals to every spotter in the South of England the arrival of Sicile Records, Nord 1000s, Wassmers and all the other French types that no spotter's log book should be without. In the event, the spotters were disappointed – only five eventually turned up with sixteen Frenchmen. The reason was the usual one, bad weather at the French coast. Those who came were delayed by the weather and the dinner at the Royal Aero Club eventually started an hour late – a caterer's nightmare splendidly managed.

The visitors had been fortified for the journey to the Russell Hotel by a Baring-prepared punch. James spent the afternoon mixing bottles of Medoc and Cointreau, chucking in some fruit, and tasting it, with the result that he had to call for Alka Seltzer in the middle of the dinner.

He was in good hands however – for he was sitting opposite three doctors – two French and John Urmston. The meal was superb; I would tell you what we had but the menu was in French. The only word I recognised was "grouse," reputedly shot by "GB" and Veryan in Scotland and calling for some tricky translation. After the meal came the toasts and the speeches – Norman in French and Monsieur in English. Norman raised a laugh by saying (in French) that we were especially glad to see our visitors from Beauvais for two reasons, and then adding in English: "But I'm afraid I haven't got time to go into the two reasons!" After the meal we all rushed to Westminster Pier where a boat was waiting to take us on a trip down the river. The hardy ones stood on deck listening to gramophone records at Strength Five and explaining about Tower Bridge in various languages, while the less spartan and more sensible ones propped up the bar below deck. Georges Crucifix seemed to know the sights of London far better than any of the Englishmen: "Ah! Voici le Cutty Shark!" Michael produced the French for 'dry dock' at this point – most impressive . . .

Back at Redhill and lunch at the hotel – "un vrai pub anglais." Fay and John had laid on a splendid feast of cold roast beef and baked potatoes which, with a little hair of the dog, made everyone feel a lot brighter.

All that remained to do was to say all our goodbyes, to promise to go to Beauvais next year and to load all the people and baggage in the right aeroplanes – more difficult than one would have expected. Bob Winter and Michael Jones nearly got airborne on the struts of the Super Cub when the charming lady doctor in the Nord 1000 got a bit too enthusiastic over warming up her engine, but apart from that the departure went without incident. If the French enjoyed themselves half as much as the English did then they had a pretty good weekend . . .

A Normanism: Norman Jones, after his speech of welcome in French during the "At Home" dinner, uttered, with obvious relief: "I hope you understood *that*, you French people," and they applauded wildly.

At the end of the year the Club had nearly 600 members of which 400 were active pilots. At Redhill there had been a year's busy scene of aircraft taxying in and out, and the urgency in the air was often highlighted with the familiar inducement to keep the engine running and so save time – a windmilling movement of arm before the dash to take control of the throttle. The constant movement of aircraft, pilots and friends made a kaleidoscope of animated colour that bewitched.

In a tale of the Club with so much happening, how brief and blind must be the vision of just one person. Multiply my experiences 400-fold, and it makes a mockery of any attempt to portray, yet I must try. Is it not better – to paraphrase the old adage – to have tried than not to have tried at all?

Names and faces flit across my memory, cheery happy folk climbing into and out of aeroplanes in a constant stream of to-ing and fro-ing, cries for the loan of a pair of goggles, an electric hat, for early electrical intercoms were being tried out because the old and trusty Gosport tubes were getting hard to come by. Cushions in lockers and cushions under pilots, someone forever calling for a swing, a melody of sucking in and blowing out of Gipsy Majors is on every hand, an energetic concerto of compressions. Cowlings up and the wooden handle of Jim's long screwdriver clumping a casing to provoke an impulse . . . sights and sounds so familiar that even now, as I write this in sunny Spain, I have only to close my eyes to see and hear it all again.

And names. Before me I have a year's batch of *Tiger Rags* from which to glean a fraction of that which I have missed. Mac McDonald on the phone on New Year's Day asking if we were night flying that night, and Charles McKenzie, just back from East Africa and already our glider-towing champ. Young Robin Blech who the year before had flown a Turbulent to Colmar at the age of 18 and who, before the year was out, would become an assistant CFI, the youngest ever.

And letters from all over the world bringing with them the warmth of comradeship. The never-ending stream from Dave Allan over in Australia forever counting the minutes to his return. The sense of loss when Ian Trethewey crashed at Fair Oaks in a Comanche 180. And Len Gallagher, a BEA captain, who offered his services to help us brush up our IF and for his willingness was made i/c. As someone said at the time: "That'll teach him to volunteer." We had one passenger member by the name of Bill Fisher who seemed to spend all this time searching for old aircraft to preserve. I think his greatest moment must have been his organising the epic and successful return to these shores of Lancaster G-ASXX from Australia later that year. And of David Harris and Bill Goldstraw out there corresponding to keep in touch with "home" – their word, not mine. A brotherhood of flying.

Back here, Rochester had proved a friendly airfield. It was where Ted Perrin would welcome fellow Tiger Club members with a warm fire and cups of tea.

And the Women . . . There was an invitation to us all in April to the tower at Redhill to mark the presentation by the Chairman of a Rollason Condor G-ASEU to the British Women Pilots' Association. Joan Short, as tiny as her name, had married and hurried northwards, but returned in her Turbulent from Yorkshire across the Channel to Berck for lunch with Don Lovell and all . . .

The 99s (all noted women pilots) gave a Thanksgiving Party in November at which they honoured – I think – some Club members. A husband of a 99-er is called a 49½-er, and 66-er (a lady honoured by membership but who is not a pilot) can see her husband become a 33-er. Count on this occasion John Blake, Norman Ryder, Neil Harrison, Simon Ames and me (Benjy). Club members Sally Ames, Lollie Benjamin and Jill Southern became 66-ers but Sue Phillips, Dawn Turley and Joan Waugh (née Short) got the full treatment and became 99-ers. I know what I mean, they know what they mean, but the casual reader will be forgiven for thinking I drank too much.

The December Committee meeting minutes were briefer than usual. Against item 5, Annual Dinner Dance, Norman had noted: *"Dick Emery will entertain."* Norman saw nothing amusing in this statement. Norman, who'd never watched television, knew nothing of Dick's profession, only knew that he was a flying member who had volunteered to entertain, so entertain he would – and did.

1966
THE FORMATIVE YEARS AGAIN,
DAWN-TO-DUSK AND HRH

1966 AND THE TIGER CLUB'S TENTH YEAR

January: The airfield at Redhill looked wet. Seagulls circled miniature lakes knowing full well no one would disturb them. Few did, but if flying did continue throughout the month it was on a restricted scale. It's at times like this that runways begin to look attractive. Not that anyone has contemplated the thought seriously, but it would have been something of a remarkable first if the Sea Turbulent could have used Redhill's lakes for a take-off.

The Sea Turb is a reality of course. It flew last year from an estuary down in Kent until it had the misfortune to sink. By all accounts it flew very well and plans are afoot to get another afloat again in Kent. January is the Turbulent's month with the welcome report that its C. of A. should be granted. This well-deserved recognition will cheer the foreign touring boys who will soon be able to chug about Europe without the restrictive paperwork.

It's a little-known fact but the Tiger Club has established branches at three airfields other than Redhill. Fair Oaks, Rochester and the latest, Wycombe Air Park, formerly Booker. Already there is a Turbulent and Tiger at Wycombe with the possibility of a Condor very soon.

Socially December has probably been one succession of parties, but the one at Tim Lodge's deserves comment for the welcome it gave Dave Allan back from Australia, oh yes, and the party-goer who fell out of a window; it was a great evening.

Visitors to Redhill during December included Lady Aitken, David Jacobs, Donald Campbell and the American actor member Cliff Robertson. His private air force in California is impressive: Three Tigers, a Spitfire and an Me.108. He extends a welcome to Tiger Club members over there to use them. Whether the invite includes the Spitfire I'm not so sure . . .

We greeted 1966 with enthusiasm. Even though only ten years had pased since the Club's founding there were then, as now, still many unanswered questions about how the Club all began and when. Bish, in an attempt to clarify things, wrote part I of *The Formative Years 1956-1957* for the *Tiger Rag* in March, and in doing so added to the confusion.

In the January issue of the *Tiger Rag* it was suggested that this month might not really be that of the tenth anniversary of the formation of the Club. In point of fact it is and this is how it came about.

During the racing season of 1955 there had been talk amongst those racing Tiger Moths that a Club should be formed for those so doing, and at the Annual Racing Dinner held at the Royal Aero Club on the evening of January 24th 1956, Norman Jones saw to it that a number of those who favoured the idea should sit at his table. In addition to himself these included Jimmy Denyer, Basil Maile, Bev Snook and the Hon. Peter Vanneck, who had all been racing during 1955; also there was "Chris" Wren. During the evening the matter was further discussed and it was decided to proceed with the organisation. It was originally proposed that to be eligible for flying membership a member would have to have "owned a Tiger Moth and/or to have raced one in the Kng's Cup Air Race" whilst two of the future events proposed were to hold an annual dinner and to present the member who had made the best showing of the year whilst flying a Tiger Moth with a Tiger-skin flying helmet and the rather unofficial title of "Tiger Tim"! The annual subscription was to be 10/-. These qualifications were later amended to "anyone who has flown a Tiger Moth in the King's Cup or the British Lockheed Aerobatic contest." In the event, the six mentioned above became Founder Members of the Club, plus veteran pilot J.M. Donald who was then 68 years of age and the new Club's 'elder statesman.'

At this time Norman Jones owned a number of Tiger Moth aircraft and certain of these were loaned out to members of No. 601 Squadron, Royal Auxiliary Air Force (of which Norman was a pilot in the twenties) and which included Peter Vanneck, Desmond Norman and Tony Oldham. The aircraft were G-AOAA, 'OAB, 'OAC and 'OAD and at the first round of the National Air Races flown at Yeadon on Whit Monday 1956, Tony Oldham scored a victory in 'OAC.

Later, at the Coventry meeting which of course included the King's Cup race and Lockheed aerobatics, these aircraft were joined by G-ANSH and 'NZZ, the former of which was flown in the races by Basil Maile and in the Lockheed by your present scribe who Norman Jones had very kindly asked to fly in the Contest and had been entered by him . . .

On July 30th Norman wrote to me and officially asked me to become Hon. Secretary of the Tiger Club and from then onwards we commenced to organise, although we were still flying as individuals in Norman's aeroplanes, rather than as Tiger Club members. For a start we arranged by stages some Tiger Moth racing at the annual Summer Convention of the Association of British Aero Clubs, that year being held on Sept. 4th at Elstree, together with solo aerobatics by yours truly. (In those days I virtually had the monopoly in aerobatics for the Tiger Club, a monopoly which I am very glad to say was soon challenged – as you will all know!)

We made one more "appearance" in 1956, this being at Sandown during the weekend of September 21-22, the occasion being a meeting of the British Women Pilots' Association. There in their own right were Mavis Harriott in 'NSH and Margo McKellar in 'NZZ whilst the mere males in the shape of Norman and myself arrived in 'ODR.

Once again there were aerobatics and racing – display No. 2?

On November 23rd was organised a second of our objects – that of holding an Annual Dinner, this being by present standards a very small affair held in the dining room of the Royal Aero Club in Piccadilly. This gathering also included an Annual General Meeting – the first and only one so far – at which Norman Jones was appointed Chairman and myself Honorary Secretary. The Committee was organised early in the following year.

Came that said year and on January 20th the first official flights by aeroplanes of the Tiger Club. These took the form of formation dual and practice flights with Wilfred Fitzmaurice and Ken Smith in two Tigers. The Club book of membership, now in 1966 a volume of over 500 names, was first issued in 1957. It contained 31 names of members, 14 of whom are still with us. The cost of flying a Tiger was fixed at 27/6 per hour; happy days made possible by the fact that we did not have the big overheads and first costs that now beset us! . . .

It's interesting to note that although Bish became Secretary, and presumably was responsible for the membership booklet, he failed to recognise Chris Wren as a Founder at the time, or indeed in subsequent years, in spite of what he wrote in '66. Perhaps he left him out because he wasn't a pilot. And then too John Donald, an endearing man, also seemed to be dropped early on as a Founder although he was certainly present at that first Dinner, as an old envelope which still exists will confirm. Norman had jotted down on it the names of those around him.

The Tiger Tim helmet vanished sometime in the early sixties. Bev wore it in '58 and handed it over to me during the '59 Races. It was by then weary and moth-eaten. Sad to relate I can't remember what happened to it. Borrowed and not returned was a helmet's usual fate. In May Bish followed up with Part 2 of *The Formative Years*:

. . . At the start, the club fleet consisted of the tried and trusted 'NSH, 'NZZ, 'OAA and 'ODR, and I am very glad to say that 'OAA and 'NZZ are still with us, albeit in a very different guise than originally. These were shortly joined by 'ANHI and AOXS, the first listed being classed as a 'photographic type,' which had an aperture on the floor of the front cockpit through which camera shots could be taken, whilst the second was the 'Taxi-Tiger,' which had the front cockpit enclosed by a perspex canopy which kept the passenger in comparative comfort, but left the poor pilot out in the cold. Towards the middle of the year the famous G-ACDC joined the fleet. She also is (more or less) still with us.

Our first organised event was a celebration of the fact that in March '57 the Tiger Moth would have had a C. of A. for 25 years and a party was held at Fair Oaks to commemorate this event. Unfortunately, whilst the weather was very fine locally, mist was prevalent over much of the British Isles on that day, which cut down the number of visitors somewhat. However, about 25 Tigers were present so it was quite a good party. A second celebration for the Tiger Moth was held at Sandown during Easter when the race for the "Tiger Moth Silver Jubilee Trophy," which had been very kindly given to us by the then Mayor of Croydon, Alderman Basil Monk, was flown off. This race attracted 15 entries, the final being won by Dennis Hartas in 'NHI. Yet a third celebration for the year was the holding of what was to become the main annual Tiger Club Aerobatics contest, that for the "de Havilland Aerobatic Trophy," a silver model of a Tiger Moth, very kindly presented to us on extended loan by the de Havilland Aircraft Company Ltd of Hatfield. This Trophy had been got for us through the good offices of Wing Commander Pike who has been a member of the Club almost from the start, and the first contest was held at Sywell Aerodrome on May 5th in the usual cold conditions that seemed to coincide with our shows just then. At that time the competition was restricted to pilots with a certain minimum hours and was won by a local member, Charles Boddington, who was later to go from strength to strength aerobatic-wise. We performed the usual formation and racing items which were now beginning to be our main stock in trade. And we WERE getting known, for about this time we received a request to put on our acts at Swansea where the airport was about to be officially opened.

June 10th 1957 saw the first (and only as far as I can remember) open British Aerobatic Competition held by the Royal Aero Club at White Waltham. This was also one of the first official outings of one of our new toys, which was 'NSH, now fitted with a special auxiliary petrol tank and air pump, with the aid of which the engine would run for a short while inverted, this greatly helping aerobatics. Unfortunately this could not be made to function with the ease of that on the present-day Super Tigers and it meant the working of a second throttle lever, opening whilst you rolled to the inverted position and closing as you rolled out! Or so we had thought so far; we later discovered that if you opened the second lever whilst right side up and left it there the motor would run for several minutes without cutting, whatever position you were in. But on the day of the contest we had not discovered this, so those who flew 'NSH did not do so well, most especially myself, who completely messed up my show! The ultimate results showed that David Phillips in 'NZZ had been adjudged the winner . . .

Glad to say that de Havilland never did ask for their beautiful Trophy back and I suppose now that de Havilland no longer exist, except in our hearts, we will ever retain it.

In February came the news that HRH The Duke of Edinburgh was going to support the Dawn-to-Dusk Competition. Mike Jolley, who had succeeded James Gilbert as the Club's PRO reported:

DAWN TO DUSK COMPETITION

The Tiger Club's annual Dawn-to-Dusk competition, devised to test a pilot's navigational skill, airmanship and the aircraft's performance and efficiency, will be extended in scope for the 1966 competition. This year any pilot holding a current Private Pilot's Licence may enter for the competition and competitors may enter any aircraft so long as it is solo.

The Duke of Edinburgh has consented to support the 1966 competition. The winner will receive the Duke of Edinburgh Trophy, an award in the form of a clock and £100 prize. There will be second and third prizes of £50 and £25. In addition, special commemorative certificates will be awarded to competitors who perform well.

Competition regulations will require competing pilots to take off from Redhill airfield after 0400 hours BST to fly the greatest distance within the UK and then land back at the same aerodrome before 2130 hours the same day. (Last year's winner covered more than 1,300 miles in a single seater Volkswagen-engined Turbulent aircraft.)

As in previous years, the competition will take place during the week before and after mid-summer's day 1966 between dawn and dusk, giving some 17½ hours of daylight, during which time the pilots will be airborne for nearly 14 hours, a real test of concentration and stamina.

The competitors will be judged by a panel of experienced pilots who will judge the entries based on the production of a written log which must be prepared within 72 hours of landing. This will give details of route, total distance covered, turning points, block speeds and fuel consumption.

Routes can be flown anywhere in the UK (excluding N. Ireland, Channel Islands and the Isle of Man) and the route chosen is to consist of straight-line tracks flown between recognised airfields marked on the latest 1:500,000 scale aeronautical map of England. Each turning point must be passed by circling the signals square or airfield buildings. No track may be repeated and any landing must entail a minimum time on the ground of thirty minutes.

The trophy, replica and certificate have been designed by Chris Wren, the aviation cartoonist, at Prince Philip's request; they are of original and entertaining design, in keeping with the spirit of the competition . . .

In February we were invited to the West German Aero Club at Osnabrück during May in connection with that city's "British Week" and to be the guests of the Aero Club's members and families. That initial invitation was the forerunner of the Club's very close association with the Osnabrückers and a friendship which happily continues in an unbroken line of alternate visits to this day. It was also the month the Tiger Club was awarded the Lennox Boyd Trophy for flying efficiency. If by 'efficiency' they meant no accidents, it was a good job it was '65 and not the year '66.

The *Tiger Rag*, apart from my log books, some odd papers and committee minutes, has been my primary *aide memoire* for these wonderful years. And since the *Rag* always showed a cheerful face – my optimism would permit nought else – accidents didn't feature very often, and if there was a real whopper that couldn't be concealed it was always written up with a studied understatement.

It became policy, and sometimes a kindness, not to reveal all, and besides to air too much was a bit like washing one's linen in public, which wasn't on. But even with my terrible memory I recall there were some real beauties that year, thoughts prompted every now and then by the cryptic comments in the monthly committee notes, and Arthur Humphrey's immortal words: "Don't bother me now, I'm crashing."

During a visit to Redhill this spring of '88 I had asked Michael Jones for some information on membership and he hunted in vain for me.

"I can't help," he finally said as he rummaged dispairingly in a hangar cuboard. "But if you want some accident reports I've got all these and more," and lugged out an armful of them.

"Now there's a book in itself," he said. "Interested?"

If this were really a history of the Tiger Club I'd be honour-bound to plod through them. Thank heavens it isn't, but this I know. More pilots than you'd ever imagine have had the proverbial egg of an accident on their faces, and the oft-quoted: "There but for the Grace of God go I" might well have been the fervent words of more than we think. If God's Grace in general missed most of us, his Grace in particular at least spared – in the most part – our life and limbs.

As the months roll chronologically by I'll pass on some incidents that I recall, but it's as well to reflect that all things are relative. We were a huge Club with an active list of 450 pilots so perhaps the incident percentage was lower than the norm? Perhaps, but Churchill's words: "There are lies, damned lies and statistics" will effectively squash whatever case I might have offered, even if one were necessary.

DISPLAY CHANGES AND THE ANNUAL BALL

The display organisation underwent a change early in the season. The Club was growing and our displays were becoming an important factor in its public recognition. We were now being asked to provide participations in ever-increasing numbers, and quite suddenly some of the members awoke to the realisation that our expertise was not only in demand, but that people paid for the privilege of seeing us.

Since many of us were not commercial pilots, we were not in the position to fly for hire or reward anyway; although at the time there was a slackness in this interpretation, no one was prepared to push for a ruling. For instance test flying professionally didn't call for a commercial rating, and I know for certain that Pee Wee Judge flew on a PPL.

So we flew for expenses, but if ever there was an overworked expression it was the word "expenses." But there can be no denying that the prospect of some extra income was raising its head, and in some quarters there were murmurs of a discontent in the Club's undemanding acceptance of the finances accruing from the Full Displays.

Much of these mutterings were in ignorance. No one really knew anything about our Display Promoter's task or outlay. On the face of it any bright day seemed to bring out the crowds. We flew up and down long lines of spectators who'd paid to see us. Mum, Dad and kids paid a fiver a car load to come in, and there appeared to be thousands of them. Promoting must be money for old rope.

For most of us it always remained a great day out and, providing we got our flying paid and some refreshment, that was enough. But, asked the voracious few, did the Club get enough back? Often hiding behind that sentiment there was the unspoken demand that substituted 'self' for 'Club.' Bill Chesson our Promoter was a patient target. Only he knew the ins and outs, and he gave an agreed amount to the Club come rain or shine. It was a regular and modest income towards the expenses of the Club from a man who never complained when no one turned up, and who in his steady unshowy way was Mr Reliable himself. If he was aware of the grumblings he made little of it, and when at the beginning of '66 the first break in the promotional routine of the previous years became apparent, he accepted the new regime with cheerful acceptance, remaining our friend and advisor. An experienced promoter, Bill had never had all his eggs in one basket, and with his Lydden Circuit near Canterbury doing well with autocross and motor-racing, I think he even welcomed the break.

The new Organiser, as Clive Francis styled himself, had recently resigned from the RAF with the rank of Squadron Leader and, whilst a fine pilot, must have proved something of a maverick in the Services. His unpredictable initiatives and occasional exhuberant flying would have made him an outstanding wartime pilot, but these very attributes must have frustrated his peacetime career. It was as if he reasoned that if the RAF hadn't the good sense to see his potential it was *their* loss; his determination to success was in no way diminished in his civilian role.

His entry into the Tiger Club was dynamic. His leadership of the nine-strong Turbulent formation was an extension of his service experience and his inspired, and mostly service-trained, "squadron" became an exceptional team, following him into exploits that on occasion took both pilot and diminutive mount into marginal situations. I recall a young Robin Blech remarking: "I like him, but I do wish he wouldn't treat me as the most junior member of his squadron!"

It was against this background that Clive decided to go into promoting air displays on his own account. His drive carried us along with him, but not without a degree of waryness, for it was not unknown to hear of ex-servicemen burning their fingers and gratuities in short time when entering civvy street. But new faces and new directions deserved support and Tiger Club Display Ltd. came into being.

Initially Clive let it be known, in February – in a letter to me – that *"all display flying would be eligible for 50% rebate and all display practice flying INSTRUCTION by the accredited team or act bosses would receive a 100% rebate. The definition of INSTRUCTION will have to be carefully delineated but I suggest the basis will be only when the leaders are flying exclusively to bring on the new boys and not when practising with their established teams.*

You were kind enough to say that you would undertake the administration of the Display Practice Fund . . . to start with I will personally guarantee that the Fund will receive £300 during the season and I would ask you to plan to limit the amount of practice expenditure to this amount until the results of the first couple of shows are in."

I remember I opened a bank account in the style of Tiger Club Flying Training Expense Fund. The idea worked for a while but eventually lapsed as other methods of repaying display and ferry pilots came into being. Many years later, James Baring, one of the signatories, and I drew out the remainder of the Fund and thankfully handed the cheque – a very small one – to Michael.

Clive Francis certainly attempted to pull things together, and under his wing he tried to coordinate, with a flurry of letters to everyone, about every participation big or small that involved Club aircraft and pilots. The venture wasn't a success. It was to prove a case of over-direction, OK when dealing with sheep, but not much use when coping with fellow pilots every bit as bright and intelligent, yes, and as individually minded, as our lot. But in the spring there were no doubts on the horizon and it was all systems go.

Tony Haigh Thomas became Display Director Elect and my understudy prior to taking over the reins in '67. Running on ahead a little, in the event Dave Allan took on the job. I have a feeling it was around that time Tony had to go and fly Lightnings for the Saudi Air Force. It was an offer he couldn't resist, apparently the money offered was sensational. He must have had kittens then when the '67 war flared up. Fortunately for Tony, the Saudis, rather than risk their prized supersonic Lightnings, grounded them, so when his tour was over he came back well pleased, and if I remember aright, bought a chain of launderettes on the proceeds.

I wrote of March:

It's been quite a month. Fine weather, loads of flying and a highly successful Dinner at the Hilton. Firstly our sincere congratulations to both Norman Jones, for his award of the RAeC Silver Medal, and Neil Williams for his RAeC Bronze. And whilst on the subject of good wishes, let me promptly offer all our congratulations to no less than four sets of proud parents during February and March. To Eve and David Phillips, a girl; Yvonne and Bob Pooley, a girl; Diana and Barry Tempest, a girl; and Lollie (and me), a boy.

Forgot to mention last month that the Club now has another Jodel. it's the DR.1050M Excellence, a souped-up version of the Ambassadeur. In outline it resembles the Mascaret but inside it's fitted with a rear bench seat . . . it's a beauty to fly and the quietest of the range . . .

The Dinner on the 18th February was the first we had at the London Hilton, then newly opened and very swish, where the rates, at least when they first opened, were reasonable indeed.

The London Hilton has, in its short existence, seen many strange things within its portals but nothing as original as a Turbulent. It stood in the foyer as proud as life – and drained of fuel. We know; more than one toyed with the idea of starting it. 350 members and friends came to enjoy themselves – and they did. We left at 1.30 am and the party was still going strong . . .

Norman Jones introduced the Trophy Winners and Margo McKellar presented the various Cups and Awards. A very popular win was the de Salis Award to "Taffy" Taylor. "Taffy" in his first year with the Club crammed in as much aerobatic adventuring as most of us in a lifetime. To Neil Williams a well deserved DH Trophy and a Tiger Club Medallion for his contribution to Club aerobatics. Charles Boddington came second followed by Taffy. Martin Barraclough was awarded the McAully Trophy and Bob Winter the Esso with Tony Haigh Thomas second. Norman, in a speech which broke from previous practice, continued to pay tribute to many Club members. Robin

Voice was awarded the Glider Towing Medal for '65. "Jacko" Jackson received a vote of appreciation for organising the glider towing so successfully. Robin Voice was again mentioned for his efforts in '65 during the Dawn-to-Dusk contest, as was Don Lovell (who won the event) and Robin Blech. Don Lovell was also thanked for his great efforts on behalf of the Foreign Touring and James Baring looked shattered as he was named Foreign Tourer of the Year. To Tony Haigh Thomas a mention on his place in the team to visit Moscow. Norman wound up by again thanking Bev Snook for organising the Dinner . . .

Norman's speech was certainly a break from tradition. Hitherto Norman, a man of few words, thanked few. He used to contend that it was enough to have had the privilege to have done something for the Club. He mellowed on this occasion.

In the middle of all this a Tiger flew in – wings and all – and tore around the ballroom uttering rude noises. The Tiger mask hid the intruder's identity but in my book he was later seen playing with a junior control-line model in the middle of the floor. This was highly entertaining, but the waiters looked most apprehensive and stood well back. Eventually, the model developed a nice line in ground hops and turned the act into a glorious prang.

The cabaret was tremendous fun. Introduced by the incomparable Dick Emery, we instantly fell in love with Jennifer Johnson, her singing and guitar. Dick, in his turn, was never better – and his singing voice surprisingly good. Later the Clark Brothers gave us a brief song and shuffle.

Norman Ryder, in a brief and charming speech, made the first announcement that Norman Jones had been awarded the RAeC Silver Medal for his services to Light Aviation . . .

Heard at the Dinner:. "The ARB is like a virgin – it shouts like mad but knows it has to give in in the end." Attributed to Norman Jones.

"I'm damned near forty," exclaimed Sue Phillips.

"You're never!" remarked someone.

"I'm thirty-one," replied Sue indignantly.

OF CHECKS, MEMORABLE PRANGS AND THE USSR

"GB," now living deep in Gloucestershire, wrote in the April to all the check pilots reminding them of their responsibilities and emphasized the need to carefully select suitable fields for forced landing practice. In fact he suggested that we use either one of two known fields in future: one was John Wright's strip at Rydinghurst Farm and the other Jack Miller's place at Slinfold. The letter must have brought grins from the knowing.

In the acceptance check it was usual to close the throttle on the unsuspecting applicant for membership at some two thousand feet or so and tell him he'd had an engine failure and to make a forced landing. He would be encouraged to drop down into a field of his choice, but to open up when he'd convinced himself and the examiner that he'd have made it. Trouble was we'd recently had two end in a crash, and another was subject to a low-flying charge, and "GB" our Senior Check Pilot was getting twitchy.

The cause of one of the incidents was a matter of a cold engine failing to pick up – in spite of engine bursts every 500 feet – and the other seemed to revolve around an appeal from the applicant, anxious to prove his forced landing would come off, and an unconvinced examiner equally anxious that it wouldn't. It didn't. Strangely enough no one ever insisted on a specific break-off height, but common practice was about 300 feet. It was now increased to 500.

May: and the hangar at Redhill seems crammed with new aircraft. To join the recent Jodel Excellence is the new Mousquetaire. It's a smooth looking ship with a more sophisticated radio than the norm. In company with the Excellence it has the Narco 360 channel . . . the new Beagle Husky looks like taking the place of the Cub. Whilst it has the added advantage of a glider tow hook, it lacks the Cub's sheer *joie de vivre* but as a robust four-seater it's going to take some beating. A twin to the well-driven Stampe 'SHS is the latest French addition 'TKC. Colour scheme is identical, a fact that will enhance its display potential. 'TKC is also a dual model which should help training.

The Active looks most dashing in its new livery. The red and white chequerboards on the fuselage, fin and wing tips made me at least think of the pugnacious Bristol Bulldog. Tiger 'CDC is now back with us, looking as good as ever, its mishap of a few months ago forgotten, although not by the Senior Check Pilot . . .

I don't think many appreciated the Club's chief engineer Frank Hounslow's part in obtaining Stampes. His journeys across the Channel were seemingly endless, but he insisted on the best, and his fluent French and technical know-how combined to give us exceptional mounts.

The first display of the season was at Panshanger in May, and successful enough to make all of us feel that the new management had things nicely in hand. In John Blake's absence, Margo McKellar had organised a terrific meal and yours truly was saddled with the commentary. The display went fine. Among the highlights was undoubtedly Peter Phillip's superlative handling of the Cosmic in the kind of performance that becomes legend, and Martin Barraclough's Active display. He put our hearts in our mouths with his startling opening – a fullblooded spin. James Baring and his crazy-flying really got the crowd rooting for him and Norman Jones' comedy taxiing went over great especially when his huge umbrella blew inside out. The programme is now too well-known to record in detail: enough to say everyone did extremely well. Must mention, however, two first public performances of Standing on Wing: Liz Barton and Sue Phillips both made a swinging debut. All in all, a successful day with a lovely sunset to fly into on our return to Redhill...

The incidents to aircraft were mounting up . . . someone had bent the Cosmic's prop and been fined £5. It had the most unusual scimitar shape, and we cheerfully caned the thing to its maximum revs blissfully unaware that back in the States they were no longer in vogue since they had a reputation for flying off on their own.

A few weeks after the Panshanger show James Baring joined Dick Emery at Wisley for the RAeS Garden Party in a command performance of two Tiger write-offs in one afternoon. Dick Emery, who was now the country's top television entertainer, owned his own Tiger and this he somehow managed to drift off the runway into a tent, winding up in the car park on top of Tiger Club member Roy Proctor's car. Roy and Ann were furious with Dick for bending their transport, and even more irate when the Press, learning the pilot was Dick Emery, tore across to take photos and to interview an unhurt Dick who, sensing some good publicity, was putting on a nonchalant air.

Just as Dick was well into his act and doing a "Mandy" for the cameras, there was another accident and everyone left an upstaged Dick Emery and rushed across to the remains of James Baring's Tiger 'CDC, written off doing his crazy-flying slot. James wasn't hurt either, but Dick never forgave him his timing. A real and loveable professional was our Dick. The incident however brought him into conflict with the Committee over the lack of compensation for Roy's bent car, and sadly his resignation was sought and accepted later in the year.

September: The sight of a perfect formation overhead one bright Saturday late last month heralded the return of the British Aerobatic Team home from Moscow. Competitions apart, the actual journey to Moscow and back was an adventure in itself . . . The Club's "At Home" was the best attended ever. The Dinner at the RAF Club was near Annual Dinner dimensions. A striking feature of the evening was the number of bilingual Club members. I could only see three who, like me, were reasonably fluent in only one tongue – English – but all this talent was in vain for the visitors all spoke excellent English. The Sunday was a sore disappointment, the wind blew lustily and the rain ringed a wet audience in the hangars. Our visitors glumly watched as their aircraft tugged restlessly at restraining ropes. They weren't to get away till the Monday.

Norman Jones entitled his tribute to the returning aerobatic team *Retreat from Moscow 1966*. In it he wrote:

. . . It is a long way from Paris to Moscow and back, as Napoleon found in 1811. It is even further from Redhill! So it was with lively pleasure that we welcomed back our aerobats and their helpers last Saturday afternoon from their Russian adventure. They arrived at the tactful time, just before tea. The champagne which was provided to celebrate their successful return was, we were told, welcome but not so welcome as their first cup of Miss Read's tea – their opinion of the Continental kind being very poor.

Very pleased we were to see them, with their aeroplanes looking as spick and span as on the day they left us three weeks ago. Everybody looking brown and well, and bringing back certainly honour as well as Russian brandy (the correct allowance, Customs please note!) if not glory.

Of the actual aerobatics in the World Championships I hope we shall have a full description in due course. But enough to say here that this is the fourth time that the Tiger Club has taken it on itself to send representatives of this country to compete against the nations of the world in the gentle art of making an aeroplane dance in the sky.

This last attempt has been our best-prepared and most successful effort; help was forthcoming from a number of well-wishers and the pilots themselves have devoted many hours to practice.

Although, as we all know, in flying there is no hard and fast division between amateur and professional, in these contests there is a vast gulf between the State-aided teams and those that fly on their own power. Moreover the difference in the aeroplanes does much to obscure the variation in pilot techniques. Therefore results tend to be of less importance than the effort which is put in to compete and improve in skill. Our pilots were far from outclassed and we finished 9th amongst the nations.

Thanks are due to everybody, not least to those on the ground who prepared the aeroplanes so carefully that mechanically the trip was without incident. And on the same afternoon that they returned, our machines were back in service again, providing sporting flying to other Tiger Club members . . .

Since everyone was clamouring for news of the journey and the wildest of stories abounded, Nick Carter the Team Manager obliged. He wrote *"The Journey Out"*:

The Moscow Competition really began with the British Team immediately after Dax, the International Aerobatic Trophy in September, 1965. It was then that Neil Williams and Taff Taylor competed so nobly against Zlins in the Stampe 'SHS and Neil got fourth place. It was obvious, however, that a well-flown Zlin will outfly a well-flown Stampe and our immediate problem then was to get hold of a Zlin for Moscow this year. It is a story in itself how the Zlin was eventually obtained, how it was financed and how it was painstakingly serviced and painted and finally approved by the ARB. It eventually shone resplendent in its British colours of red, white and blue and boldly carried its Welsh Dragon ready for the fight.

By this time, Neil Williams, Taff Taylor and Tony Haigh Thomas had trained to perfection in the Zlin and James Black and Robin d'Erlanger had toiled in the Stampe through the introduction of the Moscow sequences ready for the Competition. Dave Allan, the Australian member, also trained with us and offered himself as the Australian entry ready to accompany our Team.

The Competition in Moscow was due to start on Monday 8th August, and in the planning stages it was decided that three competition aircraft would be taken, the Zlin, Stampe 'SHS and Stampe 'TKC. We needed adequate baggage-carrying facility and the help of an engineer, and our party decided to take the Mousquetaire 'TKX as the transport and radio aeroplane. There were many arrangements to be sorted out, team uniforms and finances to be provided. The Royal Aero Club worked miracles in obtaining financial assistance, and it was at 7 o'clock on a bright morning on Saturday 30th July that the Redhill tarmac hummed with life and the game was on.

The four aeroplanes left Redhill shortly after 8.00 am on that day after having special Customs clearance and a great send-off by the Chairman downwards. We anticipated five days of flying to Moscow and our route lay Redhill–Ostende–Hilversum–Wilhelmshaven–Kiel–Maribo–Ronne on the Island of Bornholm – Lisie Katie and Olsztyn, both in Poland, and on to Vilnius some sixty miles into Russia. From Vilnius we were due to be met by Russian aircraft and led by a route of their choice to Moscow, the total distance approaching 1,800 miles.

The early part of our flight as far as Hilversum went without incident. Hilversum was notable for a good lunch in the excellent Clubhouse and also their method of stacking their aircraft in the hangars by tipping them up on to their noses, in which attitude they occupied a remarkably small floor space.

From Hilversum to Wilhelmshaven the weather was heavily stormy and we landed just as the clouds parted to give us a good reception and the tail end of the broadcast of the World Football Series whilst we had tea. It was remarkable how much glory rubbed off on us as a result of the British triumph in the Football Cup and this eased us on our way quite surprisingly. That night was spent in somewhat shakedown fashion at Kiel aerodrome and all should take warning that the road around the aerodrome is not intended as a peritrack. However, no incident, and after a somewhat uncomfortable night, we were on our way again for the mysteries of much farther afield.

Maribo is a tiny strip cut into a cornfield. Not the easiest place to find, but when found quite enchanting for its farm attached and the comfort of the farmer's dining room and excellence of his coffee. Refuelling completed, we were on our way again for the Baltic and the thrill of crossing so much water. Now we were at Bornholm, a pleasure island, prosperous and clean, a friendly airport with all mod cons. We thought we had earned a rest but this was not to be. Neil could not see his beloved Zlin picketed in the open if there was even the slightest chance of a hangar. There was a hangar. Full of debris and an old car. Its doors did not work and they were not wide enough for the Zlin anyway.

After we got the Zlin in this hangar – and picketed the other aircraft down – we headed for our much-needed baths in a hotel already kindly laid on by a very kindly Niels. We never did ask the host his surname. It was here that John Blake, our Team Manager, Neil Harrison and James Gilbert met us, having started that day from Gatwick in the *Flight* Baron, and eleven of us sat down to dinner that night in fine spirits on this enchanting island.

Monday morning early saw us again airborne, this time over the Baltic sea, heading for Poland and a not too well-established airfield position of Lisie Katie which had been given us by lat. and long. some forty miles different from its more likely position. On landing at Lisie Katie, we were taken for refreshment to a sort of monastery building quite free of charge and with impressions of handshakes and farewell waves that proved that they had not seen visiting aircraft for many years. Another forty minutes and we were at Olsztyn, our second Polish airfield. This one again long grass, gliders and crop-spraying aircraft. Here we were taken into the local town by a bus which mysteriously arrived for that purpose and we were given a free civic reception and taken back to our aeroplanes ready for the final hop into Russia. Our engines started and we were ready to taxy for take-off when we were told that Russian Vilnius had not yet agreed to our arrival. We did not know that they had been asked and we feared the worst. A lot of running backwards and forwards, and suddenly we got the "off." We were away.

The Iron Curtain really exists. We left and crossed the frontier which was so evident by the winding scar which crossed the countryside. It must be a cleared width of at least twenty yards with a continuous wire barricade, and as Westerners we felt a little insecure as we crossed it. Loud Russian voices growled on the Vilnius radio frequencies, and we were sniffed at by the odd military aeroplanes as we progressed.

Our own radio call to Vilnius was met with some silence, but eventually a female voice answered our call in English. Our terms were obviously not familiar and in answer to my "negative" as to whether we wished a met. report, we nevertheless received a full string of details from thirty thousand feet downwards. We shortly landed at Vilnius and were marshalled to a point where we saw the *Flight* Baron already parked. Our passports were demanded before we left the aircraft and there was a feeling of rather rigid control that worried us. We were moved across the tarmac to the aerodrome building and each of us received detailed currency investigation and a warning that we must not buy roubles. Gradually the pressure lifted and by the time we were having a meal in the airport restaurant we had already made friendly contacts. The clock was two hours on in Vilnius and we were late in finally getting to our hotel in the town. A perfectly comfortable place but with a serious and unbending administration that made long delay in room allocation, but we finally got our heads down.

In the morning we were taken by coach back to the airport and to our surprise were received by about twenty little Russian girls, all in national costume and carrying flowers which they loaded on to us. How graciously we received this favour I cannot say, but some well known figures in the Tiger Club looked very strange with an armful of flowers. We had a coach trip around the town which was full of historic interest. There was a prosperous nature generally to be seen and we were well received wherever we went. The day finished with a civic dinner for those competing teams who had arrived at the Vilnius entry point, and we started to take a liking to Russian food and their excellent drink.

The following morning we met our Russian escort who were to take us on to Moscow. The arrangement was that the formation would be led by a Russian paratrooping biplane, an Antonov, and that the British and Polish teams would take up designated stations in formation on this aircraft and that the rear of the convoy would be covered by a Russian Yak 18. The whole convoy would have to fly at the speed of the slowest aeroplane which was the Stampe's about 95 miles per hour.

It was uncanny to find oneself in moderately close formation on a Russian aircraft for the next two days. We landed at Minsk, nightstopped at Vitesbk, landed at Smolensk and what appeared to be a closely-guarded military airfield at Vyasma, and finally reached Moscow in the evening of

Thursday 4th August, after a total flying time of approximately eighteen hours . . .

To this day I can find nothing of the individual placings, or of the fun they had returning. I suppose it was sufficient to see them all back in one piece, but I do remember no one was anxious to do it again.

Bunny Bramson: "And what did the Russians think of John Blake?" James Black: "I don't really think they could make him out." Norman Jones: "I am not surprised. They probably thought it was the return of Peter the Great."

THE SEA TURB, FAIR OAKS AND BILL'S BEECHERS

Bish was nothing if not the compleat enthusiast. His Seaplane Section news each month radiated an optimism hard to ignore– although most of us did, as much for the reason that Lee-on-Solent was a long way to go when in no time at all one could get airborne at Redhill without getting wet.

In July he wrote:

The Seaplane Section recommenced operations towards the end of April last.

All in all, the section is very much better equipped than ever before thanks to the generosity of a number of members. Firstly Norman let us have a second caravan and this is now set up as a proper Clubhouse in miniature, all stores and kit being banished to the old one. Light refreshments are provided at midday and teatime by Mrs Colin Newnes who is ably assisted by volunteers from the Girls Venture Corps from Gosport and Emsworth. Thanks to George Eyston (who for the past two seasons has let us have the use of his Jeep for aircraft launching) we now have a really serviceable beaching gear trolley, one which has taken away most of the enforced bathing carried out by launching crews in the past. Not only has George provided us with this, but he has also managed to acquire a small mechanical digger, the presence of which is very much welcomed by those who in the past suffered with shovels and subsequent backache on Sundays.

Ivor Falconer has found the trials of running the Seaplane section AND four farms in the Isle of Wight rather too much of a strain and his place has been taken as Hon. Secretary by Colin Newnes as from this month.

Members who have this year gained their seaplane rating include Tom Freer, Colin Newnes and Bob Harper, whilst "Jacko" Jackson is well on the way to this. There was rumour current a few weeks ago that it was going to be necessary to take out a Student Pilot's Licence and pass the whole eight-question written examination on lights and risk of collision at sea, which latter can be taken on the premises at Lee . . . Don't forget we are open from 1100 hours until 1800 on Sundays for conversion courses and are now ready for another intake.

It was a typical Norman gesture to saddle the willing Bish with a delightful but quite unsuitable aircraft for the Solent and in double quick time, but Bish cheerfully accepted the situation and wrote it all up in the November issue of the *Tiger Rag*, but a bit late for '66.

THE SEA TURBULENT

At the beginning of July, while on a visit to the Seaplane Club at Lee, the Chairman told us about a Turbulent-on-floats that had been tried out in 1965. Would we like to have it at Lee? I like flying Turbulents! So by the middle of August G-ARJZ was sitting on its floats in the hangar at Lee.

The history of the aeroplane is that Dr Urmston, with the hindsight of a Wet Wot, designed and built a pair of floats; Rollasons modified a Turbulent to take them; and the whole went to Hamford Water in Essex for trials. "The Smallest Seaplane in the World" appeared to have great promise, and the team – Norman Jones, Margo McKellar, Tony Haigh Thomas and Dr Urmston – learned about floatplane water-handling. At that time water-rudders were not fitted (if the significance of this escapes you, you need to visit Lee-on-Solent on a fine Sunday), and during an enthusiastic step-turn downwind the aeroplane capsized, giving Dr. Urmston a different view of the problems involved in seaplaning. With enthusiasm only a little dampened, the aeroplane was sent back to Croydon to be dried out, and the season's experiments ended.

This year a set of water-rudders were made and fitted at Lee. To avoid mods to the existing air-rudder control system, the water-rudders are steered by tiller-lines, the ends of which are anchored with bungee rudder strops just outside the cockpit, at the wing-root. The method of steering is similar to that used by the cox of the Oxford "Eight," or rather, the coxes of both the Cambridge and Oxford "Eights" lashed side by side to form a catamaran. Taxying trials were successful, and the Turbulent proved to be an interesting floatplane, as it exhibited characteristics of water handling that cannot be demonstrated in the Sea Tiger but only read about in books. For example, during a turn to the right to a downwind course – on the water – the air-rudder has to be put to the left (to reduce the effective fin area). This showed why Dr Urmston's trials the previous season had been difficult. It also showed that we had been lucky in NOT connecting the water and air rudders as in the Sea Tiger, since in the Turbulent they need to be used, at times, in the opposite sense.

Hugh Kendall of the Air Registration Board made a visit to Lee, and after 40 minutes of eyeball engineering pronounced the Sea Turbulent reasonably safe to fly. He left the impression that the worst could only happen at less than waterskiing speeds, and after all we did have a rescue boat! The aeroplane was weighed, and the AUW at take-off was found to be 100 lb heavier than the wheel version, with the C.G. close to the rear limit.

The first flight at Lee was made in a 10-12 knot wind which is probably the limit for the Sea Turbulent on open water, because the length of the waves is then approaching the length of the floats (11 ft). The take-off looked very exciting from the safety-boat, clouds of spray, very similar to the Supermarine S.6 in the film *50 Years of Powered Flight*. In the cockpit it felt quite safe, although it obviously tested the accuracy of the designer's stressing, and the standard of the workmanship in the construction of the floats and struts. Take-off power was marginal (chiefly due to the use of a small diameter propeller, to limit spray problems), and the aeroplane only became airborne after three premature bounces. The aeroplane handled in the air just like an ordinary Turbulent, and after cautious stalls and some gentle turns, a single final landing was made. The landing was so simple and easy that it caused great surprise to both pilot and safety-boat crew.

During the following weekends in September the flight tests were continued by Air Commodore Paul, Colin Newnes and Tom Freer. Each in turn was surprised and delighted with the little aeroplane, which not only retained its "fun to fly" qualities, but even added to them! Handling in the air is not noticeably different to the land Turbulent, even if it can be measured. The floats were designed with adequate side area aft of the C.G., and the directional stability has not suffered.

Stall and post-stall behaviour in straight and turning flight is unaffected by the floats. The aeroplane was found to stall at the unexpectedly high speed of 47 knots indicated; however it was fitted with a non-standard pitot static head projecting from the leading edge of the port wing, and it was found later, when the floats had been replaced by wheels, that it stalled at the same speed.

Performance has suffered due to the increased weight, but after the first few flights, a larger diameter fine-pitch propeller was fitted to the engine (which has a higher compression ratio than standard); take-off performance was greatly improved, and the aeroplane now climbs at 375 ft/min.

It was apparent that the aeroplane was dragging its heels on take-off and landing, and during some calm-water take-offs it was confirmed by the safety-boat crew that the floats and struts need to be re-rigged so that the aeroplane is floating on the water at about 5° greater incidence. The extra lift from the wing should then improve the take-off performance. With the floats at the present angle the attitude on landing appears to be exaggerated – the aeroplane gives the impression of a swan landing on water – and there is none of the long-distance 'speedboating' of a 'real' seaplane as it settles into the water. The landing is made at about 50 knots with a little power on, and as Tom Freer put it: "before it seems reasonable, one can feel the float-tails touch the water, but since one's own end of the aeroplane is obviously still flying one ignores it, until three or four wave crests later one disbelievingly shuts the throttle and the aeroplane lands itself." After a flight from smooth water it was found that one of the rear struts, which by all the laws should have been in tension, had buckled in compression. It gave Dr Urmston an opportunity to display his skill with a welding torch, and the strengthened strut survived until the end. The end of the test came when it was discovered that the floats had cracked at the step joint.

It is hoped that new floats will be built incorporating the lessons learned from this season's tests, and then if you live in the Lake District or even Lee-on-Solent, there is some interesting flying awaiting you . . .

It wasn't quite the swan song for the little Turbulent, but the writing was on the wall. She flew a happy and eventful three hours that year against her bigger sister's 38; but what an adventure.

FROM THE CHAIRMAN

In the Tiger Club we have as few rules as possible. But one of our most important ones is that anybody who takes a plane away from its home base is responsible for it until it is returned.

It therefore follows that whilst the machine is away it cannot be flown except by the person who is responsible for it without his permission.

(Which if you read it carefully was exactly what Norman meant. i.e. "You're in charge, make the most of it." We did, gratefully.)

August and 'SKP, our latest Tiger to return to the fold has, painted low on the rudder, the words 'rebuilt by Rollasons.' Some wit has now carefully inserted the one word – 'twice.' Fair Oaks was a gem of a display but not without incident. Ron Jacobs reported that during the crazy-flying display one elderly lady got so excited that she fainted away, to recover in the first aid tent and be quite upset she had missed the end of the act.

Fair Oaks has always been a winner. One of those memorable days and the sort of occasion that tends to come up in later years as an example of how things used to be. Memory does that – it overlooks the present until the facts are forgotten and only the nostalgia remains. Fair Oaks reverses the process. It was a day of good weather – a Sunday instead of a traditional Monday (a fact to stand in our favour, the Monday's weather was awful) and a day to which much of the success was owed to the unsung members, like Frank Hounslow and Roy Davis. Imagine a goodly crowd and, just as the balloon bursting item begins, the word is hastily

220

passed (and whoever passed it forgot the mike was live and several thousand enjoyed the panic!) that the unopened and sealed hydrogen bottle was empty. Hydrogen, who's got hydrogen? Yet Frank suddenly thought of the kindly balloon seller in the crowd who promptly gave us all the balloons and gas we wanted. The crowd who were in on the act from the start warmly applauded him and his sales soared. So to all the helpers, to Gavin Dix, Brian Smith and Stephen Thompson our heartfelt thanks. Peter Phillips' flying in the Cosmic surpassed his previous best. It was an unsurpassed display of verve and grace.

The opening formation was one of perfection and the brief interludes of the Tigers and Turbs were little cameos of precise dancing colour. The audience's enthusiasm for these tiny craft never wanes; it may be the knowledge that it's within their reach to fly one. Aerobatics by newcomer James Black and Neil Williams were delightful and the commentary by Taffy Taylor exactly fitted the bill. He later "talked" Neil in the Zlin around the sky in Neil's Moscow free sequence. One felt that Taff and Neil were as one – so often have they liaised on this sequence and the public appreciated the finesse of the complicated manoeuvres as never before. This and so many of the other acts were warmly applauded. For real spectator participation though, James Baring's crazy-flying was top. The "oohs" and "aahs" and the thousands of sighs of relief when he finally rolled to a stop must have sounded good to James. It did to the rest of us. Top marks to actors Dave Allan as CFI and Taffy as his assistant in the opening illusion – both fell off the Tiger realistically, only apparently they weren't acting. Flour bombing, parachuting – (from three Tigers for a change and expertly led by Bill Laslett) and a neat little show by Joan Hughes in the Pfalz replica from the film *The Blue Max*.

The display ended and for many pilots it was a signal to snatch a quick cup of tea, refuel and press on up to Wolverhampton for the Goodyear races. The rest of us lounged back to Redhill in warm evening sunshine. A perfect day . . .

Tiger Club "At Homes" have long been a popular feature but very often the support they deserved wasn't forthcoming. Unlike our visitors, who would come from tight flying communities, where all the members not only knew each other well but lived in the same town, we in the Tiger Club were a scattered lot, which made the family-based hospitality so welcoming and financially viable whilst abroad a near impossibility here. Strange as it may have seemed to bemused visitors, few of our members lived near Redhill, and long journeys to homes wasn't on within the parameters of time and togetherness.

It was always a point of embarrassment that there was no option in most cases but to convey our guests to hotels, and, no matter how modest, we were always aware of the expense they would incur. So we tried especially hard to make up for this by a great deal of entertainment and a good dinner. Few years succeeded as well as 1966 when in September Don Lovell arranged the best ever occasion. He wrote:

"This year, for the first time, we received friends from three countries, France, Holland and Germany. Although not all those expected arrived, 39 guests were received and entertained for the weekend. There were 11 visiting aircraft, 4 Pipers, 1 Cessna, 4 Jodels, 1 Sipa, 1 Nord, and with our own fleet they made a spendid scene in the sunshine of near-perfect weather on Saturday.

The first to arrive were our visitors from Osnabrück, in time for a late lunch; all but one aircraft arrived in time for the now famous punch prepared by James Baring.

While awaiting the arrival of our Beauvais and Rotterdam visitors, the Tiger Moth was seen to be in great demand for some local familiarisation trips, and joyriding Jodels also took to the air. A surprise visit from Pee Wee Judge and a Beagle formation of four aircraft arrived about 3 o'clock, adding interest and four twins to the gathering. They remained for about an hour and departed in great style to continue practising for the Farnborough show.

Dinner at the RAF Club was well supported – a total of over 100 people attended, and all our guests were accommodated in the Russell Hotel, members with cars arranging for all transport requirements.

Sunday arrived, and with it some really foul weather which held all but one fully-equipped Piper at Redhill until Monday. The one exception was able to file an IFR Flight Plan and returned via Gatwick to Osnabrück in 1 hr. 40 mins. – some tailwind.

Lunch at the local pub was again a great success, after which followed a very intensive period of rearrangements for our guests now requiring hotels, locally, at Brighton and London. A few were found scheduled flights from Gatwick to Le Touquet but since all flights from Lympne and Lydd had stopped, only very few reservations were available. The remainder of our guests enjoyed themselves in smaller groups at various restaurants on Sunday evening.

Monday morning saw the departure of our visitors, the first off at 7.30, the last at 11 o'clock, some, no doubt, not very late at the office after all.

In all, this was for me a busy and enjoyable weekend. I hope it was the same for you.

Still in September and continuing the Club News. The hangar was full, yet we missed the Cosmic Wind. Its final demise was a week earlier whilst racing at Halfpenny Green. Bill Innes must have sat mesmerised as they both went full tilt through a thick hawthorn hedge. Tom Storey said the aftermath looked like Beechers. Bill has asked me to thank everyone for their tremendous support and sympathy. The hospital switchboard was so jammed with well-wishers that when I rang the operator replied: "Yes, I know you wanted him – everyone does – is he famous?" He wasn't in hospital long enough to benefit, but his convalescence will take a spell.

"But the question is, Norman, will you ever make money out of the Condor?"

"Oh yes, I've got it all worked out; I've only got to make them twice as fast and spend half as much on materials and I'll do it!"

THERE WAS I . . ., ALAS 'PG AND AT PEACE

October. Misty mornings and still warm days; that's how most of us will remember September. And with it some of the year's loveliest flying weather. Tiger 'CDC is back again; in fact the complement of Tigers has never been higher. Robin Voice wants the new Spot Landing Contest off the ground quickly. To those of you who haven't tried this annual event, I urge you to have a go – it's tremendous fun. Robin got the job by proxy.

Said Norman Jones at the Committee meeting: "Who'll run the Spot Landing Cantest?"

Someone looked at Robin d'Erlanger, who was busy looking at the ceiling, and said: "Robin."

"Robin," said Norman. "Good idea; write to him, Michael."

So Robin Voice got a letter.

Robin wrote: "Have you ever felt that you were tired of warm coffee and baked potatoes in the Clubhouse? Thought, perhaps, that winter had more to offer? Well this year we are resurrecting the spot landing contest. Not a short landing competition or anything dangerous like that, but merely a test of accuracy. As always, the scheme is a ladder, up or down which one progresses as a result of challenge contests. There is a big prize and Michael will accept a 'minimum' flight time of five minutes although it should be possible to make the flight in even less than that."

The big prize was £5.

The Clem Pike Trophy came to us that month. It remains to this day the highest award the Club can give to a member, but originally it was, as Bish pointed out, offered to the Seaplane Club. He wrote:

The Tiger Club has been presented with a very nice silver Trophy by Wing Commander C.A. Pike, one-time Chief Flying Instructor of No. 1 EFTS Hatfield and a past Master of the Guild of Air Pilots and Air Navigators. This Trophy will be awarded periodically to the Member of the Tiger Seaplane Club who has in the opinion of the Tiger Club committee rendered signal service to the art of seaplane flying or the organisation thereof. This is the second time that Clem Pike has been instrumental in helping our movement in this manner, the first being when he obtained permission from de Havilland's for the indefinite loan of the de Havilland Trophy."

The "Over Sixties Crowd," as "GB" called them, later gave Clem a party at Redhill to celebrate the 50th anniversary of his first solo. Among those assembled were Hubert Broad, George Lowdell, Cyril Arthur (who had just retired as the CFI at Fair Oaks) Titch Holmes, George Eyston, Bish, Norman and of course "GB." Great names from a great past.

In the September I had appealed for more copy. Finding some 4,000 words a month was at times an effort, so in an attempt to talk members into putting pen to paper I had written: *"I can't believe nothing out of the ordinary ever happened to you, let's have a report on that 'there was I, nothing on the clock but the maker's name' tale."* The following month Chris Paul with his tongue happily in cheek opened the series and virtually closed it at the same time. Judge for yourself.

"I cannot ignore your 'There was I . . .' appeal in the News Letter. Actually this happened to a friend of mine who owned a DH.53. Arriving back in the early dawn of a summer Sunday from a Saturday night out, he shattered the cool, early calm of his home station by shooting up the Mess. In a subsequent interview with the Station Commander, his DH.53 was forbidden to fly from that aerodrome any more. My friend, therefore, wheeled it out through the main gates, pausing only to insist upon proper compliments from the guard, and into a field adjoining, whence he took off and shot up the Mess. Not unnaturally, his subsequent circuit and field landing was a well-attended performance. Unfortunately, a misjudged approach removed his undercarriage, compelling my friend to open up and go round again, without undercarriage, but with a gaping hole in the fuselage floor; this proved his salvation for on finals he lowered his legs through the hole and, by running very fast, was able to use his own undercarriage in place of the original de Havilland structure. He ended his landing run, panting and exhausted, in front of his purple-faced Station Commander, and in his own words: "There was I with my aeroplane around my neck too puffed to say a single word!"

November. Good news for the vintage contingent. The Puss Moth is soon to be back on the Club strength and with it a magnificent Fox Moth, one of those hardy aircraft that flew from the Southport beaches for so many years. Although it is a full five seater, it's likely to be limited to four to help keep it healthy in its old age. Both aircraft will be flown on a limited basis and used mainly for display work. Two more Stampes have been bought – bringing the total to four. It is likely though one will be kept in reserve. That, and the likelihood of at least one Zlin, is going to make 1967 a year to remember . . .

It's easy with hindsight to mock at our optimism then. At least one Zlin! But twenty years ago nothing seemed impossible. Who could have foreseen too, that once the Fox Moth was available for all to fly, no one would bother?

1966 wasn't always Mike Jolley's year. On the up side he was our popular and thrusting PRO and had got engaged to a lovely Judy, but on the reverse side he'd written off our beloved Mascaret. He bravely wrote a tribute.

"Papa Golf's career with the Tiger Club started on May 4th 1964, when Michael Jones took delivery of G-ASPG at Bernay and ferried it home to Redhill. It was·the 41st Mascaret to have been built and despite innovations, including a swept fin and all flying tailplane, the distinctive cranked Jodel wing easily identified it as a descendant of the 117 and Ambassadeur.

With 'ASPG the touring pundits really had a new lease of life; with a cruising speed of 130 mph plus at 2,600 rpm those with strong bladders could, if necessary, stay airborne for 6½ hours.

James Gilbert was the first to take Papa Golf abroad; his trip to Cannes included the first of a total of 80 Channel crossings made by the Mascaret. Altogether she flew 850 hours and covered more than 100,000 air miles – most of them abroad. My own association with the aeroplane began with a holiday trip I made to the Mediterranean in September '64. At that time the stage lengths seemed pretty ambitious, but since then James Baring has made even Gatwick-Majorca and back seem old hat. Anyway, the route is reproduced below to show how far one can go in 2½ weeks and still have plenty of time for sunbathing.

GATWICK-INNSBRUCK	575 s.m.	4:40
INNSBRUCK-DUBROVNIK	470 s.m.	4:25
DUBROVNIK-CORFU	250 s.m.	2:30
CORFU-PALERMO	350 s.m.	3:20
GAGLIARI-AJACCIO	190 s.m.	1:45
AJACCIO-CANNES	145 s.m.	1:10
CANNES-LYON	208 s.m.	2:00
LYON-BEAUVAIS	315 s.m.	2:40
BEAUVAIS-GATWICK	153 s.m.	1:15

The Mascaret concept was a classic example of how a basic and simple design could be continually improved upon, but it still amazes me how that cranked wing works so well in terms of weightlifting and speed. Isn't it a pity though that our friends at Shoreham haven't been able to emulate this light aircraft design concept. Anyway, this is a short tribute to a very popular little aeroplane whose career ended very sadly in the prime of its life. Let's hope that another Tiger Club Mascaret arrives from Bernay in the not too distant future . . .

December. As I write this, I am all too conscious of Xmas just around the corner, and with Xmas a spate of parties and dinners. One such Dinner was held in mid-December by the RAeC in honour of the British Aerobatic Team and was a great success. The Ford film of the Competitions was well-received – some of the aerobatic sequences were poetry indeed. Team Captain Neil Williams chose not to speak and instead team-mate Tony Haigh Thomas did the necessary. He was in good form. It was rumoured he'd been practising his speech in his bath, and had given instructions for all to applaud when he mentioned yaks. He needn't have bothered, the story went down very well. Apparently the Russians in their generous hospitality had introduced some charming Bolshoi chorus girls to the competitors, and because Neil was married they offered him a Yak. (To help those who no longer remember, a Yak was a Russian aerobatic aircraft). The story goes that Neil was delighted. The unrehearsed bit was the rejoinder from James Black in the body of the hall: "Sure, but was the Yak?"

Clive Francis, who was looking for experienced volunteers for the Turbulent team, turned to Barry Woodhouse, who was known to have a service background, and asked: "Will you fly in the Turb formation?"

"Yes," said Barry.

Clive was delighted. "And aircraft you flew?"

"Helicopters," replied Barry.

In looking back over the year my thoughts keep returning to Redhill which stealthily had become the centre of our world.

It was the year Dev Deverell finally won his two-year fight with the American FAA that ended in the certification of the Cliff Robertson Tiger Moth and a lead for the others that followed. His fighting letters won the day. The stupidity of the FAA had stung Dev into action. Surely they must have laughed too at one of their proposed restrictions: "shall not fly on Sundays." And we heard from Frank Tallman over there. His new leg worked well, he wrote, he'd got his Airline Transport rating back, had flown the P.51 Mustang, F.8F Bearcat and a Boeing F.481 Hot Air Balloon.

The last bit raised eyebrows. Sadly he wasn't to be free of trouble, but at the time we cheered his recovery.

It was the year when all our Club aircraft including the Turbs were finally equipped with two lots of landing cards. The Aerodrome Owners'

Association one permitted us to land at any aerodrome of theirs for 9/- (45p), and the best value of all, the Air Ministry card which permitted us to land at one of theirs for free – if you could find one. Taffy Taylor's booklet *Aerobatics as a Hobby* was a sell-out in June at 1/- a time. He ventured a second lot at 2/- a time and they went quickly too. He must have kicked himself. Paul Poberenzy, the President of the American EAA, flew a Turb at Redhill and John Ayres hit the National Press twice. The first time when he completed successfully trials in a Lightning – short stops in a gravel pit – and again when he joined the British Antarctic Survey flying the more mundane Pilatus Turbo Porter in the Falklands. After the gravel pit business we reckoned he went to the Falklands to recover.

Back at Redhill Robin Voice won the Dawn-to-Dusk in a Turbulent, 1,158 miles at an average speed of 88 mph for 38 mpg. And Roy Davis finally got the first lot of Tiger Club car badges sold at 30/- a time. In the August Don Robertson, sailing this time, came second in his beautiful catamaran Snow Goose in the Round British Race, Brian Healey became Editor of a new monthly, *Light Aeroplane,* and John Urmston, flushed with his success at building a Wot, sent everyone stationery headed "Bespoke Aeroplanes and Purveyors of Wots!" December and a record of 1,500 aero-tows in one year. "Jacko" Jackson could be, and was, proud. And before the year ended Sheila Scott had confounded us all with her tremendous Round-the-World Flight. Sheila was on the way . . . and so were we.

The year ended, as all good years should end, with no regrets and an impatience for the year to come. A direction had entered our lives and it showed. It showed in the confidence we had in ourselves and between ourselves and without being aware of it – for all true confidence comes naturally – we had unlimited confidence in our Boss and his generosity.

And generous he had been. The new aircraft, and the promise of more to come, had given us a taste of a flying experience few outsiders could possibly have known. He widened our horizons, saw that we polished our skills, was forbidding and encouraging as the moment demanded. We relished our time at Redhill, even at times to the point of straining a home life, but Redhill was a home too.

For it was there that we moved and thought freely. It was where the hangar doors and the aircraft were moved at will. It was where we could drink tea and philosophize and no one ever said nay. No one threw us out, then no one let us in. One speaks of freedom as though it's an old friend, but the reality is often an illusion. For real freedom is of the mind and our minds were at peace at Redhill.

Ten years of the Tiger Club was behind us. Seven hundred members faced the future with a well-grounded assurance. In the years to come few would be disappointed.

INDEX

TIGER CLUB MEMBERS 1957-1966

A

John Ayres	1957	The Hon. James Baring	1959
Roy Allen	1958	D.B. Baker	1959
Cyril Arthur	1959	Earl of Bective (later Headfort)	1959
Ray Atwood	1959	Bill Bedford	1959
Rose Ayres	1960	Leon Biancotto	1959
Stanley Allen	1960	Paul Boyce Mears	1959
W. Armstrong	1960	P.D. Breen	1959
Ishan Ali	1960	Harvey Britten	1959
T. Attley	1960	Peter Brooks	1959
Robin Adeney	1961	David Brown	1959
John Airey	1961	Neal Baldwick	1960
Marcus Anwyl-Davies	1961	Matthew Banks	1960
Cyril Audrey	1961	G.A.P. Barlow	1960
Charles Austin	1961	D. Barnato-Walker	1960
Don Ayres	1961	William Booth	1960
David Allan	1962	Peter Brittan	1960
Sally Ames	1962	A.E. Brown	1960
Alfred Adams	1963	H. Browning	1960
Dennis Allen	1963	Neville Browning	1960
Doreen Audrey	1963	Keith Bryant	1960
Douglas Ayer	1964	Y.D. Butterley	1960
Christopher Amoore	1964	Stephen Baillie-Reynolds	1961
John Anning	1964	Arnold Barclay	1961
David Austin	1965	Ernest Barnes	1961
S. Albrow	1966	Pat Bellin	1961
Peter Arnold	1966	John Berkeley	1961
Peter Ashton	1966	Frank Bigger	1961
Gilbert Aspin	1966	Ronald Bishop	1961
		Milton Blair	1961

B

		George Blackburn	1961
Bill Bailey	1957	Max Bonney	1961
Jimmy Basnett	1957	Jack Brabham	1961
J. Baynes	1957	P. Brennan	1961
Lewis Benjamin	1957	Norman Brett	1961
D. Bevis	1957	Rosemary Brittan	1961
K. Bevis	1957	R.C. Browne	1961
C. Nepean Bishop	1957	C.G. Burton	1961
Gladys Bishop	1957	John Baker	1962
John Blake	1957	P. Banister	1962
Charles Boddington	1957	Lionel Bee	1962
George Bottomer	1957	Juanita Benjamin	1962
Stand Brant	1957	Eric Blacklock	1962
Charles Brown	1957	James Blake	1962
Sammy Banting	1958	G. Booth	1962
Elizabeth Brandwood	1958	David Bulnois	1962
Sue Burges (Phillips)	1958	Henry Bramwells	1962
M.F. Butterworth	1958	George Bancroft	1963

Martin Barraclough	1963	**C**	
G. Barraclough	1963	Peter Clifford	1957
K. Beale	1963	Clive Compton	1957
J. Blondel	1963	Peter Cameron Webb	1959
F Bongiene	1963	Bill Chesson	1959
Alan Bramson	1963	Teddy Cleven	1959
Miriam Bramson	1963	Mark Colbeck	1959
Brian Bramson	1963	Mike Conry	1959
B. Brownlow	1963	Peter Coyle	1959
Geoffrey Buckett	1963	Francis Couesnon	1959
R. Barclay	1964	Arthur Crowhurst	1959
Keith Barrow	1964	C. Curtis-Nuthall	1959
Elizabeth Bennett	1964	Peter Carr	1960
T. Beverley Smith	1964	Chris Carver	1960
Robin Blech	1964	Grace Coddington	1960
John Brown	1964	Richard Collard MP	1960
Colin Bryant	1964	Vic Collin	1960
John Bryant	1964	Paul Conyers	1960
Alain Buloz	1964	John Cook	1960
Ambrose Barber	1965	Peter Corlett	1960
Richard Bishop	1965	Peter Coyle	1960
Thomas Bishop	1965	Bruce Cousins	1960
James Black	1965	Donald Campbell	1961
Gloria Blake	1965	John Carter	1961
Philippe Boulanger	1965	Robert Carter	1961
Martin Brewer	1965	Peter Chapman	1961
Leonard Briars	1965	Susan Chapman	1961
Kenneth Brissenden	1965	David Checketts	1961
Tom Brooke-Smith	1965	Sam Clutton	1961
Kenneth Browne	1965	Denis Crabb	1961
Cyril Bryan	1965	Georges Crucifix	1961
P. Buckley	1965	A. Campbell	1962
A. Burns	1965	Ann Carter	1962
W. Butcher	1965	Robert Carter	1962
John Bamford	1966	Gillian Cazalet	1962
Kenneth Barker	1966	S. Chenoy	1962
Roger Barnes	1966	B. Collins	1962
Keith Bawtree	1966	K. Couling	1962
Arthur Bell	1966	J. Freeman Cowen	1962
Nigel Biggs	1966	Richard Cox	1962
Roger Blackburn	1966	Gordon Crabb	1962
John Blackmore	1966	E Carter	1963
Enid Blech	1966	S. Carter	1963
Wilfred Blowers	1966	John Childs	1963
Ronald Boland	1966	Winston Churchill	1963
Nicholas Bowden	1966	C. Clabaugh	1963
Nicholas Briggs-Adams	1966	Mark Tim Corbett	1963
Robert Brown	1966	John Crewdson	1963
Robert Butler	1966	Julian Carbo	1964
		Brian Chadwick	1964
		Michael Canning	1964

John Cochrane	1964	G. Dix	1963
Malcolm Cockburn	1964	Marian Driessen	1963
John Colban	1964	Jennifer Dudley Fletcher	1963
Betty Cones	1964	Peter Dirs	1964
Maurice Cronin	1964	R. Domas	1964
Keith Crosby	1964	J. Doyle	1964
Graham Crowther	1964	Anise Driessen	1964
Roy Cuthbert	1965	Robert Dunlop	1964
Albert Carlyle	1965	Robert Damon	1965
Gosta Cassel	1965	Stefano Donghi	1965
Andrew Chadwick	1965	A. Dotiwala	1965
Mrs. M. Channing	1965	Christopher D'Oyly	1965
D. Charity	1965	T Duhig	1965
John Christie	1965	R. Dunn	1965
David Cole	1965	P Dyer	1965
Michael Cole	1965	William Driver	1966
Donald Connolly	1965	R. Druce	1966
Cyril Coppleman	1965	Walter Drury	1966
Mrs T. Corbett	1965	Peter Dryden	1966
Valerie Crown	1965		
J. Crawford	1965	**E**	
Victor Cannock	1965	Clive Elton	1957
James Carter	1965	G. Ealson	1958
Peter Clarke	1965	John Elmes	1958
Tom Conner	1965	HRH Duke of Edinburgh	1959
Joyce Crabb	1965	John Elverston	1959
Jean Crabb	1965	D.P. English	1959
		Mrs Clive Elton	1961
D		Dick Emery	1961
Jim Denyer	1957	P. Evendon	1962
J. Donald	1957	Joseph Elliott	1963
A. Deverell	1958	P. Empson	1963
Sam D'Arcy	1959	Carl Ebersole	1964
Arthur Downes	1959	Lewis Ellison	1964
R. Diggins	1959	Eric Eadie	1965
A. Driessen	1959	James Early	1965
B. Davey	1960	Jimmy Edwards	1965
A. Davis	1960	Angus Eggleston	1965
M. Davis	1960	William Elliott	1965
Derek Dempster	1960	Robert Emerson	1966
H. Donovan	1960	Colin Evans	1966
T. Davey	1961	Wynn Evans	1966
Roy Davis	1961	George Eyston	1966
Robin d'Erlanger	1961		
V. Derrington	1961	**F**	
H. de Salis	1961	Janet Ferguson	1957
J. Van Dam	1962	Peter Fitzmaurice	1957
S. Dalzell-Smith	1963	W.V. Fitzmaurice	1957
K. Davies	1963	Denis Fox	1957
Peter Davies	1963	Edward Fox	1958
C. Dennis	1963	Rachel Fox	1958

A.E Fish	1959	Jack Gravely	1957
Joan Fish	1959	J. Greenhead	1957
Ian Fish	1959	A. Golding Barrett, "G.B."	1958
Trevor Fish	1959	John Garood	1959
Clive Francis	1959	F. Griffiths	1959
Jean Francis	1959	Barry Griffiths	1960
James Fahy	1960	Raymond George	1960
Michael Fanthorpe	1960	James Gilbert	1960
John Fell	1960	Keith Goldie-Morrison	1960
Malcolm Fisher	1960	George Greenwood	1960
Antony Fletcher	1960	Ronald Goodchild	1960
Kenneth Freeman	1960	Christiana Griffiths	1960
Peter French	1960	Elizabeth Griffiths	1960
George Fry	1960	John Gunner	1960
Ronald Fry	1960	Gerard de Guitaut	1960
Edmund Fane	1961	William Gill	1961
Ernest Farrell	1961	Len Gallagher	1962
Alan Frost	1961	Tom Geake	1962
P. Farquhar	1962	Bill Goldstraw	1962
R. Fairrie	1962	K. Grundy	1962
Mike Forge	1962	Robert Gairns	1963
John Fairey	1963	Daphne Gardiner	1963
Ivor Faulconer	1963	R. Garnier	1963
Ronald Fautley	1963	Michael Golby	1963
Frederick Fox	1964	Robert Gorton	1963
Terence Fellingham	1964	Patrick Graham	1963
Anita Fisher (Baring)	1964	Mogens Green	1963
John Foaden	1964	Richard Griffiths	1963
Arthur Fuller	1964	Hugh Gardiner	1964
Mrs M. Fuller	1964	David Gaster	1964
Ian Fairhurst	1965	Norman Gibson	1964
Kenneth Fenton	1965	Keith Godfrey	1964
Anthony Fetherstone	1965	Jean Gordon	1964
Sheila Fennell	1965	Luis Gordon	1964
Manfred Fistler	1965	Denis Greene	1964
W. Foster	1965	John Greenhill	1964
Harry Foules	1965	Marianne Greuter	1964
Tom Freer	1965	Diana Griffiths	1964
Cordon Ferriman	1966	Roman Garby-Czerniawski	1965
John Firth	1966	Rosemary Gardiner	1965
Zandra Fisher (Barraclough)	1966	Horace Glassborow	1965
Leslie Foreman	1966	Charles Gordon	1965
Tom Foxworth	1966	Horace Gray	1965
David Frankel	1966	Herbert Greb	1965
John Fricker	1966	David Green	1965
Ian Frow	1966	Angela Gleave (Lodge)	1966
Arnold Frutin	1966	Robert Good	1966
		Arnold Green	1966
G		Donald Green	1966
James Gibbons	1957	C. Griffiths	1966
Peter Gibbs	1957		

239

H

Name	Year
Geoffrey Hancock	1957
Mavis Harriott	1957
Jack Harris	1957
Dennis Hartas	1957
'Titch' Holmes	1957
Brenda Horsfield	1957
Harry Hall	1958
Mike Hawthorne	1958
Peter Hearne	1958
E. Hewitt	1958
Jon Hutchinson	1958
Robert Harrop	1959
James Hoseason	1959
Elizabeth Hyams	1959
Graeme Hamilton	1960
Bob Hamilton	1960
Harold Hargreaves	1960
Marie Hargreaves	1960
David Harris	1960
Charles Harrison	1960
Neil Harrison	1960
Robert Hart	1960
Henry Hartley	1960
Pauline Hawley	1960
Ray Heath	1960
Michael Higginson	1960
Eric Hillyard	1960
Betty Holmes	1960
T. Howie	1960
George Humphrey	1960
Arthur Humphreys	1960
Sally Harper	1960
Philip Harrison	1960
Jacques Heuillard	1961
D. Hewitt	1961
Peter Hoar	1961
George Hoult	1961
Peter Houston	1961
Hugh Hughes	1961
J.J. Hughes	1961
Christine Hunt	1961
David Hunt	1961
John Hurrell	1961
Fred Harries	1962
Peter Harrison	1962
John Heath	1962
Alan Hodson	1962
John Hounsfield	1962
Frank Hounslow	1962
Nicholas Hughes	1962

Name	Year
Hugh Hutton	1962
Sheila Hands	1963
Victor Hargreaves	1963
Mrs P. Hargreaves	1963
Robert Harper	1963
Roger Hastings	1963
A. Hueurtz	1963
Stuart Hiller	1963
R. Houselander	1963
Richard How	1963
Peter Hussins	1963
John Hugo	1963
Tony Haigh Thomas	1964
John Hamblett	1964
Lloyd Harding	1964
Gordon Harmen	1964
Donald Harnsberger	1964
Henrik Heden	1964
Jean-Pierre Hilly	1964
Anthony Huggins	1964
Phillippa Hughes	1964
Philip Hamblett	1965
Douglas Hamilton	1965
Trevor Hampton	1965
Neil Harrison	1965
Ralph Hart	1965
Dagmar Heller	1965
Lizzie Hermansen	1965
Frank Hewitt	1965
Robert Hill	1965
Brian Hockley	1965
William Holden	1965
Robin Hood	1965
George Howe	1965
Roy Hubble	1965
Mrs. C. Hughes	1965
Denys Hamilton	1966
John Hanley	1966
T. Harries	1966
William Hasker	1966
Brian Healey	1966
Rodney Hill	1966
David Hood	1966

I

Name	Year
Maurice Imray	1957
Brian Iles	1959
Bill Innes	1961
Phil Irish	1961
Pat Iles (née Peacocke)	1961
Frank Irving	1962

Alfred Indyk	1965	**L**	
Tony Iveson	1966	Pete Langstone	1957
		J. Leckie	1957
J		Colin Labouchere	1958
A.J. Jackson	1957	John Le Claire	1958
Mrs. M. Jackson	1957	Sir Alfred Le Maitre	1958
Johnny Johnston	1957	J. Ladeveze	1959
Norman Jones	1957	Marcus Langley	1959
Michael Jones	1958	John Lee	1959
Pee Wee Judge	1959	John Lemon	1959
Ron Jacobs	1960	John Lothian	1959
John Johnson	1960	Duncan Lacey	1960
Sally Jones	1960	Robert Lewin	1960
D.R. Jackson	1961	John Lake	1961
William John	1961	Bill Laslett	1961
Derek Johnson	1961	Louis Lawes	1961
Michael Jolly	1962	David Lloyd	1961
O.P. Jones	1962	Don Lovell	1961
Claes Jacobsson	1963	Tessa Lovell	1961
Ian Jago	1963	Alec Lumsden	1961
Gordon Janney	1964	Mark Lambert	1962
Cyril Jones	1964	R. Le Brocq	1963
C. Jeffery	1965	John Lewis	1963
Alan Jackson	1966	Tim Lodge	1963
David Jarvis	1966	Peter Van Lonkhuyzen	1963
Michael Jarvis	1966	Frederick Landau	1964
Peter Jarvis	1966	Jean Leek	1964
		Veslemoy Lien	1964
K		George Lowdell	1964
Rosemary Kirby	1957	Alan Lassiere	1965
D. Kly	1957	Douglas Laurie-Lean	1965
H. Knight	1959	Andrew Lavies	1965
Denis Kirkham	1960	Donald Le Clair	1965
M. Kardar	1961	Bob Lees	1965
Manx Kelly	1961	Keith Lelyveld	1965
Peter King	1961	Gerald Lewis	1965
John Knowles	1961	Graham Lewis	1966
David Kyle	1961	J. Lewis	1966
David Kerridge	1962		
Sam Key	1962	**M**	
Hugh Kendall	1962	Margo McKellar	1957
Ken Kneen	1962	Basil Maile	1957
Gerald Kear	1963	John May	1957
Roy Kitch	1964	Mrs. B. Mackenzie	1957
Edna Kneen	1964	Miss E. McPate	1957
Ludmila Kolobov	1964	Tony Miller	1957
William Knowles	1964	Basil Monk	1957
Richard Kingsmill	1965	T Moulson	1957
Michael Knight	1965	Brian Martin	1958
Frank Kinder	1966	Yvonne Middleton	1958
Carol Koczon	1966	H.T Molyneux	1958

Dennis Monkton	1958	Edgar Mills	1964
Elwyn McAully	1958	John Mimpriss	1964
Yvonne Marcus	1959	Edward Mole	1964
Peter Masefield	1959	Edwin Mullis	1964
George Mayhew	1959	Graham MacDowell	1965
John Mercer	1959	Terence Martin	1965
Paul Minton	1959	John McRae	1965
Phil Moore	1959	Jorge Muñoz	1965
Eric Murray-Smith	1959	Gillian Mackay	1966
Tony Mabelis	1960	Elizabeth Manning	1966
Saleigh MacGowan	1960	William Merchant	1966
William Massey	1960	Terence McGee	1966
Richard McCullough	1960	Miss E. McSkimming	1966
Timothy Melville-Ross	1960	David McWilliams	1966
John Miller	1960	Suzanne Metz	1966
Claire Montbron	1960	Roy Mills	1966
Terence Murphy	1960	Edward Mitchell	1966
Archie MacDonald	1961	Hamish Moffatt	1966
Alvin Martin	1961	Peter Morgan	1966
Brian McAlister	1961		
Barbara McAully	1961	**N**	
William McKinnon	1961	Nancy Newman	1957
Mark Milburn	1961	Desmond Norman	1957
David Morgan	1961	Jack North	1957
Alan Morries	1961	Pessy Nye	1957
Mrs M. MacDonald	1962	Miss J.C. Nicholson	1958
Don Mallette	1962	R. Naylor	1960
C. Manley	1962	Hugh Niel	1960
Malcolm Mann	1962	Roger Neaves	1961
Fred Marsh	1962	D.A. Newby	1961
Charles Masefield	1962	Faith Newmark	1961
D. MacRae	1962	Colin Newnes	1961
G. Monk	1962	Mrs. E. Neild	1963
A. Montgomery	1962	James Nichols	1963
Michael Moore	1962	Leslie Neeves	1964
John Morris	1962	Sam Newington	1964
Henry McKinnon	1963	Ian Napier	1965
Frances MacRae	1963	Philip Norris	1966
Brian Marikin	1963		
Cecil Matthews	1963	**O**	
Robert Matthews	1963	Leslie O'Connor	1957
Susan McCully	1963	Mike O'Dell	1957
Charles Metz	1963	Audrey Ogilvy	1957
Lorna Minton (Proctor)	1963	David Ogilvy	1957
R. Moehl	1963	Tony Oldham	1957
Colin Morley	1963	Jack Overbury	1957
Charles MacKenzie	1964	Mike O'Brien	1958
Bernard Manning	1964	Ken O'Rourke	1958
William Mares	1964	Patricia O'Brien	1960
Alan Middleton	1964	Aubrey Offen	1960
Pamela Middleton	1964	Derek Offen	1960

Shaun O'Connor Parsons	1964	Brian Pleasance	1963
Victor Ovenden	1964	Gillie Potter	1963
		Daphne Poynter	1963
P		Ron Payne	1964
Avis Phillips	1957	Arthur Penzer	1964
David Phillips	1957	Ted Perrin	1964
Jack Piercy	1957	Zena Perrin	1964
Clem Pike	1957	Frank Peterson	1964
John Pothecary	1957	Peter Pledge	1964
W.R. Parkhouse	1958	Brian Plendereith	1964
Chris Paul	1958	Mrs. E. Plendereith	1964
Joan Piercy	1958	Alvena Pocock	1964
Barry Purcell	1958	Sidney Parker	1965
Barbara Paice-Watson	1959	Joseph Pease	1965
Pat Peacocke (Iles)	1959	Anneliese Pinto	1965
E.R. Perreaux	1959	William Prestwich	1965
Stanley Ferry	1959	Michael Parker	1966
Phil Phillips	1959	Jack Pickrell	1966
Jim Phillips	1959	Alan Plumstead	1966
Peter Phillips	1959	Iris Poole	1966
William Pine	1959	Edward Prestwich	1966
Lew Pond	1959	E Prince	1966
Michael Popoff	1959		
Hazel Prosper	1959	**R**	
John Packer	1960	Jock Renton	1957
Gerhard Pawolka	1960	Tony Richmond	1957
Nick Pocock	1960	R. Rimington	1957
Ronald Potter	1960	Mike Reilly	1958
Malcolm Preskett	1960	J. Rey	1958
Nigel Pritchett	1960	H. Reynolds	1958
Mervin Palmer	1961	Ken Rawles	1959
Ronald Palmer	1961	Buck Reeve	1959
Frank Parker	1961	Michael Reid	1959
Richard Parkhouse	1961	Pat Robinson	1959
Alec Parkinson	1961	Valerie Robinson	1959
Derek Pickup	1961	John Robson	1959
Bob Pooley	1961	Graham Rich	1960
Ronald Porteous	1961	Clive Roberts	1960
Anthony Preston	1961	Malcolm Rostron	1960
Edward Price	1961	Desmond Rees	1961
Frank Price	1961	David Rhodes	1961
Roy Proctor	1961	William Richardson	1961
H. Pattison	1962	Don Robertson	1961
D. Peacock	1962	David Rowse	1961
Desmond Penrose	1962	Peter Reiss	1962
R. Phillips	1962	Mervyn Ricketts	1962
John Page-Blair	1963	John Riseley-Prichard	1962
Lily Page-Blair	1963	Colin Rosborough	1962
Robert Parker	1963	James Rose	1962
David Parsons	1963	Hans Ruesch	1962
Mrs. Eve Phillips	1963	Jeremy Renny	1963

James Richardson	1963	Gordon Smith	1961
D. Robinson	1963	Tony Southerland	1961
Denis Robson	1963	Gordon Stanley	1961
Jane Robson	1963	Dick Stratton	1961
Michael Riley	1964	Michael Streeter	1961
Williams Roberts	1964	John Swift	1961
Norman Ryder	1964	Beryl Sanders	1962
Rad Radwanski	1965	France Seignol	1962
Peter Reilly	1965	Bernard Sedgewick	1962
Anthony Roberts	1965	John Smith	1962
Ronald Roberts	1965	Peter Sterry	1962
Cliff Robertson	1965	Adrian Swire	1962
Howard Rose	1965	A. Segall	1963
Stanley Rice	1966	Sylvia Shelley	1963
Benjamin Riseborough	1966	David Simpson	1963
Bernard Rose	1966	Christopher Singer	1963
David Runnalls	1966	David Smith	1963
		Ellis Somake	1963
S		Tom Storey	1963
David Scallon	1957	William Scorse	1964
Trevor Sharwell	1957	Sue Singer	1964
Joan Short (Waugh)	1957	Brian Smith	1964
Jean Smith	1957	Maritz Soland	1964
Ken Smith	1957	Nat Somers	1964
Mary Smith	1957	Gordon Spreckley	1964
Bev Snook	1957	Michael Spence	1964
F.S. Symondson	1957	John Symonds	1964
John Schooling	1958	Alan Sim	1965
Ian Scott-Hill	1958	Charles Sims	1965
John Severne	1958	Mrs. J. Smith	1965
Jacob Shapiro	1958	S. Smith	1965
Robert Simpson	1958	Jill Southam	1965
Richard Sivyer	1958	Richard Steil	1965
John Skinner	1959	Anthony Stracey	1965
Nicholas Snook	1959	Fred Stringer	1965
Pauline Snook	1959	Michael Stroud	1965
K. Swain	1959	John Sanders	1966
David Scott	1959	Julian Sandys	1966
Sheila Scott	1960	George Scarborough	1966
Katherine Severne	1960	Carl Schofield	1966
Anthony Shall	1960	C. Seager-Thomas	1966
A.J. Spiller	1960	John Shaw	1966
Robert Stephenson	1960	Bernard Simpson	1966
John Stevens	1960	Ross Skinner	1966
B. Stramik	1960	John Slessor	1966
Peter Sullivan	1960	Anthony Smith	1966
Lewis Schwarz	1961	Clive Smith	1966
John Serrell	1961	Donald Smulian	1966
Peter Sivyer	1961	Dennis Sole	1966
George Slavin	1961	Hilary Somake	1966
Ernest Smith	1961	Charles Spiteri	1966

Rowarth Spurrell	1966	Charlotte Vanneck	1961
Cecil Stewart	1966	Yvette Vallois	1963
John Stewart Wood	1966	Rene Vallois	1963
Vivian Stewart Wood	1966	Robin Voice	1964
		Rein Van Dyke	1966

T

Joe Taylor	1957	**W**	
Bill Tomkins	1957	John Wardley	1957
Barry Tempest	1959	E. Wild	1957
W Tonkyn	1959	Ron Willbie	1957
John Taylor	1960	Chris Wren	1957
Ian Trethewey	1960	Bob Weeks	1958
James Thayer	1961	Eileen Wardley	1959
Richard Thoma	1961	Bill Waugh	1959
Charles Thomson	1961	A. Weston	1959
Peter Treadaway	1961	Bryan Winslett	1959
L. Tappenden	1962	R.H. Wood	1959
Anna Tarleton	1962	Neil Wates	1960
David Thomas	1962	Emanuel Wein	1960
Ronald Thompson	1962	Peter Welch	1960
Lord Trefgarne	1962	R. Weston	1960
Sally Trethewey	1962	Timothy Whitaker	1960
Claude Trethewey	1962	Lou Wilber	1960
Arthur Tyrrell	1962	Robin Windus	1960
Norbert Theisen	1963	Moira Wilson	1960
Helmet Toenges	1963	John Winters	1960
John Tullett	1963	John Wise	1960
Alan Turley	1963	John Wadman	1961
Nick Turvey	1963	Diane Wale	1961
David Timmis	1964	Donald Warburton	1961
Frank Tallman	1965	Alfred Warminger	1961
Charles Taylor	1965	Michael Warner	1961
Stephen Thompson	1965	Ann Warren	1961
Christopher Trew	1965	Kenneth Wilkinson	1961
Peter Tanner	1966	John Williams	1961
John Taylor	1966	Neil Williams	1961
Christopher Tilney	1966	Bob Winter	1961
Michael Townsend	1966	Clive Wren	1961
		John Wright	1961
U		D Wiggins	1962
John Urmston	1963	John Winslow	1962
Betty Urmston	1965	R. Woodhouse	1962
Bryan Upton	1965	William Wallace	1963
Jack Upchurch	1966	Don Wetherilt	1963
Christopher Unitt	1966	Dennis Wiggins	1963
		Alan Wilson	1963
V		Keith Warton	1964
Peter Vanneck	1957	David Weber	1964
Cordelia Vanneck	1957	Nigel West	1964
Robert Vaile	1959	Frederick White	1964
M. Votier	1959	Graham Wulff	1964

Neville Wynn	1964	Roger Whittle	1966
Ronald Wakely	1965	Roy Williamson	1966
Alan Walker	1965	Frank Wolfson	1966
Michael Watts	1965	Barry Woodhouse	1966
George Webb	1965	Henry Wright	1966
Jurg Weber	1965	Robert Wright	1966
Carol Williams	1965		
Mrs. P. Wilson	1965	**Y**	
Mrs. Jean Withers	1965	James Young	1961
Charles Woodham Smith	1965	Mrs. Joan Young	1961
John Ward	1966	Harold Young	1966
Alan Wersha	1966	William Younger	1966
Roger Westwood	1966		
Simon Wheeler	1966	**Z**	
Arthur White	1966	Julian Zuromski	1960
Alistair White	1966		

TIGER CLUB AIRCRAFT OPERATED 1957-1966

TIGER MOTHS

G-AOAA	Modified as Super Tiger later
G-ANHI	
G-AOXS	Taxi-Tiger with canopy over front cockpit
G-AODR	
G-ANSH	First Tiger to be fitted with inverted fuel and oil systems
G-ACDC	
G-APDZ	Super Tiger
G-ANZZ	Super Tiger
G-AIXD	
G-ANMZ	Super Tiger
G-APRA	Modified for paradropping
G-ANDA	
G-ARAZ	First Tiger to be used for SOW
G-ASKP	
G-AIVW	Sea Tiger

JACKAROOS

G-ANZT	
G-APOV	Thruxton version modified by Rollasons

STAMPES

G-AROZ
G-ASHS
G-ATKC

PUSS MOTH

G-AHLO

HORNET MOTHS

G-ADNB
G-AEWY
G-AHBL

CONDORS

G-ARHZ
G-ARVZ
G-ASEU

JODELS

G-APOZ	D.117
G-ARNY	D.117
G-AOVZ	D.140 Mousquetaire
G-ARDZ	D. 140A Mousquetaire
G-AROW	D. 140B Mousquetaire
G-ATKX	D. 140C Mousquetaire
G-ARFT	DR.1050 Ambassadeur
G-ARUH	DR.1050 Ambassadeur
G-ASAB	DR.1050 Ambassadeur
G-ATLB	DR.1050M Excellence.
G-ASPG	D. 150 Mascaret

BEAGLE

G-ATMH   Husky

ARROW ACTIVE

G-ABVE

COSMIC WIND

G-ARUL

PIPER SUPER CUB

G-ARAM

TURBULENTS

G-APBZ
G-APIZ
G-APLZ
G-APMZ
G-APNZ
G-APVZ
G-APZZ
G-ARCZ
G-ARGZ
G-ARIZ
G-ARJZ
G-ARLZ
G-ARMZ
G-ARNZ
G-ARRZ
G-ARZM
G-ASAM
G-ASDB

COMMENT: Many of these aircraft were sold through Rollasons during the decade to Club Members, in particular the Tigers and Turbulents.

248